Nou

Social Welfare in
Latin America

Comparative Social Welfare Series

Edited by
John Dixon

Social Welfare in Asia
Edited by
John Dixon and Hyung Shik Kim

Social Welfare in the Middle East
Edited by
John Dixon

Social Welfare in Africa
Edited by
John Dixon

Social Welfare in Developed Market Countries
Edited by
John Dixon and Robert P. Scheurell

Social Welfare in Latin America

Edited by

John Dixon

and

Robert Scheurell

R

Routledge
London and New York

First published 1990
by Routledge
11 New Fetter Lane, London EC4P 4EE

Simultaneously published in the USA and Canada
by Routledge
a division of Routledge, Chapman and Hall, Inc.
29 West 35th Street, New York, NY 10001

Printed and bound in Great Britain by Mackays of Chatham PLC, Kent

British Library Cataloguing in Publication Data

Social welfare in Latin America. — (Comparative social
    welfare series).
1. Latin America. Welfare series
I. Dixon, John II. Scheurell, Robert P. III Series
361'.98

ISBN 0-415-02401-3

Library of Congress Cataloging in Publication Data
Also available

CONTENTS

ACKNOWLEDGEMENTS

As this book goes to press we wish to acknowledge the help we received from a variety of quarters. A special debt is owed to Mr Hyung Shik Kim, a co-editor for the first volume in this comparative studies series - <u>Social Welfare in Asia</u> (1985) - for his crucial contribution to the conceptual framework that underlies the series.

To Mrs Cheryl Leeton go our thanks for typing the manuscript in its various drafts and in its final form. The artwork was done by Mr Karl Rudeiger of the Instructional Media Centre at the Canberra College of Advanced Education, to whom go our thanks.

Publication of this book, indeed the entire comparative series, would not be possible without the support received from the International Fellowship for Social and Economic Development Inc. (IFSED), a non-profit organisation. Further information about IFSED can be obtained from the Director, Mr John Dixon, PO Box 228, Belconnen, ACT, 2616, Australia.

To our wives, Tina and Sally, go our thanks for putting up with our idiosyncrasies throughout the preparation of this manuscript.

For any errors of fact and for all opinions and interpretations, the authors and the editors accept responsibility.

John Dixon   Robert P. Scheurell

PREFACE

This volume on Social Welfare in Latin America is one of six volumes which encompass all of the regions of the world. The other volumes in this series are:

. Social Welfare in Asia (1985)

. Social Welfare in the Middle East (1987)

. Social Welfare in Africa (1987)

. Social Welfare in Developed Market Countries (1988)

. Social Welfare and Socialism (forthcoming)

There are a variety of publications focussing on comparative public policy and in-depth studies of specific regions. What makes this series unique? Firstly, a similar model is used in each volume and for each country in order to develop as much consistency and uniformity in content as is feasible. Secondly, the system of co-editing attempts to develop consistency and uniformity in writing style. Finally, the global perspective encompasses the entire world. The chapters on various countries are both descriptive and evaluative of the social security and personal social services provided.

Social security is defined as:

> the whole set of compulsory measures instituted to protect the individual and his family against the consequences of an unavoidable

interruption or serious diminution of the earned income disposable for the maintenance of a reasonable standard of living (Rys 1966, p.242).

Thus it includes compulsory employer liability (with or without insurance); provident funds; social insurance (benefits subject to contributing conditions); social assistance (benefits subject to residence qualifications and an income or means test); and universal programmes (benefits subject only to residency qualifications). The social security boundary is, however, blurred in many countries, for elements of fiscal welfare (that is, a system of tax rebates or taxable income deductions that reduce the tax liability of particular target groups) and occupational welfare programmes (for example, occupational superannuation, non-statutory sick pay entitlements, free or subsidised health care for employees and their dependents) may impinge on social security in some instances. Where this is significant, details are included. Health insurance arrangements are also included.

The personal social services are characterised by service functions that have a major bearing upon personal problems, individual situations of stress, inter-personal helping or helping people in need, and the provisions of direct services in collaboration with workers from statutory and voluntary agencies. Accordingly, the term 'personal social services' will be used in such a way as:

. to distinguish them from cash benefits;

. to refer to various forms of services in kind that are provided, in the main, in response to recognised 'personal' needs; and

. to include service provisions that usually require the assistance and help of qualified personnel, such as social workers or probation officers.

It should be noted, however, that the adoption of this terminology in the context of a developing society may cause some conceptual and practical problems. Thus it is necessary to be eclectic in what should be included under the rubric 'personal social services'.

Preface

There are a variety of approaches one can take in studies of comparative public policy such as descriptive, analytical, quantitative and conceptual. The descriptive-evaluative approach as used in this volume allows one to review a variety of countries and look for salient general trends. As the editors reviewed the contributions, a number of general trends were present in all of the countries, although varying in degree. These themes can be classified into three broad areas (for convenience), although there is some overlapping of the classifications: demographic, social and economic, and social security and welfare trends.

Demographic Trends. Six of the nine countries have a high proportion of individuals under age 18, 40-50 per cent, and an annual growth rate of 1.9 to 3 per cent which means a doubling of the population every 23-35 years. These demographic trends have tremendous implications for basic services, such as health, housing, education, employment without even considering the need for personal social services, such as child care, day care, family and marital counselling, unwed mothers, and so forth. The resources of these countries are already strained, and this problem will become more acute in the near future.

Three of the countries (Argentina, Cuba and Uruguay) had a declining birth rate and an ageing population. However, in these countries the economic resources are limited. All of the countries had a distinct difference in the provision of services between urban and rural populations, with the urban areas receiving more adequate services than the rural areas.

Socio-economic Trends. All of the countries are heavily Roman Catholic in their religious preference and have remnants of the padrone/ hacienda system (from the colonial era), scarce and limited economic and industrial resources, extensive poverty (50-60 per cent of the population) and a small upper and middle class and a large lower class. The only exception is Cuba as a result of their income redistribution policies.

Of interest in looking at the economies of these countries is the fact that four have been attempting to industrialise (Argentina, Mexico,

Puerto Rico, and Uruguay) and in all four countries, the progress toward economic industrialisation has stagnated in the 1980s. In fact, all countries are dependent on developed market countries for financial assistance.

Social Security and Welfare Trends. All of the countries have a minimal or non-existent concept of the personal social services as discussed in the developed market countries. In all countries the social security programmes were established by the 1940s. All of the countries have an extremely complex form of social security administration as a consequence of different (and competitive) levels of administration.

Part of the administrative complexity of social security is a result of a variety of special interest groups having their own pension or social security system. These special interest groups are usually occupationally oriented, such as politicians, military personnel, university professors, jockey club members, glass makers and so forth.

Three significant social problems which all of the countries are facing include inadequate health facilities, a growing problem of unemployment and child poverty, and an urban/rural differential in the provision of services. Health facilities of a curative type (hospitals) are adequate in urban areas, but not rural areas, and preventive medicine is generally inadequate. In all of the countries there is a growing concern with unemployment and underemployment (working poor) and in some cases homeless youth.

In all of the countries, there is a theoretical coverage of the entire population for social security and the health programmes. However, the take-up rate of the eligible population participating in these programmes is extremely variable for most countries (except Cuba and Puerto Rico). Many rural residents do not receive services. In all of the countries, the Roman Catholic Church and mutual aid groups, including the family, attempt to provide needed services.

Monetary Units. All monetary units are expressed in natural currency units. No attempt has been made to convert these into a common unit by means

Preface

of official currency exchange rates. The currency
units for the countries included in this anthology
are:

Argentina	:	Argentine Peso
Brazil	:	Cruzeiro
Chile	:	Chilean Peso
Colombia	:	Colombian Peso
Cuba	:	Cuban Peso
Guatemala	:	Quetzal
Mexico	:	Mexican Peso
Puerto Rico	:	US Dollar
Uruguay	:	Uruguayan New Peso

REFERENCE

Rys, V. (1966), 'Comparative Studies in Social
  Security: Problems and Perspectives', Bulletin
  of the International Social Security
  Association, 19, 7-8 (July-Aug), 242-68.

CONTRIBUTORS

Dr Marian Angela Aguilar is an Assistant Professor in the Worden School of Social Services at Our Lady of the Lake University of San Antonio, San Antonio, Texas, USA.

Dr Roberto Arias Perez is the Presidente de Caja Columbiana de Subsidio Familiar, Bogota, Colombia.

Dr Silvia Borzutzky is in the University Center for International Studies at the University of Pittsburgh, Pittsburgh, Pennsylvania, USA.

Dr Grace Keyes is a lecturer in Cultural Anthropology at Our Lady of the Lake University of Texas, San Antonio, San Antonio, Texas, USA.

Dr Celso Barroso Leite is in the Centro de Estudios de Previdencia Social, Pro de Janeiro, Brazil.

Professor Carmelo Mesa-Lago is the Distinguished Service Professor of Economics and Latin American Studies at the University of Pittsburgh, Pittsburgh, Pennsylvania, USA.

Dr Irene Queiro-Tajalli is an Assistant Professor in the School of Social Work at Indiana University, Indianapolis, Indiana, USA.

Professor Sergio G. Roca is in the Department of Economics at Adelphi University, Garden City, New York, USA.

Dr Rodolfo Saldain is in the Banco de Prevision Social, Montevideo, Uruguay.

Professor Raquel M. Seda is in the Graduate School of Social Work at the Unversity of Puerto Rico, Puerto Rico.

For

Tina, Piers and Aliki

and

Lynn and Laura

ARGENTINA
Irene Queiro Trajalli

THE WELFARE SYSTEM ENVIRONMENT

Ideological Value Environment

The Spaniards reached Argentina in 1516 while
searching for a passage to the west. This was 24
years after Columbus arrived at the American
continent. In 1536, one of the conquistadores
founded the city of Buenos Aires. However, it was
not until 1580 that the Spaniards succeeded in
establishing a permanent city in the great estuary
of the Atlantic now known as Rio de la Plata. The
Spaniards ruled the land for almost 300 years.
Argentina began its struggle for independence in
1810, but the formal declaration of independence
was made in 1816. For 40 years two main groups,
'federalists' and 'unitarians', struggled to
impose their ideological ideas on the organisation
of the republic. In 1853 national unity was
achieved and the Constitution signed. From about
1880 Argentina began a period of economic growth.
The political elite of Argentina believed in both
economic and political liberalism which would
bring benefits to itself and simultaneously enrich
the country.

From a historical, geographical and cultural
perspective the Argentine society is based on four
pivotal elements: God, family, homeland and
freedom. According to Matera and Serrano (1986)
love for God is the result of the assimilation of
the Christian influence brought to the land by the
conquistadores and missionaries. The family is
another important and stable institution with deep
roots in the Spanish and Italian groups arriving
in Argentina. The concept of homeland is rooted
in the identification with the community as a

1

system where people mold their characters and develop a sense of unity. Finally, the concept of freedom is closely related to the gaucho, the cowboy of the pampas, who loved the land and recognised no boundaries but the sky as the limit. Overall, the nature of the welfare system in Argentina has been shaped by a number of groups with different ideological orientations, the most important of which are discussed below.

The Roman Catholic Church. During the Spanish colonisation of 1516-1816 the Jesuits played a key role not only in christianising the Indians, but also in providing education and assistance to the needy. In the following centuries, the Roman Catholic church was the main community institution for people from which to seek spiritual comfort and economic help.

Mutual Aid Societies. Argentina had a heavy influx of Italian, Spanish, Polish, German, French and Russian immigrants between 1880-1920. In order to provide support for each other in a new country, immigrants organised social clubs and mutual aid societies. Some of these original groups developed into formal organisations which, at present, provide comprehensive services to their members.

Organised Labour. The urban working class represents one of the main forces in the struggle for social reform in Argentina. Through the decades, labour has been successful in organising itself and demanding social policies comparable to those in industrial countries.

Political Parties. During the 1880s the political sphere was dominated by the liberal politicians who had control of the only authentic political party, the Partido Autonomista Nacional. The most important national decisions were made by consensus or informal agreement among officials of the executive branch of government. In 1890 the Radical Party was created, which represented a population from the elite, who were dissatisfied with the ruling group. The Radical Party targeted its attacks against the government by pointing out the lack of democracy and public morality. The party, known later on as the Radical Civil Union, has played a key role in twentieth century politics. Soon after the creation of the Radical

Party, the Socialist Party emerged. The Socialist Party supported the workers in the struggle for improvements in labour laws. The Peronist Party is another political group which has played a major role in twentieth century Argentine politics. The Peronist Party developed the 'justicialist' doctrine, the label used to describe the social welfare policies aimed at helping the urban labour groups. In 1985 there were 30 political parties and coalitions each one of them having specific ideas about the direction the country should follow. Undoubtedly social welfare policies have suffered from the lack of consensus among political parties as to the type of welfare state Argentine should have.

The Military Establishment. The liberals who came into power in 1852 strongly believed in a professional army to bring order to the country. From that time to the present, the military has perceived itself as the safeguard of the country. The military has ruled the country at different times in Argentine history. During those periods, the military prevented a radical lobby from developing a political base for needed welfare reforms.

Historical Origins

Soon after their arrival in 1516, the Spanish conquerors began to create social institutions resembling those in Spain. In this way, a number of programmes emerged to provide assistance in society.

Public assistance programmes developed to 'correct' and help the needy. A hospital for orphans was established to protect abandoned babies. In the late 1700s a 'correction house' was created to shelter street women of 'doubtful' behaviour. During their stay, women were supposed to work both to shape their characters and support the agency.

The private sector was active in providing welfare assistance. In 1727 the city of Buenos Aires suffered from an epidemic of yellow fever, which resulted in a significant number of deaths. Consequently, a group of people conceived the idea of creating an organisation that would help the city, one of its objectives being to bury the dead of poor families. In this way the Charitable

Brotherhood was founded. This organisation was, in addition, responsible for opening a women's hospital, a school for orphans, and a number of other institutions. This organisation came to an end in 1822 when its various institutions became property of the central government.

In 1823 the government gave authorisation to establish a women's society, the Charity Organisation Society. This organisation had responsibility for the administration of children's institutes, women's hospitals and any other public organisations devoted to the welfare of children, women and the needy. The Charity Organisation Society operated for 125 years. During its life-span the Charity Organisation Society became a powerful organisation due to the number of institutions under its administration. The organisation was supported with monies from the government and private sources. Many of the institutions, once created, were transferred to religious groups. In 1948 the Charity Organisation Society was dissolved and became part of the 'National Department of Social Assistance'.

Considering the number of welfare organisations operating in the country in a rather decentralised fashion, the National Register of Social Welfare was created in 1937 under the auspices of the Ministry of Foreign Affairs. This Register and Central File was to coordinate all the welfare services provided by national, provincial, municipal and private entities. The organisations included under the centralisation programme are all those charitable organisations aimed at helping persons in need of social, economic, recreational and health services, mutual aid societies, and private schools with 20 per cent or more of indigent student populations.

In 1943, all activities related to welfare, hospitals, orphanages, homes for the aged, social assistance, public health and hygiene became part of the Ministry of Interior. As a result, the National Directorate of Public Health and Social Assistance was created under the auspices of the Ministry of Interior. In this manner, all the institutions of health and social assistance were under the umbrella of the same organisation. In addition, the Secretariat of Labour and Social Provision was created in 1943 to defend the working class, improve their standard of living and working conditions, and promote access to housing. A year later the General Directorate of

Social Assistance, a unit within the Secretariat,
was created. Therefore, all activities related to
health remained within the auspices of the
National Directorate of Public Health and Social
Assistance (later named Public 'Health), and all
areas relating to charity, residential homes, and
social assistance were transferred to the new
General Directorate of Social Assistance.

In 1944 a Social Service Commission was
created and chaired by the Vice-President to
encourage the development of social services in
factories and other work places. Annual bonuses
were given to those businesses that would provide
benefits such as free medical care, medicine at
low cost, groceries, clothing at low prices,
meals, and educational programmes to prevent work
accidents. Different structural changes occurred
in the following decades even though the
activities and services provided remained
basically the same.

Historically, welfare services in Argentina
have been provided through the efforts of the
government, charity organisations, religious
groups, ethnic organisations, private enterprises
and labour organisations. The help provided by
charity organisations had the quality of serving
the 'deserving poor', abandoned children, single
mothers, and poor older adults. The services
provided by the ethnic organisations were geared
to help their own people to adjust to a new
environment. The religious groups were guided by
the concept of help in the Judeo-Christian
tradition. Finally, the labour organisations,
have provided services to their members as a right
of the working class.

The Political and Socio-economic Environment

Argentina is one of the largest countries in South
America. It covers an area of 1,072,749 square
miles. It has a population of 30.7 million
people. The major city is Buenos Aires with 10.7
million inhabitants. Immigration has played an
important role in the socio-economic and political
structure of the country. According to the first
national census, there were less than two million
people in 1869. It was evident to the government
that more people were needed to populate the land
and to improve the agricultural sector that was so
crucial to the country's development. Immigration

was therefore encouraged. Between 1880 and 1920 4.5 million immigrants entered the country, with the majority consisting of Italians and Spaniards, and a significant number of Polish, Germans, French and Russians.

At the present time, 97 per cent of the population is of Spanish and Italian origin. The Spaniards in 1516 brought their culture, including their religion, which was imposed on the Indians. Currently, 92 per cent of the population is Roman Catholic. In some parts of the country the rituals of the Roman Catholic church have been influenced by those of the Indians. This can be observed in some of the religious rituals.

Argentina is a unique country. It is one of the few countries in the world that has a surplus of food and it is virtually self-sufficient in energy. Unfortunately, Argentina has always been an exporter of primary products which created a peripheral economy and one that heavily depends on the international market and trade with industrialised countries. In recent history, Argentina has experienced economic and political turmoil. According to Aldo Ferrer (1983), the economy in Argentina was weaker and more backward in 1982 than it was in 1975. Between 1976 and 1983 Argentina suffered the highest inflation, with an annual rate of over 600 per cent. High rates of inflation have weakened the purchasing power of all sectors of the population, mainly the rather large and highly heterogeneous middle class (35 to 40 per cent of the national population) which has been unable to keep its previous comfortable standard of living.

It is impossible to talk about the Argentine economy without making reference to the external debt. In 1986, the external debt reached over US$50 billion. It is said that each person in Argentina owes more than US$2,000 at birth.

Argentina is a federal republic. Currently the executive branch of the government comprises the President and an appointed cabinet of eight ministers. Historically the various ministries have been restructured several times reflecting the orientation of the ruling class at the time. The latest revision took place in 1983 when the existing ten ministries were collapsed into eight. These ministries are: (1) Interior; (2) Foreign Relations and Worship; (3) Defence; (4) Economy; (5) Public Works and Services; (6) Education and Justice; (7) Labour and Social

6

Security; (8) Public Health and Social Action.
The legislative branch of government is the
bicameral National Congress; the Senate and the
Chamber of Deputies.

In summary, the long process of the declining
socio-economic situation and political upheaval
has weakened the social institutions of Argentina
including the welfare system.

THE WELFARE SYSTEM: AN OVERVIEW

The welfare system in Argentina is mainly provided
for by central, provincial and local governments,
labour organisations and charitable private
institutions. As a result, some welfare
programmes are highly centralised and have the
same characteristics across the country while
others depend on the specific characteristics or
needs of a given province and/or community.

Social Security Administration

The goals of social security in Argentina are
based on the 1853 National Constitution and
government planning. The major social security
benefits fall into four categories: (1) Old-Age
and Survivors' Insurance, (2) Disability
Compensation, (3) Family Allowance, and (4) Health.

Service provision is the responsibility of the
Ministry of Labour and Social Security. This
ministry is divided into two departments, the
Department of Social Security and the Department
of Labour. The Department of Social Security is
the body responsible for formulating the overall
plans and overseeing the social insurance
programme, including old age, death, invalidity,
disability, and survivors' insurance, as well as
work injury compensation and family allowances.
The Department of Labour regulates the policies
related to labour-related benefits and
unemployment.

Overall, social security policies have
proliferated during the last 50 years.
Unfortunately, they have not been extended equally
to all sectors of society because these policies
are closely related to the urban labourer and his
retirement. As a result, the seasonal and rural
workers, as well as the underemployed, do not

receive the same extensive benefits as the urban-working class.

Labour Organisations. Traditionally, the labour organisations have provided health and social services through their Obras Sociales (Social Security Organisation). These are another important component of the social security system in Argentina. According to present public legislation these organisations provide preventive and palliative health services and related social services to their members. These organisations are not a recent creation but rather they can be traced to mutual aid institutions of the mid-nineteenth century. At that time, they were voluntary organisations which provided medical and pharmaceutical services to their members.

Between the 1850s and the turn of the century, hundreds of new societies were created. The first formal labour union, the Buenos Aires Printers' Society (Sociedad Ripografica Bonaerense) was formed in 1857. The proliferation of the mutual aid societies was a direct result of industrialisation, which took place in Argentina in the nineteenth century when the country ceased to be predominantly agricultural. Even though these organisations were landmarks in the delivery of social services to the people, they were not regulated by the government. Regulation became a concern of the Socialist Party. Mainly, the party was concerned over the quality of services and the motives of some of the organisations since they were not fulfilling their stated social objectives. The need for legislation to regulate these groups was obvious. As a result, in 1913 the Socialist Party submitted to the Congress a bill to regulate the functions of the mutual aid organisations. In that piece of legislation the idea of national health insurance similar to those emerging in England, France, Belgium and Germany was clearly stated. However, it was not until 1946 that a law was enacted to regulate the functions of these organisations.

During the 1940s these social security organisations were a powerful political resource for the labour groups to provide the working class with health and social services similar to those available to the more affluent classes.

Between 1945 and 1955 the government exercised an active role in the organisation and control of

the health and social insurance organisations.
After the military revolution of 1955, the
government relinquished its active role and
workers' unions became once more responsible for
providing health and social services to their
members. As a result, the type of coverage and
quality of services became dependent upon the
economic power of each one of the unions.

In 1970 the National Institute of Health and
Social Insurance was created, where all the health
organisations were to be registered. The overall
goal of the Institute was to provide the necessary
planning, coordination and control of the various
Health and Social Insurance Plans.

In 1971, 231 Health and Social Insurance Plans
were registered at the National Registry, a
department within the National Institute of Health
and Social Insurance Plans. Apart from health
services, the Plans provide social services
according to their financial capacity. These
Plans provide coverage for workers, retirees and
their dependents and are financed by the
contributions of employers and employees.

Unfortunately, in recent years the health and
social insurance organisations have undergone a
process of impoverishment which resulted in less
coverage and more out-of-pocket expenses for the
members. Several factors are responsible for this
outcome, such as devaluation of salaries and a
decrease in personal income.

Personal Social Services Administration

<u>Government</u>. The Ministry of Public Health and
Social Action assists the government in the areas
of health, environment, social assistance, family
protection, housing, tourism and recreation.

<u>Sectarian and Non-sectarian Social Organisations</u>.
The private sector has played an important role in
providing social services. As we have seen the
Charity Organisation Society helped to meet
particular problems of children, women and the
needy. In addition, denominational charities have
provided care for orphans, recreational and
educational activities for children, hospitals,
homes for the aged and handicapped, shelter for
women, children and the homeless.

Argentina

Financing Social Welfare

Expenditure by the central government on social security and welfare represented 30 per cent of total government spending in 1983, while expenditure on health services accounted for a further 1.2 per cent. In addition to general revenue sharing, the central government transfers resources to the provinces via some 30 earmarked funds - housing, welfare, health and so forth - each of which has its own semi-autonomous administrative agency at both national and provincial levels.

Social Security Finance. The retirement plan is financed by employers (11 per cent of payroll), employees (3 per cent of wages) and government (70 per cent of the employees' contribution). Sickness and maternity benefits are paid for by employers (3 per cent of payroll) and employees (4.5 per cent of wages). Work injury benefits are the employers' responsibility alone. The cost of unemployment benefits and family allowances are shared by the employer and the government.

Health and Social Insurance Plans. The services provided by these Plans are financed by contributions of employers and employees. Currently the contributions are 4.5 per cent of employee's salary paid by employer and 3 per cent paid by employee (plus 1 per cent for each additional dependent).

Personal Social Services Finance. Personal social services are provided by public, sectarian and non-sectarian organisations. These services are funded with monies from the government and donations.

THE AGED

In 1950 Argentina was categorised as a country with a young population; today its population is ageing. It is estimated that by the end of this century 14 per cent of its population will be 60 years and older with a life expectancy of 71 years, some 4.6 million people.

As a country, Argentina presents character-istics of traditional societies, especially in the rural areas, as well as strong elements of

10

industrial modern societies. In the first
instance, the extended family is very strong, and
three generation households are not uncommon.
This is true in some northern provinces where
traditions are held strongly. In other parts of
the country the nuclear family is the norm.

The combination of an ageing population,
increased life expectancy, and societal values in
transition, has brought calls for higher
allocations from the government to the aged area.

Social Security

Old Age and Survivors' Insurance. This is the
responsibility of the National Retirement System;
it is mandatory and is based on work
contributions. Nonetheless, any person can become
a member by joining the National Fund for the
Self-employed. Furthermore, the social assistance
pension system, a non-contribution benefit, covers
those people in need who are not eligible for the
national retirement system.

The concept of the retirement system dates
back to colonial times (1516-1816) when certain
government officials and those people who fought
for the country would receive pensions and
donations. Concurrently, another system began to
emerge based on professional identities and group
solidarity. Later on, retirement plans were
created for the members of the Supreme Court and
area judges, teachers, staff members of the public
administration, and government officials.

The retirement system was organised in a
systematic manner in 1904 when the retirement and
pension fund was created to cover public
employees. Later on, funds were created for other
employees in such areas as railroads (1915),
public services (1921), banks (1923), journalism
(1939), commerce (1944), industry (1946), rural
sector (1954), executives (1954), university
professors (1954), self-employed (1954) and
domestic service (1956).

In 1969, the numerous retirement plans were
grouped into two systems: one for employees (Law
18.037) and one for self-employed (Law 18.038).

All workers, both self-employed or employed by
others, are covered by the national retirement
plan on a compulsory basis. Furthermore, there is
a voluntary retirement plan for those persons
under 55 years who do not hold gainful employment

11

- such as housewives, and those persons who are covered by other retirement plans but want to increase their retirement savings.

Retirement benefits are provided at 60 for males and at 55 for women who have worked for 30 years. Retirement contributions should have been made for a minimum of 15 years. The retirement age for the self-employed is 65 (male) and 60 (female). When workers reach retirement age they are entitled to a monthly income for life. The average monthly earning is computed for the three years in which the worker's earnings were the highest during the 10 years prior to retirement. The amount of the monthly earnings is 70 per cent to 82 per cent of the amount the worker had received during those selected three years.

Furthermore, the retirement plan provides benefits due to old age. Under this category, coverage is provided at age 65 to those who were employed by others if they can prove 10 years of service and have made contributions to the retirment fund for at least five years. The benefits are 60 per cent of the highest three-year income received in the last five years of employment. The self-employed can receive this benefit if the worker is 70 years of age and can prove 10 years of service, and payments have been made to the retirement fund for five years within the period of eight years immediately prior to the request for retirement.

In case of death of the retiree or an active member of the retirement plan the following relatives are eligible to receive the benefit:

. widow/widower
. single children under 18
. single daughters 50 years of age or older who were living with the deceased
. daughters who are widowed, separated or divorced
. grandchildren under 18, who are orphaned
. surviving parents
. single under 18 who are orphaned brothers or sisters.

With the exceptions of the spouse and children under 18, the rest of the eligible relatives have to prove they were dependents of the deceased. The 18 year age limit is not applicable when the beneficiary is disabled, or is pursuing high school or college education. In the latter case the limit for receiving any benefit is 21 years of age.

In 1946, the minimum retirement and pension benefits were uniformly established and they are updated periodically. In 1958, the maximum benefit was determined, with periodic readjustment of the benefit. In 1984, it was ruled that the maximum benefit would be 10 times the minimum retirement payment.

Personal Social Services

<u>Resources for the Elderly</u>. This is the responsibility of the National Institute of Social Services, a branch of the Ministry of Health and Social Action. This institute has as its main goal the provision of social and health services to older beneficiaries in a comprehensive manner.

The specific objectives of the Institute are to:

. promote preventive recreational group activities geared to enrich the psycho-social and physical functioning of the elderly;
. prolong the stay of the elderly in the family environment by providing home services;
. provide economic support to those older persons who want to continue living in their social environment;
. support the extended family when it provides assistance to the older adult;
. provide medical care services to older adults suffering from long-term or short-term illnesses;
. provide transitory or permanent institutionalisation with individualised health care to older adults with pathological disorders, who cannot be assisted in any other way;
. promote activities which strengthen inter-generational ties; and
. develop a range of services for older adults, taking into account the socio-cultural characteristics of the population in different geographical regions of the country.

Institutionalisation is perceived as the last alternative, once other approaches have failed or do not answer the bio-psycho-social needs of the older person.

Institutionalisation. The responsibility for long-term care facilities (nursing homes) is divided between the national, provincial and municipal governments on one hand and the private sector, charitable and profit-making organisations on the other. As of 1979, there were 567 nursing homes in the country. These homes are heavily concentrated in the capital city of Buenos Aires, surrounding areas, and three other provinces.

Many homes are run by ethnic groups. Some model nursing homes belong to ethnic groups such as 'Israeli and Argentinian Home for the Aged and Children', 'The Pines Home' (German Society), and 'Geriatric Institute Agustin-Roca' (Italian Society).

According to Passanante (1983) those homes under the auspices of the municipalities are hospital-like settings with a capacity for 200 residents or more. Even though occupational therapy and recreational activities are offered, a large number of the residents remain uninvolved. Except for a few residents, they do not share the activities of the communities where the homes are located.

Health Institutions for the Elderly. Geriatric hospitalisation is provided in three different ways: (1) geriatric wings within general hospitals, (2) general hospitals, and (3) day hospital (private). Unfortunately, geriatric hospitals are practically non-existent, and geriatric wings within hospitals are not able to respond to the needs of the aged. The day hospitals which have been developed by the private sector can be afforded by only a small percentage of the population. Home health care is provided to those elderly people who cannot come to the doctors' office and in emergency cases. Homemaker services are provided on a very limited scale to older people who are homebound and do not have relatives.

Evaluation

The retirement system in Argentina has two main problems. Firstly, the amount of minimum monthly payments received by retirees is too low considering the rising cost of living; and secondly, the retirement plans have shown deficits at several points in time since 1962.

Argentina

The reasons for these problems are several. One of them is the increase in the numbers of retirees drawing retirement benefits; for example, in 1962, the retirement funds supported 850,000 beneficiaries while in 1977 the figure had increased to 1,847,075.

With respect to the personal social services, institutionalisation is the approach for the aged person who lacks relatives' support to remain in the community. Unfortunately, the large institutions are characterised by an atmosphere of passivity and uniformity. At the same time alternative programmes and model institutions run by the private sector have not reached the total population.

Alternative solutions to institutionalisation are available on a limited scale with the support of local governments. Some of the services include recreational centres, hot meals, and adult day shelters. Ethnic groups and religious organisations provide day activities for older adults.

THE DISABLED

It is estimated there are 700,000 disabled people in Argentina. Unfortunately the resources allocated to this group are quite limited. The budget of the Department of Protection to the Disabled, which is a branch of the Ministry of Health and Social Action, was roughly 2,100,000 Argentine Pesos in 1987.

Social Security

Disability Compensation. According to national policies all of the worker's economic losses due to work-related accidents and occupational illness are transferred to the employer by means of a workmen's compensation scheme when the disabling condition lasts more than four days. Compensation for permanent disability (partial or total) is paid by the employer or insurance companies to employees or their survivors. The amount of payment is determined by multiplying by 1,000 the daily salary of the worker, or considering the reduction in salary as a result of the disability. The maximum grant payable is 120 times the legal minimum monthly wage. In

15

addition, a constant attendance allowance equal to 50 per cent of the benefit payable is also provided.

Temporary disability payment is equal to 85 per cent of the daily salary. If the disability exceeds 30 days the payment is equal to 100 per cent of the employee's salary. In all cases, the employer has the responsibility of paying for medical expenses, prescription drugs, and orthopedic equipment.

Invalidity Insurance. Where a non-occupational invalidity causes too large a reduction in a worker's earnings capacity then an invalid pension is payable equal to 70 per cent of average adjusted earnings received during the highest three of the last 10 years. This is subject to minimum and maximum pension rates and is adjusted for changes in general wages. A means-tested allowance is payable to any needy invalid ineligible for invalidity insurance.

Personal Social Services

Institutional Care. There are public as well as private, charitable institutions to house the disabled who cannot remain within the family system. In addition, there are educational institutions to train the disabled and help them to become active members in society.

Evaluation

Overall, there are gaps in the provision of services to the disabled. Monies allocated by the government to serve this group do not enable the organisations to offer the required quality services. Furthermore, discrimination still exists toward hiring of the disabled which prevents them from breaking the dependency cycle. This is true although there exists a national law that requires hiring disabled in public institutions.

NEEDY FAMILIES

The family is a basic social unit in Argentina. For the family to fulfil its socialisation, educational and economic functions, it requires help at different stages in its development or in crisis situations.

Social Security

Maternity Insurance. All female employees have the right to receive maternity leave. Maternity benefits amount to 100 per cent of monthly earnings. The maternity leave is for 90 days. The maternity leave could be taken for 45 or 30 days before the date of delivery, and it extends to 45 or 60 days after delivery. Maternity leave is coupled with prenatal care benefits, and benefits for birth of a child. Health care services are provided during pregnancy, childbirth and after delivery through the public health care system, mutual aid societies, and 'obras sociales'.

Survivors' Benefits. In the event of a worker suffering an occupational death eligible survivors (spouse, children and other dependent relatives, according to inheritance laws) receive a lump sum of 1,000 days of the deceased's earnings, up to a maximum payment of 120 times the legal monthly minimum wage. In addition, a funeral grant is also provided, equal to three months' minimum wage.

Personal Social Services

Families with few or no resources are assisted by public and private organisations. They provide day-care services, recreation, home appliances, furniture, and prescription drugs at a minimum price; others provide legal advice, scholarships to needy students, and so forth.

Evaluation

In general, community services to the family have developed under a variety of auspices, mainly sectarian organisations and public institutions. Furthermore, the quality and availability of services depend on the resources of the region, province and or local communities. The most significant benefits to preserve the family are those provided by social security.

CHILDREN AND YOUTH

Comprehensive protection to the family - which in Argentina is a constitutional mandate - has as one of its goals the protection of minors. In this respect, the labour benefits provided to the family promote the necessary socio-economic conditions required for a healthy development of the child. Furthermore, minors are protected by a number of institutions created by law. One of these institutions is 'patria potestad'. According to P.L. 23.364-art.264 of the Civil Code patria potestad is the sum total of the rights and responsibilities that parents have over the person and estate of their minors who are not legally emancipated, in order to protect them and provide the means for a healthy bio-psycho-social development.

Personal Social Services

Guardianship is another institution with deep roots in Argentine legislation. Guardianship could be defined as the rights and responsibilities given to a person by the law to represent and protect a minor and his/her estate, when the parents are dead, absent or incapable of performing parental duties.

Care for orphans and abandoned children was provided during colonial times. The Spanish King was the authority in charge of appointing guardians of children and orphans to the colonies. By 1821 the responsibilities assigned to the guardians were transferred to court judges and juvenile defenders. By the mid-1800s the role of the government had diminished and the heavy responsibility of protecting children fell within the boundaries of religious organisations and rich families. As industrialisation and modernisation took place, the need of children and youth for protection and more specialised welfare services was recognised. From 1919 the country experienced rapid growth in the numbers of public and private children's institutions, created to provide comprehensive protection to children and youths. Child and youth services include educational and recreational programmes, services for crippled children, maternal and child health services, institutional care and foster care.

Argentina

Adoption. This institution was incorporated into Argentine legislation in 1948. A minor can be adopted by a married couple or a person (35 years of age or older) when the minor is not emancipated or under patria potestad.

Patronato. Patronage is the governmental function of protecting those minors without a normal family environment and/or a legal guardian. The function is overseen by national and provincial judges.

Social Security

Family Allowance. Family coverage is a mandatory benefit which covers all employees, in the private or public sector, with the exception of domestic service workers. The coverage includes one-time payment benefit for marriage, birth of child, or adoption of a child. Furthermore, the employee receives a yearly sum of money for each child attending primary school to cover some educational expenses. Prenatal care coverage is provided monthly to a female worker during the pregnancy period. The same benefit is provided to the male worker when his wife is pregnant and she is not employed. In addition, employees receive a monthly compensation for the spouse, and for each child under 15 years of age, or 21 if they are in school. There is no age limitation if the child is disabled. Those employees with three or more children receive an extra monthly benefit for each child starting with the third child. The employers are responsible for family allowance coverage.

Evaluation

A wide variety of preventive and palliative services address the growing needs of children and youth in Argentina. The majority of the family programmes have direct impact on the healthy development of children and youth. In those instances where the family is not capable of providing a positive environment for the child, or when the child's behaviour cannot be managed within the family system, the government intervenes to protect and/or rehabilitate the minor.

In general, the labour laws protecting family welfare, and as a result child welfare, have been progressive and preventive in nature. At the same time, a number of pitfalls have surfaced in the area of protection and rehabilitation. For example, several writers (Raffo, Rodriguez & Berrosteguieta 1986) have voiced concern about the lack of interdisciplinary team work in the field of rehabilitation. At present, problems affecting minors have multiple dimensions. As a result, the solutions should be comprehensive and should focus on the psycho-social-economic needs and aspirations of minors and significant others. Undoubtedly, such approach requires the active participation of professionals from different disciplines working together to develop and provide high quality and relevant services to all sectors of the population.

THE SICK AND INJURED

Everyone in Argentina is eligible to receive free medical care from health institutions run by national, provincial and local authorities. At the same time, workers are covered by health plans. Employers are asked to provide pre-admission and periodical check-ups for workers. Also, workers are required to have medical check-ups regularly.

Social Security

In case of sickness employees are assured of receiving their salaries during a period of three to six months, depending upon the years of employment with the same employer (less than five years, or more than five years). If the above mentioned period is over, and employees cannot return to their job, employers have to keep their position for a year. Furthermore, if workers cannot return to their position as a result of the sickness, employers have to offer them a less demanding position without reducing their salary. Otherwise the employer should provide financial support for lay-off.

Personal Social Services

Health care for the sick and injured has been the responsibility of different institutions in the public and private sector. In 1985, Buenos Aires and other larger cities in the country were the best served in the area of health care. Undoubtedly, access to health services and quality of care varies greatly according to geographical region. Traditionally, municipal and provincial hospitals have provided free services to anyone in need of health care.

In 1978, 67 per cent of hospital beds were in public facilities, 28 per cent in private institutions and 5 per cent in facilities sponsored by <u>Obras Sociales</u>. Public health centres provide outpatient services to community residents, such as immunisation, check-ups, prenatal care and emergency care.

The primary approach to the organisation of physicians, dentists and optometrists is private practice. In 1977 there were 55,000 physicians working in Argentina, equivalent to one physician for every 430 inhabitants. There were 16,000 dentists, an estimated ratio of one dentist to 1,400 inhabitants. Unfortunately, the same year showed an estimated ratio of one nurse to 800 inhabitants.

Evaluation

In Argentina, sickness and injury benefits and health care for older adults are the direct result of the efforts and struggles of the urban working class and labour legislation.

In general, public health institutions tend to be large, oriented towards low income groups and towards the training of health care providers, while private institutions are smaller and more business-oriented. Over the past decades improvements have been achieved in medical care. Many diseases, such as smallpox, yellow fever, diphtheria, have been controlled. The death rate has been lowered and people are living longer. In spite of the progress made in health care, many concerns still exist. Rural people do not have easy access to medical services; the lack of sufficient nursing personnel has a direct impact on the quality of medical care; and monies for needed health research are not available.

THE UNEMPLOYED

In 1985, Argentina had a highly skilled labour force that numbered 11.9 million. Approximately 37.9 per cent of the economically active population (total population aged 10 and over) participated in the labour force in 1983.

The total unemployment and underemployment averaged about 10.4 per cent during 1983 and 1984.

Social Security

The 1853 Constitution contains an amended Article 14 (1957) which introduced workers' protection against arbitrary discharge.

The Department of Labour regulates the subsidies to workers in case of involuntary occupational interruptions. According to labour laws those employers who are unable to keep a labour contract have the responsibility to give advance notice of the lay-off to the worker and pay indemnisation benefits according to seniority.

Argentina does not have unemployment insurance. As a result, certain measures have been created to provide assistance to the unemployed but their scope is quite limited. For example, in 1967 an unemployment fund was created by Law 17.258 for workers in the construction industry. In some labour sectors, such as the shipping industry, workers are guaranteed a minimum salary if the number of working hours is reduced due to lack of work. In 1984, by Decree 3984, a transitory system of protection for the unemployed was signed. According to this regulation the unemployed are eligible to receive any applicable family allowance, a cash benefit equivalent to 70 per cent of the minimum salary, and continuation of health care coverage. Unfortunately, this decree and many other unemployment laws created since 1984 have not been implemented.

Personal Social System

In Argentina, there is an emphasis on employment- and labour-related services, rather than on unemployment services. The unemployed can gain access any personal social service offered to the rest of the population. Specifically

unemployment-related services are those provided
by employment offices. A small number of them
have a national scope, such as the employment
offices sponsored by the National Department of
Human Resources and Employment, and the National
Department of Protection of the Minor and the
Family. The former assists the unemployed to seek
employment, informs government about workers'
migration patterns and makes public announcements
of job opportunities. The latter assists minors
(14-21 years of age) who are under government
custody to seek employment and periodically
controls their place of employment to verify the
employer's compliance with labour regulations
covering minors. Other employment offices are
managed by municipalities and private charitable
organisations. Furthermore, some of them provide
emergency assistance to help the unemployed with
their immediate needs.

Evaluation

The operation of unemployment compensation
programmes is deficient. Benefits are at a
minimum, do not replace lost wages and are not
tailored to deal with long-term unemployment.

ASSESSMENT OF THE ARGENTINE WELFARE SYSTEM

Social welfare policies require an examination
within the complex context of social and political
events that have dominated Argentina since the
mid-nineteenth century. During this period, from
being a highly developed country in the 1920s
Argentina became a so-called Third World country
in the 1980s. This decline explains, to a certain
extent, the existence of advanced policies in
areas related to social security and less
developed policies in areas related to the
personal social services, especially
institutionalisation of the homeless, foster care
and the handicapped to mention a few.

Despite this decline, social indicators show
signs of improvement in social conditions. For
example, infant mortality rates decreased markedly
from 87 per 1,000 live births in 1940 to 35.3 in
1985. Life expectancy in 1945 was 59 years while
in 1985 was 71 years of age. According to
estimates by UNESCO, the illiteracy rate in 1985
was only 4.5 per cent.

Argentina

Beyond the positive results of the welfare policies, there is a need to re-examine the goals of existing policies and develop new ones to answer the needs of the people of Argentina as they prepare to enter the advanced world of the twenty-first century.

REFERENCES AND FURTHER READING

Corradi, Y.E. (1985), The Fitful Republic: Economy, Society and Politics in Argentina, Boulder: Westview Press.

D'Antonio, D. (1973), Derecho de Menores, Buenos Aires: Abeledo Perrot.

Di Tella, T. (1984), 'The Popular Parties in Brazil and Argentina', Government and Opposition, 19(2), 250-68.

Ferrer, A. (1983), La Posguerra Programa para la Reconstruccion y el Desarrollo Argentino, Buenos Aires: El Cid Editor.

Hodges, D.C. (1976), Argentina, 1943-1976: The National Revolution and Resistance, Alburquerque: University of New Mexico Press.

Matera, R. & Serrano, M. (1986), Cual es el Futuro del Pais de los Argentinos? Buenos Aires: Plus Ultra.

Passanante, M.I. (1983), Politicas Sociales para la Tercera Edad, Buenos Aires: HUMANITAS.

Raffo, H., Rodriguez, M. & Berrosteguieta, Y. (1986), La Proteccion y Formacion Integral del Menor, Buenos Aires: Plus Ultra.

Rock, D. (ed.) (1975), Argentina in the Twentieth Century, Pittsburgh: University of Pittsburgh Press.

Rudolph, J. (ed.) (1985), Argentina, a Country Study, Washington, DC: The American University Press.

Skidmore, T.E. & Smith, P. (1984), Modern Latin America, New York: Oxford University Press.

World Bank (1985), Argentina, Economic Memorandum, Vol. 1, Washington, DC: The World Bank.

BRAZIL
Celso Barroso Leite

THE WELFARE SYSTEM ENVIRONMENT

Ideological Environment

Brazil was discovered in 1500 and subsequently settled by the Portuguese. It is basically a Latin country, which some regard as an environmental factor, although it is not clear exactly what is implied by such an observation. In regard to the Portuguese influence, it is often pointed out that Brazil inherited from its settlers an excessive involvement of the state in its political, economic and social structure (Malloy 1979, p.3).

Brazil was organised as a political state before it had become a cohesive nation. The result is the acknowledgement and acceptance of an excessive intervention of the state which is aggravated by the lack of a solid national basis for it.

To the extent that this is true, it can be inferred that the improper position of the state in Brazil often leads people to perceive it as a potential instrument of oppression and injustice, or as a possible source of benefits and privileges. This perception also applies to welfare measures, which frequently leads individuals, groups and even the government to try to resort to welfare solutions for problems which are more directly related to the economic structure, the production policies (or the lack thereof), the very low level of wages in general and other factors. Indications of this can be found in the early colonial days, after independence (1822), when Brazil became a monarchy, and in the current republican period

25

(since 1889). This situation, while far from typical in Latin America, certainly exists in Brazil.

There is a lack of community-mindedness in Brazil, resulting in a parallel exacerbation of the notion of individual rights and interests.

As a consequence of its Portuguese and Latin origins, Brazil is predominantly a Roman Catholic country, which has had a clear infuence on the welfare environment. Numerous welfare initiatives, particularly in regard to social services, are chiefly due to religious motivations, evidenced by the fact that many pious institutions have been named after Roman Catholic saints. More recently, the Catholic Church is less relevant than in the past, and is increasingly turning toward social and sometimes political action.

Naturally, there exists in Brazil Left, Right and Centre political influences, with different degrees of political power. However, it would seem hardly accurate to say there is a clearly articulated ideological value system underpinning social welfare as such. It would also be difficult to single out, among the various value influences mentioned, a clearly predominant one.

Historical Origins

The historical origins of welfare in Brazil become clearer when we analyse separately its three basic sectors: social insurance, medical care (now predominantly included in social insurance), and the personal social services. Figure 1 summarises the evolution of social insurance programmes in Brazil.

The origin of social insurance can be mainly ascribed to the great expansion of the programme soon after the First World War. The influence of the International Labour Organisation, especially through its activities related to social security, on the fabric of the social insurance system in Brazil, should not be forgotten. The country's industrial development in the first two decades of this century, no matter how modest, created at least minimal conditions for the adoption of social insurance, under the influence of the demonstrated effect of its rapid expansion in Europe, as well as of its inception in other Latin American countries.

FIGURE 1: EVOLUTION OF SOCIAL INSURANCE IN BRAZIL

Legislation	System Covered	Target Group Covered
Law 4682, 1923	First institutions	Railroad workers
Law 20465, 1931	Other institutions	Public utility workers
Several laws, 1932/1937	Bigger institutions	Commerce, bank, merchant marine, industry, transportation (other than railroad) workers
Law 3807, 1960	Uniformisation of schemes	Urban workers
Law 72, 1966	Unification of institutions	Urban workers
Law 11, 1971	Rural social insurance	Rural workers
Law 6036, 1974	Ministry of Social Insurance and Assistance	Workers in general and entire population
Law 6243, 1975 (and Decree 89312, 1984)	Consolidation of urban social insurance legislation	Urban workers
Law 6439, 1977	National Social Insurance and Assistance System - SINPAS (new administrative structure)	Workers in general and entire population

Surprisingly enough, social insurance appeared first in the non-rural sector (railroad workers in 1923), although Brazil's economy was then, and to a great extent still is, predominantly rural. Perhaps an explanation for this can be found in the fact that most of the agricultural production was exported and thus depended upon the railroads for transportation from the rural areas to the urban seaports. The rural social insurance scheme is still quite modest as compared to its non-rural counterpart.

Medical care started as early as the mid-sixteenth century, in the form of religious hospitals designed to provide individual medical assistance, or curative services to the Portuguese seamen, military, and initial settlers. In Brazil, like other former European colonies, the development of public health lags behind curative medical facilities. This has much to do with those original hospitals servicing transient patients. Later on, more medical societies of a private nature, who owned their own hospitals, were established to serve the well-to-do families of Portuguese extraction (Abel-Smith 1976).

The origins of personal social services, to use a term that is gaining in popularity, are far from precise, but it seems likely that this sector evolved mainly from mutualistic initiatives, promoted at first by predominantly religious groups and later by labour unions and other groups.

The Political and Socio-economic Environment

Brazil is a federal republic comprised of 23 states, three territories and a federal district, where its capital Brazilia is located.

In addition to the existence of three levels of government, frequently leading to administrative and political complications, an important political factor - and certainly a negative factor - is the growing excess of political interference in the administration and management of welfare programmes and institutions.

In addition to the generalised occurrence of the 'spoils system', key positions are openly traded by the government with the political parties, at the expense of the stability of their holders and the continuity of policies. This inevitably reflects on the quality of the welfare programmes and services.

Brazil

Brazil has a population of 140 million, which is very unevenly distributed over its 8.5 million square kilometres. Brazil has a multi-racial mixture, where the caucasians and quasi-caucasians are the largest and dominant group. Almost 50 per cent of the population is below the age of 20, but this cohort group is rapidly declining, owing to a decrease in the birth rate. Indeed Brazil has a growing number of people aged 65 or more. These demographic changes have important implications for welfare and especially social insurance policies.

In broader terms, what is really relevant about Brazil's population in relation to welfare is the enormous contrast between its lower and upper socio-economic groups.

Moreover, the general socio-economic conditions are quite precarious. Although Brazil was ranked eighth in 1986 among the world's national economies, its social and economic inequalities and socio-economic conditions in general displace it to a much lower level in terms of the standard of living and other indicators of the quality of life.

More specifically, a substantial part of Brazil's population has a very low standard of living and faces a severe scarcity of food, housing, medical services, schools, transport-ation, and employment. Unemployment is hard to fight, largely owing to illiteracy or the lack of professional skills. Underemployment or participation in the significant hidden sector of the economy does not contribute much to the alleviation of the welfare costs of unemployment.

The very low wages earned by most of the workforce stand in stark contrast to the high incomes received by the privileged, educated upper-class minority. It is worth mentioning that Brazil is known to be one of the five countries where income concentration is most acute.

Indeed the current political order in Brazil, is a transitional one seeking to bridge 20 years of authoritarianism and fully-fledged democracy. Brazil might eventually be disrupted by rapid deterioration of the economic situation, where inflation and its subsequent economic hardships play a crucial role.

Paradoxically, according to Mesa-Lago (1978) welfare programmes, or at least some of them, can be a negative factor. He also points out that in spite of its pivotal economic, social and political prominence in Latin America, social security has rarely been included in national planning and has received scant attention in social science literature.

His comments apply to Brazil and although the situation is changing they remain valid.

A 1985 survey concluded that it would be necessary to allocate each year an additional two per cent of the Gross Domestic Product (GDP) to social programmes in order to substantially reduce destitution and extreme poverty, and to raise the socio-economic conditions in general, by the turn of the century, to the levels now prevailing in Southern European countries like Spain and Greece.

Obviously, the unfavourable socio-economic conditions pose a serious dilemma for Brazil. On the one hand it is necessary for it to improve and expand its social programmes; but on the other hand this is extremely difficult in the absence of adequate economic means.

THE WELFARE SYSTEM: AN OVERVIEW

The Structure and Administration of the Welfare System

In 1977 Brazil established a Social Insurance and Assistance National System (known as SINPAS, its abbreviation in Portuguese), although not all welfare programmes and institutions come under its auspices.

SINPAS is conducted, coordinated and controlled by the Ministry of Social Insurance and Assistance, and comprises three autonomous bodies: National Social Insurance Institute (INPS), National Social Insurance Medical Assistance Institute (INAMPS), and Social Insurance and Assistance Financial Administration Institute (IAPAS); two foundations: Brazilian Assistance Legion Foundation (LBA), and National Foundation for the Welfare of Minors (FUNABEM); and a public corporation: Social Insurance Data-Processing Company (DATAPREV).

SINPAS is the basic federal welfare structure, covering, at least in theory, the entire population and especially through social insurance, the urban and rural workers in the private sector.

The temporary unemployment insurance benefit is administered by the Labour Ministry, rather than SINPAS, although Brazil's Constitution quite properly includes unemployment insurance among the social insurance programmes it prescribes.

The government at all levels provides pensions and other benefits to their statutory personnel, and sometimes to the non-statutory personnel as well, who otherwise are covered by the SINPAS social insurance programmes.

In addition, there are special schemes for specific groups, such as the members of the Armed Forces, the Legislature (at all levels of government) and the Judiciary (at the federal and state levels). SINPAS benefits and services vary greatly from those targeted for these specific groups. Moreover there are differences between the benefits granted under urban and rural social insurance schemes.

The federal, state and in some cases municipal governments, administer or subsidise a variety of programmes in the area of personal social services. State and municipal social programmes do not form part of SINPAS and the same is true of several federal ones.

The voluntary, non-profit programmes and institutions are a significant part of the Brazilian welfare system. In 1986 there were 40,000 institutions registered with the National Social Service Council, including a small number of educational and scientific institutions. The federal, state and municipal governments grant subsidies and tax exemptions to those which are registered institutions. In some cases the tax exemption applies even to the social insurance contributors, for example, to employers that provide welfare programmes for their employees, such as free or subsidised meals.

In the private sector, an important occupational welfare measure is the pension fund. A growing number of corporations provide pensions as fringe benefits to their employees. These are legally defined as being complementary to social insurance. The National Confederation of Industrial Employers administers a national welfare institution for industrial workers, the Industrial Social Service (SESI), which has state and municipal branches. The National Confederation of Commercial Employers does the same for commercial workers through its Commercial Social Service (SESC).

Brazil

Other occupational welfare plans featuring retirement and death pensions, other cash benefits, and health care have a welfare and mutualistic character but are commercially operated by private companies, much in the same way as the health plans.

Social Welfare Finances

Aggregate data referring to the financing of the personal social services are not available, since a significant part of these services are provided by agencies affiliated to SINPAS or with its participation. Since social security is the most important welfare programme in Brazil, it is appropriate to focus attention on the financing of SINPAS, with its three basic programmes: social insurance, medical assistance, and the personal social services.

SINPAS is financed by monthly social contributions which account for 88 per cent of its revenues. The balance comes from the federal budget (9 per cent), and the remainder from other sundry sources (3 per cent).

The social insurance contributions are levied on wages up to 20 times the designated minimum, and are paid by the employers and employees. The employer contributes 10 per cent of their payroll, the employee contributes from 8.5 to 10 per cent of their salary depending upon the salary level. The self-employed contribute 19.2 per cent of a designated basis that varies according to the number of years of contribution paid.

In addition, the employer contributes other payments which include financing the rural social insurance scheme and work injury disability insurance (according to occupational risk) which may raise their total contributions to 20 per cent of the payroll.

The employer deducts the employees' contributions from their salary and deposits them and their own contributions in the bank of their choice not later than the tenth workday of the month following that to which the contributions correspond.

The rural workers (both employees and self-employed) do not contribute towards their social insurance protection, but the rural employers must contribute 2.5 per cent of the commercial value of their production. The rural individual employers have a separate social insurance scheme.

There are fines and other penalties for arrears in payments of contributions and other irregularities connected with the deduction and deposit of the contributions.

The contributions and other revenues received by SINPAS are then distributed among its institutions, according to a Multi-year Financing Plan, by a board composed of their presidents and chaired by the Minister of Social Insurance and Assistance. Usually the distribution is as follows: social insurance cash benefits (INPS), 69 per cent; medical care (INAMPS), 22 per cent; personal social services (LBA and FUNABEM), 2 per cent; and administration (IAPAS), 7 per cent.

An important aspect of the financing of SINPAS is that the federal government not only is in charge of the payment of its personnel and administrative expenditures in general, but also acts as a guarantor in the event of a financial deficit.

Unemployment insurance is financed through the Fund for Assistance to the Unemployed, which receives part of a compulsory trade union contribution payable by all workers (one day's salary a year).

THE AGED

Brazil's population is ageing, but very slowly; people over age 65 are still only a little more than 4 per cent of the total population, therefore their numbers are currently not much of a problem.

Social Security

<u>Old Age Pensions</u>. The urban workers in general at age 65 (men) or 60 (women) or over are entitled, through social insurance, to an old age pension. Eligibility for the programme requires the payment of at least 60 monthly contributions. After age 70 years for men, or 65 for women, the urban workers can be compulsorily retired.

The urban old age pension is equal to 70 per cent of the average pensioner's salary in the last 36 months prior to retirement (the benefit salary), plus 1 per cent of the benefit salary for each year that contributions have been paid up to

25 years. Thus the maximum is 95 per cent of the benefit salary. If this benefit salary is over approximately nine times the minimum wage, the excess is computed somewhat differently. To compensate for inflation the salary of the earliest 24 months is adjusted according to official inflation indices. No old age pension can be less than 95 per cent of the minimum wage; moreover, the amount of the pension is adjusted for inflation in accordance with salary adjustments.

Special Retirement Pensions. In the rural sector the required minimum age for the old age pension is 65 years for both men and women; the qualifying period is three years of rural activity, and the pension is equal to half the minimum wage. There are other small differences between urban and rural pension schemes.

Length-of-service Retirement Pensions. The statutory civil servants in general retire after 35 years of service, regardless of their age, but there is compulsory retirement at age 70 regardless of their length of service. In the Armed Forces the retirement age is related to the specific post. In both cases the pensions are non-contributory.

Similarly, private sector employees are eligible for length-of-service retirement pensions.

Age Allowances. Another significant programme for the aged is the so-called 'olds' law, whereby every person over age 70, or invalided, is entitled to an allowance equal to half the minimum wage, provided they do not have an income above 50 per cent of the prevailing minimum wage, and they are not covered by social insurance, nor maintained by a person on whom they are legally dependent. This programme can be considered as a step forward in the gradual evolution of Brazil's social security system from its social insurance basis to a more generous form of social protection to cover those individuals in need but not receiving benefits from the insurance system.

Fiscal Welfare. Income tax deductions are granted to people over 65 years of age.

Brazil

Personal Social Services

Social insurance programmes provide personal
social services to the aged. Basically, INPS' and
INAMPS' social workers focus their efforts on
eligibility for benefits and utilisation of
medical services.

In addition, LBA and other agencies have
regular and special programmes geared to the aged,
who are the object of growing attention by such
agencies, as the number of the aged increase.

Evaluation

In financial terms the chief problem for social
insurance (cash benefits and medical care) is the
impact of longevity on pension costs. Life
expectancy has increased from a little over 40
years in 1940 to about 78 years in 1987; however
the pensionable age is between 60 and 65 years.
This means a longer pension duration, more medical
care, heavier expenditures and a less favourable
dependency ratio (inactive/active economic
population).

As for the broader aspects of the question,
such as welfare and ultimately the quality of
life, it seems safe to say that, since the aged
and especially the very old are to a great extent
concentrated in the upper levels of society, their
average financial situation is better than that of
the population in general.

The lack of a minimum retirement age in Brazil
has social security implications of potential
significance.

In Brazil the private urban workers can retire
after 35 years of service for men and 30 years for
women, although the limit can be lower in the case
of arduous occupations (25, 20 or even 15 years).
While the general length-of-service retirement
pension is not subject to any age limit at all,
some of these special retirement pensions for
arduous occupations are subject to the age limit
of 50 years. Because Brazil's Constitution
establishes that a person can start working at 12
years of age, a woman can theoretically retire at
42 and a man at 47, and receive 95 per cent of
their benefit salary as a pension. Although this
does not happen often, because no-one is allowed
to work in an arduous occupation before they reach
age 18, it is technically possible for a miner,

for example, to retire at 33, if he started working at 18. This situation has numerous disadvantages in theory and in practice, as well as from the viewpoint of social justice. For instance: a person less than 50 years of age who holds a pension can work for a lower salary than others, which means unfair competition in the labour market; similarly, it is not fair to grant a costly social benefit to a person who does not need it. As a consequence, many specialists recommend at least the reinstatement of the 50-year age limit established when the length-of-service retirement pension was created in 1923.

A provision to establish a minimum retirement age has been included in various projects for improvement and reformulation of the social insurance legislation. But this essential correction is a very sensitive political question, and nothing concrete has been achieved, although there is a growing consciousness of the importance of the matter.

THE DISABLED AND HANDICAPPED

In Brazil's welfare terminology - disability (or invalidity) - is more closely associated with a complete loss of working capacity, whereas a handicap is usually a congenital impairment.

Regarding the incidence of disability, SINPAS figures indicate that from 1975 to 1986 the number of the corresponding pensions increased from 699,565 to 1,103,581 in the urban sector and from 80,975 to 463,324 in the rural sector.

Social Security

Invalidity Pensions. An invalidity pension is payable after 12 monthly contributions have been paid by the employer (the qualifying period) to a worker considered by a social insurance medical inspector as unable to work. This may be due to a non-occupational injury or disease which is not curable, even after rehabilitation efforts, for the worker to earn sufficient for his maintenance. There is an extensive medical procedure, involving specific medical assessment standards, to determine the degree of incapacity. In the case of some very severe diseases the qualifying period is waived including cases of diseases where segregation of the patient is required.

This invalidity pension for urban workers is equal to 70 per cent of the worker's average salary in the last 12 months (the benefit salary), plus 1 per cent of the benefit salary for each year that contributions have been paid, up to 30 years. The maximum pension is thus 100 per cent of the benefit salary. If the benefit salary is above approximately nine times the prevailing minimum wage, the excess is computed somewhat differently.

The invalidity pension for rural workers is equal to one-half of the prevailing minimum wage.

This benefit is due from the sixteenth day after the worker stops working, and is paid while they remain unable to work. It is usually a lifetime benefit and the disability pensioner is not allowed to work. If they do the benefit is cancelled.

Up to 55 years of age the invalidity pensioner must undergo examinations required and the treatments and rehabilitation services provided by the INAMPS, but any surgery is optional.

Invalid Allowances. Under the 'olds' law, low income invalids not covered by social insurance, are entitled to an allowance one-half the minimum wage.

Benefits to Invalid Dependents of Covered Workers. Invalids who are the dependent sons, daughters, or spouse of a covered worker are entitled to medical care and, after the worker's death, to a survivor's pension.

Work Injuries Disability Pension. In 1919, some four years before the creation of the social insurance system, Brazil established a work injury disability pension programme. It is currently administered by INPS as a part of social insurance.

The benefits of INAMPS and IAPAS are the victims of industrial accidents and are not subject to any qualifying period and, in the urban sector, they are determined on the basis of the last monthly salary received by the injured worker. If the employee's earnings are variable, the salary basis is their average earnings over the previous 12 or 18 months, whichever is more favourable to the worker (or their survivor).

These urban disability pensions are equal to 100 per cent of the employee's monthly salary, obtained by multiplying by 30 their salary at the day of the accident; and the amount thus found is increased by 25 per cent if they need constant attendance. In addition they receive a lump-sum benefit equal to 15 times the reference value, periodically established by the government (usually less than one-half of the minimum wage). The rural disability pension is equal to 75 per cent of the minimum wage.

The urban worker who is partly but permanently disabled by an industrial accident is entitled to an accident allowance (equal to 40 per cent of their pre-disability salary (calculated in the same way as the disability pension). This benefit is payable if they recover their working capacity but not for the same occupation at the time of the accident). A supplementary allowance, equal to 20 per cent of their pre-disability salary (similarly calculated) is payable if they recover their working capacity for the same occupation, but with limitations and therefore have some difficulty in working.

Private industrial accident coverage administratively is under SINPAS, although the benefits received are distinct from those of the other social insurance programmes. A few specialists have done their best to demonstrate the disadvantages of such dual coverage, but tradition and inertia have thus far prevented much progress towards the full integration of the two schemes.

Medical Care. The disabled and the handicappped covered by any social insurance programme are entitled to medical care and rehabilitation services under the various social insurance programmes.

Personal Social Services

Personal social services for the disabled and handicapped are mostly provided in connection with social insurance benefits, medical care and rehabilitation programmes. INPS' and INAMPS' social workers help the disabled and handicapped apply for the benefits to which they may be entitled and have access to medical and rehabilitation services. After treatment the social workers help them find jobs compatible with their reduced ability.

Evaluation

Within the limitations of Brazil's socio-economic conditions, it would be difficult to admit that its disabled and handicapped are satisfactorily taken care of.

Owing chiefly to the fact that the wages are very low, especially in worker groups who are more prone to becoming disabled, the invalidity and disability pensions and related benefits are very low. Besides, medical care is sometimes inadequate and rehabilitation services are virtually non-existent.

NEEDY FAMILIES

No matter how nebulous the category of needy families is it is indisputable that they are a sad reality in Brazil. The findings of a National Research Based on Residential Sample, completed in 1984 by the federal government statistics indicated that four per cent of the families in Brazil had no income at all, 24 per cent had incomes up to the minimum wage, which means that 28 per cent of the families were destitute. Since another 24 per cent had an income between the minimum wage and twice the minimum wage, more than one-half of all families are below the poverty line. In other words: at least 52 per cent of families are needy.

Social Security

Welfare measures for needy families are the responsibility of INPS. The family allowance programme has as its goal stability of the family as a whole, rather than focussing on children, and in some cases youth. Since the benefit is paid to the father, the mother or both, the benefit automatically becomes family income. A family allowance equal to 5 per cent of the minimum wage per child up to 14 years of age (or invalid), whatever the number of children, is payable to urban employees. If both parents are employed, with earnings below the poverty line, both are entitled to the benefit. Eligible employees receive the benefit with their salary, and the employers then deduct the amount paid from the social insurance contribution liability.

The invalidity, disability, old age and length-of-service pensioners beyond the age of 65 are also entitled to the family allowance, which is added to their pensions by INPS.

Survivors' Pensions. These benefits have a direct relationship to the welfare of needy families, since a substantial number of families receive this benefit, due to the deceased worker's dependents. These are: (a) wife or invalid husband; (b) children, brothers, and sisters; (c) mother and/or invalid father; (d) in a few cases, a person maintained by the worker and formally designated by them as a dependent. If the worker lived with a woman out of wedlock, she can be considered his dependent; in some cases this can apply to a man in relation to a female worker. Wife (or invalid husband) and children are legally presumed to be dependents; but the others have to prove their dependency. The widow (or invalid widower) is entitled to 50 per cent of the invalidity pension payable to the deceased worker at the time of the death (family share), plus 10 per cent of the benefit (individual share). If there are eligible children other individual shares are added, up to 100 per cent of the invalidity pension (five pensioners), and the total is equally divided amongst the pensioners. If death resulted from an industrial accident, the death pension is 100 per cent of the deceased worker's last monthly salary, whatever the number of pensioners.

The Brazilian Assistance Legion (LBA). This provides assistance basically aimed at poor people in general, which naturally includes needy families. The LBA sponsors or subsidises assistance programmes destined for the needy in general and especially for pregnant women, mothers, infants, children and aged. The assistance thus provided can comprise programmes and other initiatives related to food, health, education, professional training, employment placement and legal matters. LBA is increasingly intent on promoting community participation in social services, as well as developing community and private initiatives in this area. More specifically, the LBA promotes different forms of voluntary social work.

The National Foundation for the Welfare of Minors (FUNABEM). This programme is in charge of promoting the national policy for the welfare of minors.

The National Social Insurance Medical Assistance Institute (INAMPS). This programme provides free medical assistance and other health services to the needy.

Personal Social Services

Other federal, state and municipal agencies outside SINPAS administer, subsidise or promote personal social services, that, although not destined specifically for needy families, ultimately operate especially to their advantage.

At the federal level a special Department for Community Action (SEAC) was created in 1985, within the Personal Cabinet of the President of the Republic. The objective of SEAC is to channel resources to local community action programmes, restricting itself financially to complement community efforts aimed at the low-income populations in the outskirts of big cities and the rural areas.

In the crucial area of food, SEAC and the Food and Nutrition National Institute, sometimes jointly with the SINPAS' LBA and other agencies, administer, sponsor or subsidise various programmes, basically geared to needy families. The Popular Food Programme (PAP) is designed to give the neediest segments of the population access to basic foods. The Food Supplement Programme (PSA) targets pregnant women, mothers who are breast-feeding, and infants up to three years from poor families. The School Children Food National Programme (PNAE) is better known as the school lunch programme which has as its target population school age children. The Workers' Food Programme (PAT) provides employers with fiscal incentives to provide their workers with food. The National Milk Programme for Needy Children (PNLCC) is the most recent federal food programme.

Brazil

Evaluation

In assessing the support available to needy families in Brazil it seems fair to conclude that the situation is quite unsatisfactory. The basic problems of need, poverty, and destitution, especially of the needy families - more than 50 per cent of families - have yet to be solved.

The family allowance is really a social assistance measure, since the receipt of 5 per cent of the minimum wage is of little significance to well-paid workers but of great importance to low-paid workers.

The number and variety of public agencies that operate in the social protection area, erratically and sometimes even in conflict, may well be aggravating the situation.

The voluntary sector certainly contributes to the welfare of needy families, but it is fragmented and multifarious in action. The same is true at least in part of the state and municipal activities of this nature.

CHILDREN AND YOUTH

Brazil is experiencing an extremely rapid urbanisation of its population. In 1940 only 33 per cent of its 41 million population lived in the cities, whereas in 1987, when the population has more than tripled to 140 million, some 70 per cent live in cities. There are thus some 100 million people crowding the urban centres, and especially the major cities, of which an estimated 10-36 million are minors.

Some studies suggest there are less than 10 million destitute children and youth; others estimate as high as 36 million, of which 7 million are living in the streets, in total abandonment. Some authors refer to 4.5 million teenage prostitutes living off the streets. A conservative and probably correct estimate would be 12 million needy minors. The data on children, especially needy children, is unreliable and in some cases, not even available.

Social Security

Children and youth receive benefits through social insurance programmes, therefore under the auspices of SINPAS.

Survivors' Pensions. These are payable to the
dependents of an urban worker who dies after
having contributed at least 12 monthly social
insurance payments. This qualifying period is
waived if the death was caused by an industrial
accident. The dependents include the urban
worker's unmarried children up to age 18 for sons
or 21 for daughters. If the child is an invalid,
the age limit does not apply. The siblings within
the same age limits may also be entitled to the
survivor's pension, but only if the deceased
worker did not have a wife, or invalid husband,
and children. For civil servants, and especially
the military, the concept of a dependent is much
broader, and may include grandchildren.

In the event of a non-occupational death, the
amount of the pension is equal to one-half of the
covered workers' disability or invalidity pension
payable at the time of death, plus 10 per cent of
that entitlement for each dependent up to a
maximum of five dependents. Therefore the
survivor's pension can equal 100 per cent of the
disability pension. When such a survivor becomes
ineligible because of age or marriage the pension
payable to the remaining survivors is recalculated.

In the event of an occupational death, the
pension payable is equal to the deceased worker's
monthly salary calculated according to the salary
on the day of the accident. If a survivor's
pensioner ceases to be entitled to their pension,
then the amount of that pension is equally divided
amongst the remaining survivors.

Under the rural social insurance system the
survivor's pension is equal to 50 per cent of the
minimum wage or 75 per cent in the case of
industrial accident, and is payable to dependents
(defined in the same way as to urban workers).

Personal Social Services

The National Foundation for the Welfare of Minors
(FUNABEM). A 1964 law established a national
policy for the welfare of minors, and a foundation
under the administration of SINPAS, with
programmes implemented through state-based
agencies affiliated with FUNABEM. Although its
basic function is to promote the implementation of
such policy, especially by setting standards and
norms, FUNABEM operates directly a few pilot
institutions, in two states. FUNABEM subsidises

43

or otherwise develops programmes and other initiatives for church, community and other groups. At the same time some of its activities are carried out jointly with international organisations such as UNICEF. For example, UNICEF participates, with FUNABEM, in more than 400 alternative projects destined to promote exchange of concrete experiences in the crucial area of welfare of minors.

Other personal social services for children and youth include food programmes.

The role of voluntary agencies is significant in providing services for the welfare of minors. Regardless of how uncoordinated, sporadic and precarious these services may be, these agencies, campaigns, movements and other initiatives for welfare certainly have favourable effects, in the sense that they may solve or alleviate the problems of at least a number of minors.

Urban firms and employers contribute 2.4 per cent of their payroll to help finance primary education, especially scholarships for needy children. In addition there is a special programme, financed by a portion of the product of the compulsory trade union contributions, destined to provide scholarships (primary and secondary education) for workers' children, which is administered by the Labour Ministry.

Urban firms and employers also contribute 1 per cent of their payroll for the financing of a programme for professional training for young workers (apprentices) and other courses, and the Labour Ministry maintains a similar programme in the rural sector.

Fiscal Welfare. Up to 21 years of age, a youngster is considered dependent for the purpose of income tax reduction. This age limit is raised to 24 if the youngster is attending a university.

Juvenile Delinquency. Brazil has had since 1949 a Minors' Code, according to which the youngsters under 18 are judged for crimes and other forms of misconduct.

Evaluation

In spite of all these programmes, agencies, national and state policies, targeted at destitute minors, they remain one of Brazil's most serious

welfare problems. This situation has worsened
recently, with the growing deterioration of
overall socio-economic conditions. There is a
growing preoccupation with the sad lot of the
millions of minors who roam the streets and sleep
on sidewalks, half-naked, and who, in groups, beg,
assault and very likely will soon change from
marginals into criminals.

At the same time, people have begun to realise
that social programmes, especially those aimed at
children and youth in general, especially those in
low income families, constitute a sound investment
in human capital.

THE SICK AND INJURED

It is social insurance that takes care of those
who suffer a work interruption due to sickness or
injury. For dependents, there is no specific form
of social protection other than free medical care.

Social Security

Sickness Allowances. Workers are eligible after
12 monthly contributions (the qualifying period)
who are considered by the social insurance medical
inspectors to be unable to work after 15 days (the
waiting period), as a consequence of sickness or
injury. The social insurance special medical
inspection service determines eligibility for
sickness allowances, which is quite separate from
the medical care service.

In the urban sector the benefit is payable
from the sixteenth day off work and continues
while the recipient is unable to work. During
this period the worker is legally considered on
paid leave. Employers must pay their first 15
days of absence.

The monthly amount of the sickness allowance
is equal to 70 per cent of the worker's average
salary in the last 12 months (the benefit salary),
plus 1 per cent of the salary for each year of
contribution up to 20 years, that is, 90 per cent
in total. If the benefit salary is over
approximately nine times the minimum wage, the
excess is computed somewhat differently. If the
injury is the result of an industrial accident the
amount payable is equal to 92 per cent of the
worker's monthly salary, calculated on the basis

of the salary of the day of the accident, and is payable from the following day.

The sickness allowance sometimes functions as a type of informal and not quite legitimate type of unemployment benefit. Some social insurance medical inspectors, when examining a worker who is not in full health but is over 45 years of age, which greatly reduces their probability of finding a new job, may find reasons to attest to their temporary incapacity to work through illness, thus enabling them to collect the sickness allowance.

In the rural sector the sickness allowance is also payable to members of the family of a rural producer whose work, in the family economy, is indispensable for their subsistence. Its amount is equal to 50 per cent of the minimum wage or, in case of industrial accident, equal to 75 per cent of the minimum wage.

The recipient of the sickness allowance is required to undergo examinations and the recommended treatment and rehabilitation processes provided by social insurance, except surgical treatment, which is optional.

Occupational Benefits. In the public sector the federal, state and municipal governments grant their personnel, both civil and military, full paid leave during sickness, as well as medical care and, in some cases, rehabilitation services.

Medical and Rehabilitation Services. The sick or injured workers, both in the urban and in the rural sectors, are required to use the medical care and rehabilitation services available to them. The basic idea is that the workers should recover their working capacity as rapidly as possible.

The National Social Insurance Medical Assistance Institute (INAMPS) operates directly or under contract with other public health care agencies, as well as with most private hospitals and doctors in the country. Besides contracting with INAMPS the public hospitals operate their own programmes and the private medical network is also utilised by the public on a fee-for-service basis. INAMPS, directly or indirectly, provides about 75 per cent of all medical care in Brazil.

Medical care comprises out-patient services, hospitalisation, surgery and dental treatment, as well as the provision of medicines, which is a programme administered by a special agency of the

Health Ministry.
Especially in the private urban sector there are some rehabilitation centres and smaller units, but this service is provided only at very modest levels.

Maternity Benefits. Maternity, obviously, is neither a disease nor an injury, but it similarly incapacitates individuals temporarily for work. Social insurance grants female employees a maternity benefit for four weeks before and eight weeks after childbirth, or, in very special cases, in the opinion of the social insurance medical inspectors, six weeks before and 10 weeks after. The amount of the benefit is equal to the salary, and employers pay the benefit directly, and then deduct its amount from their social insurance contributions. As the maternity benefit is considered a salary, it is subject to the required social insurance contributions.

Public Health Programmes. This is under the Health Ministry, but lately INAMPS has sponsored, subsidised or promoted some initiatives in this area.

Personal Social Services

Personal social services to the sick and injured are provided primarily in connection with social insurance. INPS' and INAMPS' social workers help the sick and injured apply for benefits payable to them and avail themselves of medical services.
To those not covered by social insurance personal social services are provided by LBA and other agencies, especially in the urban areas.

Evaluation

The entire structure of medical care delivery is currently being reformulated and some of the ideas proposed are:

. to enhance the utilisation of the public medical facilities, as against contracting medical services;

. to concentrate the administration of medical services in the Health Ministry, with or without INAMPS, especially for the purpose of achieving a better balance between public health and medical care services;

. to decentralise the implementation of the medical care programmes to the municipal level as much as possible.

Because of the rapidly increasing cost of medical services, especially medical technology, health care in Brazil leaves much to be desired. In Brazil this situation is seriously aggravated by the precarious health conditions of large segments of the population, negatively affected by the present deterioration of living conditions in general, as a result of economic and other difficulties. However, income replacement programmes provide a satisfactory level of social protection to the sick and injured.

THE UNEMPLOYED

Unemployment is a relatively recent phenomenon in Brazil. Until two or three decades ago underemployment and seasonal or temporary unemployment existed, along with isolated cases of long term unemployment, but not the personal and social problems of chronic unemployment.

There are still millions of people who are illiterate and badly prepared for participation in formal employment. However, never having had any regular, formal employment, they cannot be considered as unemployed.

In the mid-1980s however, owing especially to population growth and a slowing rate of economic development, there is unemployment, that is, loss of jobs by those who occupied them.

Estimates of unemployment vary and some specialists fear that accurate statistical data are not available. A realistic estimate places the unemployment rate around 8 per cent of the approximately 50 million in the actual labour market, or about four million people in the mid 1980s. Lately labour market conditions have deteriorated further and it seems reasonable to estimate that five million people are out of work because they have lost their jobs.

There are no accurate data, however, on the additional millions who have never been employed, leading a marginal life and surviving on the basis of trivial activities of little or no economic significance.

Similarly, there are a growing number of people engaged in occupations connected to the so-called hidden or informal economy. A very important welfare implication is the fact that these informal workers, besides the precariousness of their labour relations, are not covered by social insurance. In other words, their present needs may somehow be taken care of, but their future is completely unprotected.

Social Security

At least in theory, Brazil has two forms of social protection against unemployment.

<u>Unemployment Allowance</u>. These benefits amount to 50 per cent of the minimum wage and are payable to the employees who have worked at least 120 days for the same employer, when that employer lays off, without a fair reason, more than 50 employees within a two-month period. This modest and complex programme, which is under-utilised, is administered by the Labour Ministry in cooperation with the worker trade unions.

<u>Unemployment Insurance</u>. Without eliminating the quite precarious unemployment allowance, a 1986 law created a modest form of unemployment insurance designed to provide a 'temporary benefit' to the unemployed worker who:

. has contributed to social insurance for at least 30 months during the last four years;

. is in covered employment;

. has been unemployed for over 30 days; and

. does not have a net income sufficient for the maintenance of themselves and their families.

The temporary benefit is payable for no longer than four months in an 18-month period of time; and is cancelled if the recipient refuses a similar job.

The unemployment benefit is equal to:

Brazil

- 50 per cent of the worker's average salary in the last three months provided the salary was not over three times the minimum wage; or

- 150 per cent of that salary if the worker's salary was above this limit.

Personal Social Services

The Labour Ministry has a national network of placement agencies, and various other public agencies, like SINPAS' Brazilian Assistance Legion (LBA) which offer employment services training, readaptation, placement and so forth.

The private employment services should also be mentioned in this connection, as well as the manpower companies. The latter companies operate chiefly in the area of temporary work and only recently have been legally regulated.

Evaluation

Automation begins to be felt in Brazil as a negative factor in relation to the supply of employment opportunities. As the preoccupation with automation increases, government officials, labour union leaders, and social scientists apply themselves to the search for solutions to this new and ominous problem. So far there are neither figures nor an indication of efficient and effectual ways to address this problem.

As a consequence of the high rate of population growth (over 2 per cent), it is necessary to create some 1.7 million new jobs per year. At present the reduced rate of economic development appears to be insufficient to meet this growth.

Therefore, it is feared that the current situation, already far from satisfactory, tends toward further deterioration, if the unfavourable conditions now prevailing cannot be overcome.

In the recently completed first year of operation of the temporary unemployment insurance benefit, the number of applicants grew steadily, but even in the last month of this first year only 20 per cent of the estimated unemployed had applied for this benefit, 37 per cent of whom were declared ineligible.

50

ASSESSMENT OF THE BRAZILIAN WELFARE SYSTEM

Brazil's entire population is covered by the country's welfare system, of which the National Social Insurance and Assistance System (SINPAS) is the main component.

The SINPAS social insurance scheme, the responsibility of the National Social Insurance Institute (INPS), and the state, municipal and other social insurance schemes cover practically the total economically active population. It accounts for about 5 per cent of the Gross Domestic Product. Those, however, who work in the growing sector of the so-called hidden or informal economy are not covered and their number is unknown.

The SINPAS and other personal social service programmes are targeted at all needy people (adults and minors), but again it is not known what the actual coverage is.

Social insurance, the basic welfare programme, is widely criticised, especially in regard to medical care. Surprisingly, however, the criticism comes chiefly from the press and other communication media, political candidates, and other groups who are not its basic clientele.

Its regular users are not so pessimistic in their assessment of the social insurance benefits and services provided, or even the operational procedures and administrative practices used by welfare agencies involved, although they are generally considered quite unsatisfactory by some. In a 1987 poll taken in the three largest cities in Brazil involving only social insurance users, 65 per cent of the respondents relied on the services provided, 25 per cent relied on the services with reservation, and only 10 per cent did not rely on the services. It is true that most social insurance and social services users do not have an alternative, but nevertheless the findings of this poll have some meaning.

Reassuring as these findings may be, social insurance needs improvement, as do the personal social service programmes. The survivors and invalidity pensioners must be further protected against inflation. Medical care will certainly gain from a better coordination of its provision and a closer integration with public health. The length-of-service retirement pension without a minimum age limit is costly and creates social inequities. The special conditions of the coverage of industrial accidents are anachronistic and illogical. The operation of the administrative machinery is far from efficient.

A foremost consideration in the assessment of welfare practices in Brazil is the fact that welfare constitutes only part of the prevailing socio-economic, political and cultural conditions affecting the population of Brazil and the quality of life. Therefore, welfare programmes are a reflection of the past and current conditions of the country.

In spite of the inadequacies and whatever other flaws exist in the welfare programmes and measures, clearly dominated by social insurance, these programmes are Brazil's most important social policy agent in meeting human needs.

REFERENCES

Abel-Smith, B. (1976), Value for Money in Health
    Services, London: Heinemann.

Malloy, J. M. (1979), The Politics of Social
    Security in Brazil, Pittsburgh: University of
    Pittsburgh Press.

Mesa-Lago, C. (1978), Social Security in Latin
    America, Pittsburgh: University of Pittsburgh
    Press.

CHILE
Silvia Borzutzky

THE WELFARE SYSTEM ENVIRONMENT

Historical Origins

The historical origins of Chile's social welfare system can be divided into three major periods; up to 1924, 1924 to 1974 and since 1974.

Prior to 1924. Although the first set of social and labour laws in Chile date from 1924 the origin can be found in the socio-economic and political crisis that affected Chile around the turn of the twentieth century. At this time there were fundamental changes occurring in the nature and function of the state, the enfranchisement of the working class, the acceptance of new political organisations, improvements in working and living conditions of the workers, and the passage of social legislation and labour laws.

Before 1924 Chile's social legislation was formed by a few isolated laws that dealt with specific issues. The most important of these were the Worker's Accident Law of 1916, which established a limited employers liability system and established the employer's obligation of discharging the burden of proof, and the Nursery Law, which obliged the employer to maintain nurseries in industries employing more than 50 employees. The first pension fund dates back to 1918 and was designed to provide pensions to blue and white collar railroad workers.

The need to carry out major transformations in the functions and role of the state, including the passage of social legislation, was manifest in 1920 with the election of the Arturo Alessandri to the Presidency. He campaigned for constitutional and labour reforms (Stevenson 1938). Two major bills dealing with the creation of a social insurance system were introduced to Congress between 1921 and 1924. The Liberal Bill introduced by President Alessandri proposed the creation of a national insurance scheme applicable to both blue and white collar workers and included a full range of benefits for disabled and able bodied workers. The Conservative Bill, on the other hand, was heavily influenced by the German social insurance system aimed at establishing a pension system for blue collar workers exclusively (Morris 1966). Neither bill was enacted.

In spite of the seriousness of the socio-economic crisis in Chile, the massive unemployment rate in the nitrate and copper mines, and the impact of both the Russian Revolution (1918) and the Mexican Revolution (1919) the Chilean Congress obstructed the passage of socio-economic legislation in the early to mid-1920s, thus paralysing the entire nation, all in an attempt to maintain the autocratic exclusionary system of government (Aldunate 1969; Alessandri 1952; Morris 1966). On 5 September 1924 the military acted to put an end to this paralysis by means of a coup de etat.

1924 to 1974. The development of the Chilean social security system during this period was a natural by-product of the political organisation and economic problems that confronted Chile. It represents a fundamental element in the relationships between the state and society. The system mirrored the fragmented organisation of labour and the client relationships that elements of organised labour established with particular political parties. This produced a fragmented social security system which protected the most articulate group within the political coalition. The system that evolved focussed on the protection of the dependent urban worker while excluding independent workers and rural labour. Indeed, by 1964 92.4 per cent of the wage earning population were covered by the Chilean social security system. It should be pointed out, however, that distribution of the coverage was very uneven.

The method of financing social security during this period involved contributions from employers, the workers and the state in regard to the Blue Collar Workers Fund, while only employers and employees were expected to contribute to the Civil Servant and the White Collar Workers Funds. Between 1925 and 1964 the two general financial systems degenerated into about 50 financial sub-systems, creating a totally anarchic financial structure and thus constant deficits.

The four major types of benefits provided during this period include pensions, family allowances, health and maternity benefits, and cash benefits.

In addition, a non-contributory workmen's compensation programme, which was financed entirely by the employer and administered by private insurance companies, provided benefits and health care to injured workers.

By the mid-1960s the administration of social welfare in Chile was the responsibility of 19 pension funds in the public sector and 16 in the private sector; about 50 welfare agencies in the public sector and an undetermined number in the private sector; about 24 public assistance institutions and seven workmen's compensation funds. In addition, the following public agencies were involved; the <u>Superintendencia de Seguridad Social</u>, the General Comptroller Office; the Ministry of Labour and Social Security; the Ministry of Public Health; the Ministry of Finance; and the National Planning Office. It is important to note that this dismemberment of the social welfare system was not related to any expansion of its coverage, since the five original funds had the potential of providing protection to all but the independent workers, who never received any coverage during this period.

This chaotic administrative structure, in turn, increased the cost of social welfare in Chile. By 1964 Chile's social security system was amongst the most expensive in the world. Social security revenue amounted to 12.2 per cent of Gross National Product (GNP) while expenditures were equal to 8.2 per cent of GNP (Mesa-Lago 1978).

Even more salient than the cost itself was the unequal distribution of resources and inefficiency of pensions. The Chairman of the Commission of Reform appointed by President Jorge Alessandri, Jorge Prat noted in 1965: that the present social security system is condemned to disintegration because it is unfair, because it is oligarchic, because it is discriminatory and because it is inefficiently expensive, both for the working population and for the national economy (CESSC 1965, p.xvi).

The Prat social security reform recommendations were never implemented, but his Commission's report is the most authoritative and complete analysis of the system.

Over the next six years attempts were made by the Frei administration to reform Chile's social security system. After extensive investigation, a number of reform bills were developed but their passage through Congress did not occur because the social security reform issue generated a political uproar of such magnitude that reform was impossible. In fact, the social security system had become such an intrinsic part of the entire political system that its reform was not possible unless the entire political system was reformed (Borzutzky 1983, Ch.5).

The early 1970s saw the emergence of the Allende administration. Although social security policies were not at the centre of Chile's political discussions during this period these policies were used, as in the past, by both the government and the opposition to strengthen their electoral forces. Those policies implied the expansion of the system to accommodate new pressure groups and to attempt to restructure the health delivery system.

Chile's democratic political regime was destroyed in the bloody coup of 11 September 1973.

Since 1974. The military government that replaced the Allende administration faced two fundamental tasks: the elimination of the remnants of the old regime and the reorganisation of Chilean society along new lines. The transformation followed a neo-liberal economic model and it took place under a political system that was strongly authoritarian.

The Pinochet administration decided to initiate reform of the social security system very early in its life. Between 1973 and 1974 the government replaced all the numerous family allowance programmes by a unified system, the Fondo Unico de Prestaciones Familiares. This was followed by other reforms that took away the administration of family allowances from the pension fund and gave it to a new type of organisation: the Cajas de Compensacion de la Asignacion Familiar. Moreover, in 1981 family allowances were expanded to cover children of indigents, even when they were not contributing to the social security system.

Until 1974 the majority of Chile's population did not have protection in case of unemployment, that year the government established a general and unified system of unemployment relief.

The expansion of the very rudimentary system of welfare pensions occurred in 1975.

More significant reforms occurred in 1978 when the Pinochet government decided to focus on three major problems: the insufficiency of pensions, the question of indexation, and the inequalities of benefits.

Further reforms took place in 1980 which were geared to transform not only the economic and social roles of the state in Chile but also to establish a new economic system guided by neo-liberal principles. The 1980 reform modified the nature of the pension system for all blue and white collar workers, either in the public sector or the private sector, except the military. The two most important aspects of the reform relate to financial and administrative matters. The 1980 legislative reform changed the basis of the financial system by eliminating the employer's contribution and transforming the common fund into individual funds. These reforms were aimed at reducing the cost of labour. Indeed the establishment of the individual funds and the elimination of employer's contributions are the two most essential elements of the new financial structure and the new system, which is, in fact, a compulsory private insurance system.

The 1980 legislation drastically changed the administration of the pension system. The principle of subsidiarity of the state, the need to develop the local capital market and the need to improve the administration of the social security fund, led the administration to argue that social security should be placed in the private sector. In order to achieve this goal the new law created a new organisation, the Administradoras de Fondos de Pensiones (AFP), a pension funds managing corporation, which is charged with the administration of individual funds and the provision of social security benefits established by law (D.L. 3500, ART.23).

Ideological Environment

Since the military coup in September 1973 the ideological environment surrounding the Chilean welfare system has been dominated by neo-liberal economic values and political authoritarianism. It is perhaps most aptly summed up by the words of the then Minister of Labour and Social Security in 1980, Jose Pinera, who argued that:

> the collectivist philosophy that inspired the [social security] system which is based on a false vision of men and society, creates systems that, in the final analysis, turn themselves against men and especially against the poorest and the weakest amongst them (Santiago, 29 June 1980).

Political Environment

Chile is a republic divided into 12 regions and a metropolitan area.

Until September 1973 Chile had one of Latin America's most stable democracies. On 11 September 1973, a military Junta led by General Pinochet overthrew the Allende government and began the process of dismantling the previous political system and organising society along new lines. In the new government power was concentrated in the hands of the Junta de Gobierno formed by the Commanders-in-Chief of the Armed Forces and the Director-General of the Police.

The enactment of the Constitutional Acts of 1976 was the first step in the process of institutionalisation of the regime which gave constitutional validity to the Junta, but failed to create a new political organisation. In December of 1977 General Pinochet began a process of consolidation of his own power and, invoking external aggression and conspiracy against the fatherland, called for a referendum. The plebiscite of January of 1978 allowed him to root his personal leadership in 'the will of the people' and eliminate the Junta from the governmental process.

From the end of 1978 until 1980 the political debate within the government focussed upon the constitutional process. The 1980 constitution which was drafted by a commission hand-picked by General Pinochet, and that included his closest advisors, established two political models: the transitional model to be applied between 1980-1989, but that could be extended until 1997, which maintains the personalist government, and the authoritarian model that would follow the transitional one, which calls for a very strong executive, a weak Congress and that empowers the armed forces with the supervision of the political system (Borzutzky 1987, pp.68-73).

The constitution rejects even the most basic notions of political pluralism, giving the President through the Article 24 transitory total discretion in the area of political and civil liberties, and it has banned the activities of all Marxist groups.

Socio-economic Environment

The republic of Chile is a long, narrow country lying along the Pacific coast of South America from Peru and Bolivia in the north to Cape Horn in the far south. Most Chileans are of European and Indian decent. Spanish is the language. There is no state religion but Roman Catholics represent over 85 per cent of the population.

In 1981 Chile had a population of 11.3 million people, most of whom lived in the middle regions of the country.

In 1973 the military Junta inherited an economy with an inflation rate of between 500 and 1000 per cent, no foreign reserves and a declining Gross Domestic Product (GDP). The 'shock policy' was the first comprehensive set of economic policies and it was designed to bring about a reorganisation of the economy and a drastic reduction of inflation through restrictive monetary policies, the liberalisation of foreign trade, and the reduction of the economic role of the state.

The impact of the stabilisation policies and the implementation of the neo-liberal economic model were felt throughout the economy. Regarding fiscal and monetary policies the monetarist policies eliminated the fiscal deficit, created a healthy situation in the Balance of Payments and by 1981 had brought the inflation rate down to 9.1 per cent. Regarding economic growth, the immediate effect of the programme was to produce a contraction of economic activity manifested in a decrease of the GDP of 12.9 per cent. In 1978 began a process of economic growth and for the next three years the economy grew at an average rate of 8.7 per cent. A new recession set in 1981 which culminated in 1982 when the GDP decreased

14.5 per cent, investment declined 36.8 per cent, while inflation climbed to over 21 per cent and unemployment increased to 30 per cent. By the end of 1983 the average rate of economic growth for the past ten years had been of only 1 per cent while real salaries were 14 per cent below their 1970 level (Borzutzky 1987, pp.75-9).

Between 1984-1986 the economy has grown at an average of 4.8 per cent, the average inflation rate equals 22 per cent and, officially, about 15 per cent of the workforce remained unemployed with another 5 per cent on make-work schemes. Foreign debt which was negligible at the beginning of the Pinochet regime reached US$19.4 billion by the end of 1987.

THE WELFARE SYSTEM: AN OVERVIEW

Social Security Administration

Chile is currently operating a dual social security system comprising a social insurance system, which is gradually being phased out; and a mandatory private insurance system. Under the transition arrangements all new entrants into the labour force must join the new system. Workers already covered by the old system were able to switch to the new arrangements until May 1986, receiving credit for their previous coverage.

The Ministry of Labour and Social Welfare has overall responsibility for the social insurance system with dispensing of long-term contingency pensions being the responsibility of the social security financing fund. Health Services has the responsibility for the administration of benefits and services with respect to sickness and maternity. Administration of Chile's work injury programme is the responsibility of the Social Insurance Service, Private Salaried Employees' Welfare Fund and other Social Security Funds, as well as three employer's non-profit manual insurance groups. The administration of unemployment benefits and family allowances is the responsibility of the Superintendent of Social Security. Special family allowance programmes for children and pregnant women are the responsibility of the Emergency Social Fund.

The administration of Chile's new social security arrangements rests with the Super-intendent of Pension Fund Management Companies, with individual Pension Fund Management Companies administering the programme. The National Health Fund has oversight responsibilities for Chile's new national health scheme, which divides Chile into 27 Health Service Districts. Private health insurance organisations (<u>Institutos de Salud Previsional</u>) were introduced in 1981 and constitute a form of optional health medical insurance for the middle and upper income classes. It should be noted that the government has begun transferring responsibility for public health and rural clinics to the municipalities.

Financing Social Security

In shifting from a social insurance system to a mandatory private insurance system Chile has shifted the burden of social security finance from the employer to the employee (see Table 1).

The 1980 legislation introduced two major changes in the financial structure of the social security system: the elimination of the employer's contribution and the transformation of the common fund into individual funds.

The process of reduction of the employer's contribution began in 1975 and by 1980 it had decreased from 43.3 per cent to 20.3 per cent of the gross taxable wages. The 1980 legislation totally eliminated the employer's contribution to the unemployment fund and reduced the rate payable for work injury insurance. The employee on the other hand, pays a contribution of 19.94 per cent under the old system and 13.5 per cent under the new legislation.

Among the goals of the 1980 reform was to obtain a reduction of the overall costs of the system that by 1971 amounted to 17 per cent of GDP. Social security costs decreased during the mid-1970s mostly as a result of the economic recession amounting only to 9.3 per cent in 1975. By 1980 they had increased again to 11 per cent of GDP.

The family allowance programme is entirely financed by the state.

Personal Social Services

Chile does not have a system of personal social services for the aged, the handicapped or for any other target group.

TABLE 1: SOCIAL SECURITY FINANCING IN CHILE

	Percentage of Wage
Employee Contribution	
. Old age, invalidity and survivors' insurance (old pension system)	19.94
. Mandatory private insurance (new pension system)	13.5
. Sickness and maternity insurance (old system)	5.74-6.55
. Mandatory private health insurance (new system)	6.0
Employer's Contribution	
. Work injury insurance	4.25-4.65 (according to risk)
Government Contribution	
. Deficit financing (old pension system)	
. Special subsidies to guarantee minimum pension (new pension system)	
. Partial subsidy for sickness and maternity insurance (old system)	
. Whole cost of family allowance and unemployment benefits	

THE AGED

Between 1960-1980 the percentage of the population that are 65 years or older increased from 4.3 to 5.5 per cent and is estimated at 8 per cent for the year 2010. Life expectancy for 1980 was 67.6, the sixth highest in Latin America (Mesa-Lago 1985, p.124). Thus, retirement and old age pensions are of importance to a segment of the population that is growing fast.

Chile

Social Security

Retirement and old age pensions are regulated by the D.L. 3500 of 1981 which established a general retirement age of 65 years for males and 60 years for females, and a general requirement of at least 10 years of contributions.

In the old system the value of the pension was a variable proportion of the taxable wages, while in the new one it is determined by the capital accumulated in the savings account plus the amount transferred from the old system (bono de reconocimiento).

Once the basic requirements to obtain a pension have been fulfilled the pensioner has three different options: (a) to buy an immediate life annuity from an insurance company in which case the funds accumulated in the savings account are transferred to the selected insurance company. This option is available only to those individuals that have accumulated enough funds to buy an annuity that is equal to or larger than the minimum pension guaranteed by the state; (b) to combine a temporary annuity with a deferred life annuity. In this case the AFP pays a pension for a given period of time from the funds accumulated in the account and this is followed by a life annuity bought by the insured from an insurance company; (c) programmed pensions that are paid by the AFP. In order to use this option the insured needs to have a minimum required capital that would allow him to obtain a pension that is at least equivalent to 120 per cent of the value of a minimum state pension.

The law also established that the state has the obligation of providing a minimum pension to all males over 65 years of age and all females over 60 years that had at least 20 years of contributions, in the event that the fund accumulated is depleted or if the rent produced by the fund is smaller than the minimum pension.

Evaluation

The question of the insufficiency of pensions had been a constant problem due to the form in which pensions were calculated under the old system and the constantly high inflation experienced by the Chilean economy.

63

Chile

DISABLED AND HANDICAPPED

The state provides social security protection to
disabled workers, and recently some rehabilitation programmes have been established.

Social Security

The D.L. 3500 of 1981 established that all the
affiliates to either the old or the new system
that have lost at least two-thirds of their
capacity to work are entitled to receive
invalidity pensions. The value of the pension
will be equal to 70 per cent of the worker's base
income in the last 12 months if he or she is
actively contributing to the system. If the
worker is not currently contributing to the
pension system the value of the pension is
determined by dividing the accumulated capital by
the number of years the family is expected to live.

The state provides a minimum invalidity
pension to all those workers that have lost at
least two-thirds of their capacity to work, that
have at least two years of contributions during
the previous five calendar years and that are not
entitled to an old age pension.

In the event of a partial, work-related
disability a pension equal to 35 per cent of base
wage is payable, provided the work incapacity is
between 40 and 69 per cent, otherwise a lump-sum
grant of up to 15 months' base wage is payable.

Evaluation

The major weakness of the system is the lack of a
rehabilitation policy which has negative effects
both on the economy and on the people.

CHILDREN AND YOUTH

The welfare of children and youths has long been a
high priority in Chile.

Social Security

By and large, children and youths are covered by
the family allowances programme which since 1978

is administered through the Compensatory Family
Allowance Fund.
Allowances are paid for each child, including
adopted and stepchildren, under 18 years of age,
or under 24 if student, and to all invalid persons
regardless of age. Allowances are also paid for
unborn children from the fifth month of
pregnancy. The value of the allowances is about
US$5 per month. Invalids receive a double
allowance.

Personal Social Services

A special programme focussing on the problem of
infant, children and maternal undernourishment was
created in 1954. By 1973 the programme covered
all children under 15 years of age. In 1975 the
scope of the programme was reduced to the pregnant
mother and children under six years (Lavados 1983,
p.120). The programme involves regular medical
check-ups and the free distribution of milk.
Up to 1973 this programme was entirely
financed by the state and since then it has been
financed through the National Health Service and
the Unified Family Allowances Fund.

Evaluation

The Pinochet government has demonstrated a special
interest in the welfare of children and youths.
The family allowance programme is second only to
the pension programme in terms of both cost and
impact.
In regard to the milk distribution programme
it is important to note that this is an old
programme which reflects a permanent concern with
the nutritional status of children and high infant
mortality rates. In the last 10 years the
programme has been geared to alleviate the
negative effects that the economic recession and
the high unemployment rate have had on the low
income sectors of society. Infant mortality rate
for 1985 was 19.5 per thousand live births.

THE UNEMPLOYED AND NEEDY FAMILIES

High unemployment rates have been a persistent
problem of the Chilean economy since 1976 when

rates began to climb above 15 per cent reaching 25 per cent by 1982. By 1986 the unemployment rate had declined to 10 per cent.

Social Security

Unemployment Insurance. In Chile the unemployed are protected both through an unemployment insurance system and through special employment programmes. The unemployment insurance system covers workers dismissed for no fault on their part, provided they have made payments for 52 weeks or 12 months within the two years preceding dismissal, and are listed on the register of dismissed workers of the municipality where they live. Compensation is paid for up to 360 days, but the amount received decreases during the year. In 1986 the average compensation was of about 30 pesos per month. The compensation is financed entirely by fiscal allocations (Inter-American Development Bank, pp.154-5).

Job Creation. The high rates of unemployment of the mid and late 1970s led to the creation of two special employment programmes: the Minimum Employment Programme (PEM) and the Employment Programme for Heads of Households (POJH). Their goal was to create sources of work rapidly, and provide income to low-income families, through government-financed programmes in which the workers have to perform specific tasks or services. By 1983 almost 13 per cent of the economically active population was involved in these two programmes (Inter-American Development Bank, pp.139-40). A very large percentage of the population covered by the programmes are indigents. PEM and POJH wages are far below what is needed for a basic food basket. The programmes are operated through the municipalities.

Survivors' Benefits. Under the new system survivors of deceased persons, or workers who met pension requirements receive a pension equal to 70 per cent of average wages. This pension is distributed as follows: childless widow (60 per cent), widow with children (50 per cent), mother of children without pension (36 per cent), mother of children with pension rights (30 per cent), any orphans (15 per cent to age 18 (24 if a student or no age limit if invalided)), parents (if not other beneficiaries); and invalid widower (60 per cent).

Chile

Evaluation

The unemployment insurance programme has failed to
provide adequate protection to the unemployed
because of its limited coverage and diminished
benefits.

THE SICK AND INJURED

Law 4054 of 1925 established the right of all blue
collar workers to medical attention in case of
illness and maternity, to hospitalisation and to a
subsidy. In 1938 the Law 6174 established the
obligation of all the Insurance Funds to create
preventive medical services in order to obtain the
early discovery of chronic and contagious
diseases. Simultaneously, a system of yearly
check-ups for all the insured population was
established. In compliance with the law the five
major Funds created their own medical services.
    In 1952 the National Health Service (SNS) was
created with the purpose of providing free,
comprehensive medical attention to blue collar
workers and indigents. The SNS functions were
financed jointly by the Blue Collar Workers' Fund
and the state. The <u>Servico Medico Nacional de
Empleados</u> (SERMENA) provided medical care to white
collar workers and civil servants. The SNS
provided medical attention to about 70 per cent of
the population.

Social Security

<u>Health Insurance</u>. The health policies of the
Pinochet government have been guided by the notion
of the subsidiary role of the state which has
prompted an administrative reform in 1979, the
partial privatisation of the system in 1981 and
the transfer of public health clinics to the
municipalities. Thus, today the insured receives
medical attention either through the National
System of Health Services, which is the result of
merging the old SNS and SERMENA and is financed
through state, individual and pension funds
contributions, or through private health insurance
companies, which in Chile are called <u>Institutos de
Salud Previsional</u> (ISAPRE). ISAPREs are an
optional form of medical insurance for the middle
class and upper classes. Subscribers are expected

to remit the six per cent wage tax to the respective carrier, plus a monthly fee and the obligation to pay a portion of the curative care charges. By 1984 an estimated 487,000 people had enrolled in the ISAPRES.

Finally, the indigent is entitled to receive medical attention from the public health and rural clinics which are in the process of being transferred to the municipalities.

Temporary Disability Benefits. Workers suffering a temporary disability (work injury) receive 85 per cent of their earnings for up to 52 weeks, which may be extended to 104 weeks.

Evaluation

The Pinochet government's health system reforms have shifted financial responsibility for health care from the state to the private sector. The impact of this is still unclear but it is clear that there remains a large disparity between the health care services available in urban and rural areas (Rodriguez 1985, p.10).

ASSESSMENT OF THE CHILEAN WELFARE SYSTEM

The criteria used to evaluate the pension system is the value of pensions. The question of the insufficiency of pensions had been a constant problem due to the form in which pensions were calculated under the old system and the constantly high inflation experienced by the Chilean economy. In periods of sky-rocketing inflation such as those experienced between 1973 and 1976 when inflation rates fluctuated between 365 per cent and 585 per cent it is easy to understand how inadequate an income based on a proportion of the wages obtained in the past can be. Thus, between 1971 and 1975 the real value of pensions decreased by about 40 per cent. Through a number of indexing laws the government increased their real value between 1976 and 1980, but by 1981 the real value of a pension was about 60 per cent of the value they had in 1971 (Mesa-Lago 1985, p.125). In 1978 the average monthly pension was only US$54.

One of the goals of the reform was to increase the value of the pensions and to improve the standards of living of the pensioners, who

amounted to about 10 per cent of the population.
This improvement in the value of the pensions
remains to be seen. By 1985 the value of a
pension was estimated to be 82 per cent of its
1970 value (Arellano 1986, p.85). The new system,
in turn, did not begin to pay old age pensions
until 1986; however given the nature of the new
system the value of the pension is going to depend
in large part on the real value of wages, the
economic growth of the nation, the real yield
produced by the fund and the rate of employment.
The constant decrease in the real value of wages,
which by 1985 were estimated to be 13 per cent
below the 1970 level, and the high rates of
unemployment will clearly have a negative impact
on the future value of pensions.

Between 1973 and 1974 the Pinochet government
replaced all the numerous programmes targeted at
children and youths by a unified system, it
created special funds for its administration and,
in 1981 expanded the allowances to the children of
the indigents even when they were not contributing
to the social security system.

The scope of the unemployment insurance
programme has been limited since it has benefited
only about 25 per cent of all unemployed workers
since 1980. Moreover the amount received by the
workers has declined from 25 per cent to 19 per
cent of the average industrial wage between 1980
and 1985 (Inter-American Development Bank,
pp.156-7).

Although the special employment programmes
have served a large number of people, reaching
about 500,000 participants in 1983, the
compensations provided by both the PEM and the
POJH were very small. By 1983 the PEM wage was
US$20 while the POJH wage US$40. The cost of the
basic food basket that same year was US$80 (Inter-
American Development Bank, pp.141-3).

The health system reforms enacted by the
Pinochet government are based on a redefinition of
the state's role in health care producing a number
of contradictory effects both in regard to the
health status of the population as well as the
administration of the system. Some of these
effects are:

.   A reduction in the infant mortality rate to
     19.5 per thousand live births and a decline in
     the general mortality rate to 6.1 per thousand
     inhabitants (1985).

Chile

- An increase in the number of infectious and respiratory diseases.

- A constant reduction of public health expenditures which are estimated to be between 10 and 20 per cent under 1970 levels.

- A large disparity between the medical services in urban and rural areas (Rodriguez, p.10).

REFERENCES AND FURTHER READING

Aldunate, R. (1969), Ruido de Sables, Santiago.

Alessandri, A. (1952), Recuerdos de Gobierno Administracion 1920-1925, Santiago: Editorial Universitaria.

Allende, S. (1972), Allende: Su Pensamiento Politico, Santiago: Editorial Quimantu.

Arellano, J. P. (1981), 'Elementos para el analisis de la reforma previsional Chilena', Coleccion Estudios CIEPLAN, No.6.

_____ (1986), 'Una mirada critico a la reforma de 1981', in Baeza, S. (ed.), Analisis de la Prevision en Chile, Santiago: Centro de Estudios Publicos.

_____ (1985), Politicas Sociales y Desarrolo: Chile 1924-1984, Santiago: CIEPLAN.

Borzutzky, S. (1983), 'Chilean Politics and Social Security Policies', unpublished Ph.D. Dissertation, University of Pittsburgh.

_____ (1987), 'The Pinochet Regime: Crisis and Consolidation', in Malloy, J.M. & Seligson, M. (eds), Authoritarians and Democrats, Pittsburgh: University of Pittsburgh Press.

Briones, C. (1968), 'Antecedentes basicos y analisis del estedo actual de la seguridad social en Chile', Seguridad Social, No.98.

Bustos, J. (1948), La Prevision y la Medicina Social en Chile, Santiago: Agosto.

Chile

Comision de Estudios de la Seguridad Social
    Chilena, (CESSC), (1965), Informe Sobre la
    Reforma de la Seguridad Social Chilena,
    Santiago: Editorial Juridica de Chile, v.1.

D.L. (1925), 454 & 767.

D.L. 3500, Art 23.

D.L. 3500, Arts 37-45.

D.L. 3500, Arts 51-82.

D.L. 3502.

DFL (1980), 101.

DLF (1925), 837.

Ffrench-Davis, R. (1973), Politicas Economicas en
    Chile: 1952-1970, Santiago: Ediciones Nueva
    Universidad.

Gutierrez, R. (1976), 'Acceso a los beneficios de
    la medicina socializada', in CIEPLAN (ed.),
    Salud Publica y Bienestar Social, Santiago:
    Universidad Catolica de Chile.

Inter-American Development Bank, Economic and
    Social Progress in Latin America, 1987 Report,
    Washington: Inter-American Development Bank.

Lavados, I. (1983), Evolucion de las Politicos
    Sociales en Chile 1964-1980, Santiago: Cepal,
    I'pes.

Loveman, B. (1975), Struggle in the Countryside:
    Politics and Rural Labour in Chile, 1919-1973,
    Bloomington: Indiana University Press.

Mamalakis, M. (1976), The Growth and Structure of
    the Chilean Economy, New Haven: Yale
    University Press.

Meller, P. (1984), 'Analisis del problema de la
    elevada tasa de desocupacion en Chile',
    Coleccion Estudios CIEPLAN, No.14, September.

Mesa-Lago, C. (1978), Social Security in Latin
    America: Pressure Groups, Stratification and
    Inequality, Pittsburgh: University of
    Pittsburgh Press.

Chile

_____ (1985), El Desarrollo de la
Seguridad Social en America Latina, Santiago:
Estudios e Informes de la CEPAL, Naciones
Unidas.

Miranda, E. (1965), 'El sector agricola en la
seguridad social Chilena', Boletin de
Estadisticas de la Seguridad Social, Apartado
del Boletin 27-28, Diciembre.

Morris, J. O. (1966), Elites, Intellectuals and
Consensus: A Study of the Social Question and
the Industrial Relations System in Chile,
Ithaca: Cornell University Press.

Moulian, T. (1982), 'Desarrollo politico y estado
de compromiso desajustes y crisis estatal en
Chile', Coleccion Estudios CIEPLAN, 8(July),
105-60.

Orlandini, L. (1966), Caracteristicas Basicas de la
Seguridad Social en Chile, Santiago: INSORA.

Pinto, A. (1962), Chile un caso de desarrollo
frustrado, Santiago: Editorial Universitaria.

Rodriguez, F. (1976), 'Estructuras y
caracteristicas del sector salud', in CIEPLAN
(ed.), Salud Publica y Bienestar Social,
Santiago: Universidad Catolica de Chile.

Rodriguez, J. (1985), Distribucion del Ingreso y
el Gasto Social en Chile - 1983, Santiago:
ILADES.

Romero, L. (1978), La Seguridad Social en Chile:
Incidencias Economicas en el Periodo
1958-1976, Memoria de Prueba Escuela de
Economia, Santiago: Universidad de Chile.

Scarpaci, J. L. (1986), 'Restructuring Health Care
Financing in Chile', Social Science and
Medicine, v.21(4), pp.415-31.

Stevenson, J. (1938), The Chilean Popular Front,
Philadelphia: University of Pennsylvania Press.

Viveros-Long, A. M. (1968), 'Changes in Health
Financing: The Chilean Experience', Social
Science and Medicine, v.22(3).

COLOMBIA
Roberto Arias Perez

THE WELFARE SYSTEM ENVIRONMENT

Socio-economic Environment

The Republic of Colombia is located in the extreme north-west corner of South America, bordering both the Atlantic and the Pacific Oceans. It covers an area of approximately 1.142 million square kilometres.

The population of Colombia is 32.377 million people, of which 69 per cent reside in urban areas. The annual population growth is 1.9 per cent. Life expectancy is 64 years. Infant mortality is 53 per 1,000 live births. The economically active population constitute 43 per cent of the total population.

The Colombian population is descended from the Spaniards, Nates and Negros and has many varied shades of ethnic groups. About 70 per cent of the population are Mestizos, who are mainly of mixed Spanish and Indian descent, but there are also some of mixed Black African, Indian and Spanish descent. About 20 per cent of the population are European. Indians and Negros make up the balance of the population.

Colombia is primarily an agricultural country with more than half its working population engaged in agriculture. It has vast mineral resources that have not been fully developed. The unemployed rate is 14.8 per cent, while the annual average inflation rate is 24 per cent.

Political Environment

Colombia has a highly centralised system of government. The Head of State is the President

73

Colombia

who is elected every four years by direct popular
vote. He is the head of the executive branch in
government. At the national level the executive
branch comprises 13 Ministries, eight
administrative departments, seven
Superintendencies, 91 Public Establishments, 12
industrial and commercial state companies, and 19
mixed economy companies. The national legislature
is the Congress of the Republic, comprising a
Senate and a Chamber of Representatives, both of
which are elected by direct popular vote. The
judicial branch of government comprises the
Supreme Court, the State Council, the Higher
Courts and other Court Tribunals as established by
law.

Historical Origins and Ideological Environment

The first permanent European settlement in
Colombia was established in 1525 and so began a
period of Spanish colonisation which lasted till
the end of the eighteenth century, when several
movements for independence began. In December
1819 the Republic of Colombia was established.

Two political factions, a conservative upper
class and a group of liberal intellectuals, shaped
Colombia from the beginning of the new Republic.
The conservative upper class generally favoured
the continuance of traditional Spanish values and
close ties with the Roman Catholic Church. The
liberal intellectuals, who as a rule were also
wealthy aristocrats, demanded the separation of
church and the state and other changes to
traditional Spanish social and economic patterns.
The two factions developed into the liberal and
conservative parties during the 1830s and they
have continued to dominate Colombian politics.

Since its formation, Colombia has suffered
long years of political turmoil. Banditry and
terrorism have long beset Colombia despite
military efforts to suppress them.

The historical antecedents of Colombia's
social welfare system date back to the Spanish
colonial period and the efforts of the Roman
Catholic church. Government intervention did not
occur until the twentieth century and was
initiated by the creation of a workers'
compensation programme in 1915. From 1932 social
security laws were enacted quite frequently but it
was not until 1945 that a coherent system of

social security was created. This system covered
work accidents, occupational and non-occupational
sickness, invalidity, old age and death.
Initially coverage against these risks was the
responsibility of individual employers but in 1946
responsibility was transferred to a public agency
through the formation of a social insurance
system. In the late 1960s a special social
security system was established for public
employees and official workers.

THE WELFARE SYSTEM: AN OVERVIEW

The welfare system in Colombia is dominated by the
social security system. This comprises a workers'
compensation programme established by the Labour
Code; occupational social security for public
employees and official workers and a social
insurance programme for other workers in the
public and private sectors.

Social security administration is the
responsibility of two public agencies: <u>Caja
Nacional de Prevision Social</u> (henceforth CAJANAL),
which is responsible for state-level public
employees; and <u>Instituto de Seguros Sociales</u>
(ISS), which is responsible for private sector
employees and some official workers.

Social Security Administration

<u>CAJANAL</u>. This is a public establishment with an
autonomous management structure and its own
capital. For coordination control purposes it is
attached to the Ministry of Labour and Social
Security. It was established by law in 1945. It
has branch offices and agencies throughout the
country.

At the national level CAJANAL is governed by a
board of directors comprising six members
representing the Ministry of Labour and Social
Security, the Treasury, the Public Health
Ministry, the Civil Service Administration
Department and representatives of public employees
affiliated to it. A Director and two Assistant
Directors are in charge of economic benefits and
medical health assistance respectively. There are
31 branches at the regional and departmental
level, each with its own directorship, subordinate
to the national Director's office.

As of 31 December 1986 there were 310,633 individuals covered by CAJANAL, of which 226,465 were active affiliated members, 65,832 were pensioners and 28,336 were beneficiaries (that is relatives of affiliated members and pensioners).

<u>ISS</u>. This is a legally-constituted public agency with an autonomous management structure and independent capital. It is accountable to the Ministry of Labour and Social Security and subject to the direction and coordination of the Mandatory Social Security National Council, the ISS Board and the Directors and Management Board of Economic Insurance.

At the national level the ISS is headed by a Management Board comprising eight members representing the goverment, the employers, workers, and medical and dental professionals. Under this board is a Director-General appointed by the president of the Republic. Assistant Directors are in charge of health assistance services and economic benefits. At the sectional level there are Managers who are subordinate to the national Director-General and who effect the administration of social security.

ISS affiliation is mandatory for all nationals and foreigners who work for private sector employers under a work or an apprenticeship contract, for social security employees and mandatory social security pensioners, and official workers employed under work contracts with the government. Other sectors of the population may be affiliated as optional members, such as independent workers.

As at December 1985 the ISS had 3,088,573 affiliated individuals (see Table 1).

<u>Family Allowances Funds</u>. The Family Allowances Funds are legal entities operating as non-profit organisations established by groups of employers on a cooperative basis. The establishment of a Family Allowances Fund requires a minimum of 500 employers or a group of employers who in aggregate employ 10,000 workers entitled to a family allowance. These Funds are under the control and supervision of the Family Allowances Superintendency, which is subordinate to the Ministry of Labour and Social Security. All employers, irrespective of their size, must contribute to these family allowances funds. Only the Defence Ministry, the armed forces and the

Colombia

TABLE 1: ISS POPULATION COVERAGE 1982

	POPULATION OF THE COUNTRY				ISS COVERAGE	
Years	Total Population	Other Economically Active People	Salaried Employees & Workers	Insured Population[1]	Beneficiaries	Total Population Covered
1982	26,463,667	8,044,955	4,207,511	1,834,040	932,705	2,766,745
1983	27,183,479	8,263,778	4,321,956	1,901,700	947,953	2,849,653
1984	27,922,868	8,488,552	4,439,513	1,943,016	995,501	2,938,517
1985	26,682,370	8,719,440	5,135,750	1,988,011	1,100,562	3,088,573

Note: 1 Includes pensioners.

SOURCE: Colombia, Departmento Nacional de Estadistica, 1985 (for total population).

Police are exempted. They are required to pay family allowances directly. In 1986 there were 68 Family Allowances Funds in Colombia.

Financing Social Security

CAJANAL. Benefits provided by this organisation are financed from three sources:

- contributions from insured employees and pensioners, comprising one-third of the insured worker's first month's salary and any subsequent pay increase, five per cent of their monthly salaries and five per cent of pensioners' pension income (for medical assistance);

- contributions by employers, equal to eight per cent of payroll;

- government contributions, which are paid at the discretion of the Colombian government from its national budget.

Additional funding comes from the investment returns generated from the investment of revenues received.

ISS. This organisation is funded from contributions received from employers, employees and the state (see Table 2), as well as revenues obtained from the investment of reserves and from economic activity conducted by administrative units.

Employer Liability Benefits. In Colombia employers are required by the Labour Code to provide their employees with a range of social security benefits subject only to a minimum employment period qualification. These are totally financed by the employer.

Personal Social Services

The personal social services in Colombia are only at a very rudimentary level of development. The services that are available are provided by social security institutions.

Colombia

TABLE 2: ISS CONTRIBUTIONS ACCORDING TO SOCIAL
SECURITY RISK

Social Security Risks	Contributions Payable by:		
	Employer (percentage of payroll)	Insured Person (percentage of wages or pension)	State (Percentage of insurable wage)
Invalidity, Old Age & Death	7.5	3.75	3.75
Work Accidents & Occupational Illness	Contributions determined according to five occupational risk categories	Nil	Nil
Occupational Sickness & Maternity	One-third of contributions required to cover entire cost of benefits[1]	Two-thirds contributions required to cover entire cost of benefits[1]	Nil
Family Allowances	4		

Note:

1   The ISS determines contributions on an annual
basis according to estimated cost of cash
benefits and the cost of medical services.

SOURCE: ISS.

Colombia

THE AGED

Colombia has an aging population caused, in part, by an increase in life expectancy in recent years. This has increased the importance of the aged as a target group for social security measures.

Social Security

Social security protection for the elderly is provided under three programmes.

ISS. Insured persons covered by the ISS are entitled to a monthly old-age pension upon reaching retirement age, which is 60 for men and 55 for women provided they have made 500 weekly contributions over the 20 years immediately prior to reaching retirement age, or 1,000 weekly contributions during their working life.

The amount of the old age pension payable is equal to 45 per cent of the insured person's last base monthly salary, with the following increases permitted:

. 3 per cent of the base salary for every 50 weeks of contribution over and above the first 500, but not so as to exceed 90 per cent of the base salary;

. 7 per cent of the minimum pension for each child under the age 16 or under 18 if a student, or any age if an invalid or economically dependent on the pensioner;

. 24 per cent of the minimum pension of the spouse when that spouse is not in receipt of an invalidity or old age pension, but not so as to increase the pension beyond 42 per cent of the minimum monthly pension.

The old age pension cannot be less than the minimum legal salary nor more than 22 times that salary. The benefit is automatically and periodically increased in line with increases in the minimum legal salary.

All ISS pensioners and their relatives who are dependent upon them are entitled to medical, dental, surgical, hospital, pharmaceutical, rehabilitation, diagnostic and treatment services available to affiliated members of the ISS.

CAJANAL. All affiliated members (that is public employees or official workers) who have worked for 20 years either continuously or discontinuously, for a state institute and who have reached the age of 55 (for both males and females) are entitled to a monthly retirement pension. This benefit is equivalent to 75 per cent of the employee's monthly earnings averaged during the last year of service. Those employees who have worked for less than 20 years qualify for retirement pension at age 65. Their monthly pension is equivalent to 20 per cent of their last salary, an amount increased by 2 per cent for each year of service beyond the age of 65. This is payable for as long as the recipient lacks resources for their sustenance.

Labour Code. Employees who work for large private companies that are not covered by the ISS qualify for an age pension upon reaching the age of 55 for men and 50 for women, provided they have worked continuously or discontinuously for 20 years with the same company. Their monthly pension entitlement is 75 per cent of the average salary earned during the last year of service. This life-time pension must be at least the minimum legal salary but cannot exceed 22 times that amount.

In the event of an employee ceasing to work for the company after satisfying the 20 year qualifying period, but without having reached the required retirement age, their pension entitlement comes into effect once they reach the retirement age. A worker who is dismissed without justification having worked for more than 10 years but less than 15 years for the same company is entitled to a pension upon reaching the age of 60. If dismissal takes place after 15 years of service with the company the only requirement for the pension is that the dismissed worker be 50 years of age.

Evaluation

Social security protection is only available to about 16 per cent of the Colombian population. Those that receive this protection are confronted with a multiplicity of management bodies which lack adequate integration. Those outside the social security system rely on their families for support in their old age.

THE DISABLED AND HANDICAPPED

There may be as many as two million handicapped people in Colombia, although there is no reliable data profiling this target group.

Social Security

Colombian workers are provided with a variety of invalidity and incapacity benefits from a variety of sources.

<u>Invalidity Pensions</u>. Insured persons affiliated with the ISS qualify for a monthly invalidity pension provided that their working capacity has been reduced by 50 per cent and provided that they have contributed for 150 weeks of the six years immediately prior to the invalidity, or for 300 weeks during their working life. The invalidity pension is determined in the same way as the old age pension. This pension is initially granted for one year and renewed every two years provided the condition that gave rise to the invalidity persists. Upon reaching retirement age invalidity pensioners become old age pensioners. If at the time invalidity occurs an insured person is unable to satisfy the contribution period requirement but has a minimum of 100 weeks contributions, 25 of which have been paid during the last year, then a lump sum indemnity payment equal to one month's pension for each 25 weeks' contributions is provided.

Public employees and official workers affiliated with the CAJANAL qualify for invalidity pension provided their working capacity has been decreased by 75 per cent. The invalidity pension payable is based on the degree of disability:

.   if the work incapacity is 75 per cent, then the pension payable is 50 per cent of the last wage;

.   if the work incapacity is 95 per cent, then the pension payable is 75 per cent of last the wage;

.   if the work incapacity is greater than 95 per cent, the pension is equal to the last wage.

This benefit is granted for a period of two years, at the end of which each beneficiary is

subject to a medical examination to determine
continued eligibility and the appropriate pension
payable.

Employees of large private companies receive
invalidity assistance if as a result of a
non-occupational sickness or injury their working
capacity is reduced by 66 per cent. The benefits
provided are as follows:

.   for a partial but permanent invalidity
        condition a lump sum payment of between one
        and ten months' wages is paid, as determined
        by the doctor qualifying the invalidity;

.   for a permanent and total invalidity condition
        a pension equal to 50 per cent of average
        monthly wages during the preceding year is
        payable for up to 30 months.

The invalidity pension becomes a
superannuation or old age pension if the employee
has worked continuously or discontinuously for the
same company for 15 years and if they are 55 years
of age or become so during the period of the
invalidity. This pension is provisionally paid
for one year at the end of which all beneficiaries
are subject to a medical examination to determine
continuing eligibility and the pension entitlement.

Occupational Disability. The Labour Code provides
covered employees with a range of benefits in the
event of a work-related disability, provided the
disabling accident has not occurred as a result of
the victim's serious fault. In the event of a
permanent partial incapacity the worker is
entitled to a benefit proportional to the damage
suffered of no less than one month's salary but no
more than 23 months' salary. The degree of
incapacity is determined by the employer's medical
officer, who makes reference to the Incapacity
Valuation Table to determine the percentage of
work capacity lost, according to the nature of the
injury sustained, and the benefit payable. In the
event that the injury has a special effect on the
employee's cursory type of work, the benefit
payable is increased to up to 24 months' salary.
If the worker suffers multiple injuries then the
benefit payable may be greater than that
appropriate for any single injury but cannot
exceed 23 months' salary. In the event of the
medical officer being unable to identify culpable

injuries in the Incapacity Valuation Table the case must be referred to the National Department of Medicine and Hygiene or the Ministry of Labour for determination. The base salary upon which the benefit calculations are determined is equal to that earned by the worker at the time of the accident or if the worker has been employed for less than one year the average earned during his entire time of service.

Public employees and official workers covered by CAJANAL who suffer a work-related disability receive comparable benefits to those provided to workers covered by the Labour Code. The significant difference is that in the event of work capacity being reduced by 75 per cent or more then public employees and official workers are entitled to invalidity pensions.

Workers covered by the ISS who suffer a work-related disability also have their degree of disability determined by reference to the Incapacity Valuation Table. However, when determining the disability benefit payable consideration is given to the worker's age, and his possibility of future gainful employment. The benefit payable is proportional to that which would be received in the event of a permanent total incapacity. Initially, the disability benefit is paid for a period of two years, after which a medical examination is required to determine continued eligibility. Upon reaching the age stipulated for the old age pension this benefit becomes a life-time annuity. In the event of a disability of between 5 and 20 per cent incapacity the benefit payable is a lump sum amount equivalent to three years pension entitlement. A permanent partial incapacity of less than 5 per cent is not subject to indemnity.

In the event of a work-related permanent total incapacity, defined as a situation where a worker is disabled to such an extent that he cannot carry out work of any kind, the Labour Code provides for covered workers to receive an indemnity equal to 24 months' salary.

Public employees and official workers who are deemed to be permanently and totally incapacitated due to a work injury qualify for an invalidity pension.

Workers covered by the ISS who suffer a permanent and total incapacity receive a monthly pension equal to 60 per cent of their base salary, but not so as to be less than the invalid pension. This disability benefit is paid initially for a period of two years after which, if confirmed, it continues indefinitely. It is converted to a life annuity when the beneficiary reaches the age at which, under the ISS, he would receive an old age pension.

Permanent and total invalidity pensioners also receive additional benefits with respect to dependents including children, invalids, others who are dependent economically on the pensioner, and their spouses.

Constant Attendance Allowance. Disability pensioners under the Labour Code receive an additional seven months' salary in the event of a disabled worker requiring constant attendance.

Public employees and official workers covered by CAJANAL receive the maximum invalidity pension if they require constant attendance.

Workers covered by the ISS receive a supplementary allowance equal to 25 per cent of base monthly salary.

Medical Services. All incapacitated workers are eligible for free medical care. Under the Labour Code this is provided by the employer for a period up to 180 days. CAJANAL provides public employees with medical services for up to 180 days although official workers may receive such benefits for as long as they are deemed necessary. The ISS provides free medical services for up to 360 days provided the worker has been registered with it for at least four weeks prior to disability occurring and provided that the medical prognosis for cure is favourable.

Personal Social Services

Rehabilitation Benefits. The Labour Code does not require employers to provide any rehabilitation assistance. At the termination of the incapacity period, however, the worker must be reinstated in the same position held prior to the disability occurring.

Public employees and official workers receive such devices as are necessary for the recuperation of their working capacity. This includes supply, repair and renewal of prosthesis, and orthopedic appliances.

Colombia

Workers covered by the ISS are entitled to prosthesis and orthopedic devices as well as adequate measures for the recuperation of working capacity.

Evaluation

There is a clear lack of integration amongst the health, social security and personal social services sub-systems targeting the handicapped in Colombia. Indeed, the development of health and personal social services has been rudimentary at best.

NEEDY FAMILIES

Family poverty is a serious social problem in Colombia, although there is little data available to provide reliable estimates of its extent or nature.

Social Security

Survivors' Benefits. Under the Labour Code survivors of deceased workers employed by covered employees received a benefit equivalent to one month's wage for every year of service, but not so as to be less than 12 months' wage or more than 100 times the minimum legal wage. Upon the death of a pensioner the pension entitlement is transferred to the spouse and those children under the age of 18. Where neither exists it may be transferred to dependent parents, if invalids, or dependent siblings. This pension is payable for the life-time of the surviving spouse, or until such time remarriage occurs. If the benefit is shared with dependent children, then 50 per cent is assigned to the spouse and the balance is divided amongst the children. Their eligibility ceases when they reach maturity at age 18.

When death occurs as a result of a work accident or illness the benefit payable is double that otherwise payable, but not so as to exceed 200 times the minimum legal wage. This benefit is divided equally between the surviving spouse and any dependent children. If there is no surviving spouse then all the benefit is divided amongst the children. If there are no children then all the benefit is divided amongst surviving dependent parents. Otherwise it is divided amongst surviving dependent siblings under the age of 18. If there are no dependents then the benefit is divided amongst the nominated heirs according to civil law. The payment of this benefit is made to qualified beneficiaries by the deceased's employer for a period of three years after death. If during this time no claim is made by the deceased's beneficiaries their rights are extinguished under the Statute of Limitations. Moreover, those dependents who are disinherited under civil law are excluded from receiving this benefit as are widows who have been divorced or remarried.

Public employees and official workers affiliated with CAJANAL receive similar benefits to those provided under the Labour Code. The major differences are that the death benefit associated with non-occupational death is equivalent to 12 months' salary, while the benefit associated with occupational death is equal to 24 months' salary with no upper limit specified.

Survivors of a deceased worker formally affiliated with the ISS are eligible for a pension. If death was due to an occupational injury or sickness then the survivors' pension is equal to 15 per cent of the deceased worker's base salary in respect of each dependent child. If both parents die then survivors' pension is 25 per cent of the deceased worker's salary provided the dependent children are under the age of 14 or invalid. Surviving children who are students qualify for this pension until they reach the age of 18.

When death is due to non-occupational causes a survivors' pension is payable only if at time of death the affiliated member had made contributions for 150 weeks in the last six years, or 300 weeks over any period of time.

If the deceased affiliated member was receiving a permanent partial disability pension survivors receive a lump sum payment equal to three years' pension. If the deceased affiliated member was an invalid or old age pensioner then 50 per cent of the pension entitlement is paid to the surviving spouse, 20 per cent to each orphan. If the surviving children have lost both parents then the survivors' benefit is increased to 30 per cent of the pension entitlement.

Widows of deceased affiliated members cease to qualify for survivors' benefits if they receive support sufficient for their subsistence from some third person. If a widow remarries whilst in receipt of a survivors' benefit arising from occupational death she is paid a single lump-sum equivalent of three years' pension entitlement.

Burial Assistance. This is provided to all deceased covered workers and pensioners. For those covered by the Labour Code all covered employers are required to pay the burial expenses of their deceased workers, up to a maximum equal to one month of the deceased worker's wage. A similar benefit is provided in respect of deceased public employees and official workers. Deceased CAJANAL pensioners attract a burial assistance equal to two months' pension. Deceased workers affiliated with ISS who have contributed for at least five weeks receive a burial assistance allowance of one month's wage. Deceased invalidity and disability pensioners attract a burial assistance allowance equal to one month's pension. All deceased retirement pensioners attract a burial assistance allowance of one month's pension which must be between five and 10 times the minimum legal wage.

Maternity Benefits. Female employees first received maternity benefits under legislation enacted in 1938. They have the right to paid maternity leave and cannot be dismissed from their jobs because of pregnancy or lactation.

Female workers in the private sector who are covered by the Labour Code receive eight weeks' maternity leave before and after child birth. In the event of a miscarriage or premature non-viable birth the paid leave is reduced to two or four weeks. During this period the worker's full salary is paid. In the event of the worker receiving a variable salary she is paid the average wage earned during the previous year or part thereof. Employers must also provide their female workers with two 30-minute rest periods each working day during the first six months of the infant's life. The worker receives full pay during these rest periods.

If a female worker is dismissed during the term of her pregnancy, or within three months of child-birth or miscarriage, without the express permission of the Ministry of Labour, she is entitled to an indemnity equivalent to 60 days' wages plus the equivalent in cash of eight weeks' paid leave if she has not made use of her maternity leave. These benefits are in addition to the indemnity to which she is entitled for unjustifiable dismissal.

Female public employees and official workers affiliated with CAJANAL receive similar benefits to those provided under the Labour Code, except that no leave applies in the event of premature birth.

Female workers affiliated with ISS receive eight weeks' maternity leave, during which they receive a benefit equal to their average wage of the preceding 12 weeks. In the event of a miscarriage or premature non-viable birth the length of maternity leave is reduced to that deemed necessary as a rest period, but not exceeding four weeks. To qualify for these benefits the insured person must have contributed for at least 12 weeks during the period of pregnancy.

Personal Social Services

Under legislation enacted in December 1962 the Family Allowances Funds were authorised to provide a range of family social benefits to their members. Over the ensuing years these family social benefits have come to cover: health and nutrition, adult education, library training and services, housing, home-based industries finance, and social recreation. The services provided to workers eligible for family allowances are income tested such that workers earning more than four times the minimum legal wage pay the full cost.

Evaluation

The protection offered to needy urban families by Colombia's social security institutions varies by reason of industrial concentration and population density in the various urban centres. The rural population remains outside the formal social welfare support system.

Colombia

CHILDREN AND YOUTH

Colombia has a relatively high birth rate (about 35 per thousand people), which makes this a target group of social significance.

Social Security

Family Allowances. In response to the need for re-establishing social stability and for achieving family balance the Colombian government provides family allowances to complement workers' salaries. The family allowances programme was established by decree in 1957 as a special social benefit granted to lower-paid workers in the form of cash and services, in proportion to the number of persons dependent upon them. Family allowances are paid to employees, but not to the self-employed, and do not discriminate between males and females. To qualify for an allowance workers must be permanently employed, in receipt of a salary of not more than four times the minimum legal salary, must work for a minimum of 96 hours per month and must be in charge of children, orphaned siblings or parents over the age of 60 who have no other income. The children may be legitimate, illegitimate, adoptive or step-children. The monthly family allowance payable is determined by the number of designated dependents and the amount varies from Fund to Fund. On average the payment received in respect of each dependent is approximately 8 per cent of the legal minimum wage. Where a dependent is deemed to be suffering a physical or mental incapacity greater than 60 per cent, then twice the family allowance subsidy is paid in respect of such dependents.

Family allowances are paid in respect of the same children if both their father and mother are working and if their total earnings do not exceed a sum four times the minimum legal wage.

In 1986 family allowances were paid in respect of 24.4 million dependents.

Personal Social Services

Nurseries and Child Care Centres. Employers covered by the Labour Code are required to provide nurseries to care for their workers' children.

Colombia

Employers must also contribute 2 per cent of their monthly payroll to the Family Compensation Fund, which is administered by the Colombian Family Welfare Institute and provides nurseries and child care centres for workers' children.

Evaluation

Children of working mothers covered by a social security institution receive the protection of the formal social security system. Other children are not protected. Colombia's infant mortality rate is amongst the highest in the world.

THE SICK AND INJURED

The Colombian health care system primarily focusses on those in formal employment and their dependents.

Social Security

Non-occupational Sickness. Workers covered by the Labour Code receive up to 180 days' sick leave. During the first 90 days the employer is required to pay a cash allowance equal to two-thirds of the sick employee's wage, which falls to one-half for the second 90 days. Public employees and official workers affiliated with CAJANAL receive exactly the same sick leave benefits.

Workers affiliated with the ISS also qualify for paid sick leave but only if they have been contributors for the immediately preceding 12 weeks. The cash subsidy payable is two-thirds of the sick worker's basic wage for a period of 180 days, continuously or discontinuously, so long as the work interruption associated with one sickness incident does not exceed 30 days. Should a work interruption exceed 30 days then the maximum sick leave period is extended for another 180 days. The cash subsidy payable is provided by the employer for the first four days' sickness, thereafter it is paid by the ISS. In the event of hospitalisation occurring from the first day of the sickness, the entire cash subsidy is paid by the ISS.

Occupational Sickness and Injury. Workers covered by the Labour Code who suffer a temporary

work-related incapacity or illness receive their
regular and complete salaries for up to six
months. The same benefits are payable to public
employees and official workers covered by a
CAJANAL. Workers affiliated with the ISS who
suffer an occupational injury or sickness receive
their full salary for the first 180 days of
incapacity, thereafter an amount equal to
two-thirds of their wage is paid until they
recover or are deemed to be permanently
incapacitated.

Health Services. Workers covered by the Labour
Code who suffer a work incapacity as a result of a
non-occupational sickness receive free medical,
pharmaceutical, surgical and hospital services
from their employers, for up to a maximum of 180
days a year.
    Public employees and official workers
affiliated with CAJANAL receive the same health
benefits, but their availability extends beyond
six months should they be necessary. Workers
affiliated with the ISS, who have contributed for
at least four weeks prior to the initiation of
medical treatment, qualify for the same range of
health benefits as well as dental assistance,
paraclinical services, and auxiliary diagnostic
and treatment services. These benefits are
provided for up to 180 days unless the medical
prognosis for a cure is favourable in which event
the maximum period is extended to 360 days.

Family Medical Services. CAJANAL extends the
provision of health benefits to relatives of its
affiliated members who live in Bogota. Those
covered include the spouse, children under the age
of 12 and invalids. The ISS also extends its
health benefits to dependents of its affiliated
members including wives, permanent companions (so
long as both are single and have been living
together for eight years or have children, common
to both), children (including adopted and
illegitimate children under the age of 18 and
dependent invalids), and dependent invalid
husbands. In the absence of such beneficiaries
health benefits may be granted to the mother of
the insured worker (including dependent foster
mothers), invalid fathers or fathers over the age
of 60 (including foster fathers), and dependent
invalid siblings. All these beneficiaries acquire
benefit rights simultaneously with the registered

Colombia

member. However they are entitled to continue
receiving services for up to 60 days after the
member's de-registration, which may occur as a
result of death or the termination of covered
employment.

Evaluation

The benefits of the health service do not reach
all Colombians. Only those in formal employment
receive the benefit of social security protection.

THE UNEMPLOYED

Unemployment is a major social problem in
Colombia, especially in urban areas. In 1987 the
unemployment rate was 14.8 per cent of the
economically active population, some two million
people.

Social Security

The existing social security system does not
provide any unemployment insurance, however
severance pay is provided to workers who are
laid-off.

Severance Pay. Under the Labour Code all workers
(other than seasonal transitory workers, domestic
industry workers and self-employed craftsmen
employing less than five non-family members)
receive a severance payment upon the termination
of their employment, irrespective of the cause of
that severance. In the event of a worker's death
the severance payment entitlement is transferred
to the deceased's heirs. Whilst the law prohibits
employers from making partial severance payments
to their employees prior to termination of
employment, they are allowed to make such payments
at the worker's request in order to purchase,
improve or reduce the mortgage outstanding on the
worker's house, provided that the partial payment
is no greater than the amount required for this
purpose, and provided that permission is gained
from the Ministry of Work.
    Public employees and official workers also
qualify for the severance payment if their
employment is terminated.

Colombia

The amount of the severance payment is equal to one month's salary for each year of service, pro-rataed in the event of employment periods less than one year. In the private sector this benefit is paid directly by the employer. Public employees and official workers receive their severance payments from the National Savings Fund, which was established in 1968 to promote national savings, to finance important social and economic development projects, and to solve the housing problems experienced by state employees.

Evaluation

The provision of severance payments has been a successful savings mechanism which has helped workers not only to obtain housing assistance but also to provide them with some income security between jobs. When partial severance payments are requested by workers it involves their employer in substantial additional expenses, especially where the worker has considerable seniority.

The introduction of unemployment insurance in Colombia would require a long-term political and social reform process. Until this happens the severance payment system should be maintained but the practice of paying partial advances should eliminated.

AN ASSESSMENT OF THE COLOMBIAN SOCIAL WELFARE SYSTEM

Although the Colombian social security system provides protection to workers in the event of a temporary or permanent loss of their working capacity, some of the risks are only partially or incompletely covered, and eligibility extends only to a limited proportion of the population. Furthermore, the administration of social security is through a multiplicity of management bodies, which lack the necessary mechanisms for adequate integration, even where benefits would be derived from such integration. In the private sector the ISS and Family Allowances Funds protect their affiliated members in a relatively uniform manner. In the public sector, however, there are some 200 administrative agencies that co-exist with CAJANAL. There is a lack of integration between these various agencies resulting in higher health service costs and the discouragement of worker mobility between the private and public sectors, or even within the public sector itself.

Only about 16 per cent of the Colombian population is covered by its social security system. That is, only 2.8 million workers in the formal economic sector are affiliated to the various social security organisations. Some 4.7 million people (workers and their dependents) are covered by the health services provided by the social security institutions. The public health system provides health care to the entire Colombian population, but coverage does not extend to all sectors of the country.

When considering the coverage of social security in Colombia it is essential to differentiate between the formal and informal economic sectors. The first, comprising the formal business community, provides its workers with a range of social security benefits. The second, comprising production units that have evolved outside legal regulations, does not provide the social security protection that its workers need. For this reason the social security system provides unequal treatment for workers. Coverage is also concentrated on the larger urban centres with a larger formal sector.

As an alternative to the complete integration of the various administrative units managing the social security system it has been suggested that each social security sector should carry out global activity planning and thus develop services that are common between sectors, without trying to unify the various administrative units, which would be extremely difficult in Colombia in the present time. Thus it is proposed that the functions of the various administrative agencies need to be redefined as part of the search for greater efficiency. The provision of more efficient health services must be one of basic objectives of any effective coordination.

It has also been proposed that the uniform pensionable age be set at 60 (with the idea of increasing this to 65 by the end of this century). It has also been suggested that it is necessary to eliminate retirement at any age with a pension which is currently a practice. In the area of family allowances there is a need to focus more on nutritional programmes, pre-school activities, health services and the reorientation of other activities for the benefit of the less

95

protected sectors of the Colombian society.

The classical concept of the state being solely responsible for achieving social justice has long been accepted in Colombia and is based on the premise that there exists a wealthy public treasury and an efficient administration. In fact, the Colombian treasury is weak and the greater part of its administrative apparatus is not sufficiently effective. Thus there is a need to search for new mechanisms, involving a greater level of participation by the private sector and by the social security institutions, to solve the country's myriad of social problems.

REFERENCES AND FURTHER READING

Almanza, J. M. (1985), 'Reflejos de la crisis economica en la seguridad social y sus soluciones', Revista Actualidad Laboral, 10, 22-7.

Arenas, G. (1984), 'Habla Adan Arriaga: padre del derecho laboral colombiano', Revista Actualidad Laboral, 5, 3-8.

_____ (1984), 'Alcances de la Ley 11 de 1984', Revista Actualidad Laboral, 2, 18-28.

_____ (1984), 'Aspectos practicos de la afiliacion al seguro social', Revista Actualidad Laboral, 1, 22-4.

_____ (1986), 'Las modificaciones al sistema pensional del seguro social', Revista Actualidad Laboral, 13, 4-9.

_____ (1986), 'La mision del empleo y reforma Laboral', Revista Actualidad Laboral, 18, 4-14.

Arias, G. (1980), 'La seguridad social de la mujer en Colombia', Bogota 1980, p.39. (Monografia Nacional para las Americas de la Organizacion Internacional del Trabajo).

Arias, R. (1975), 'Algunos aspectos economicos de las asignaciones familiares en la nueva orientacion de la seguridad social', Revista de la Seguridad Social, 82-4, 293-300.

Colombia

_____ (1987), '30 anos trabajando para los trabajadores Colombianos', El Tiempo, 4E-5E, c. 1-6.

Campos, D. (1981), Regimen Legal de los Empleados Officiales en Colombia, Bogota: Editorial Temis, 654.

Carrillo, J.C. (1984), 'El concepto de salario y la telarana fiscal", Revista Actualidad Laboral, 1, 25-30.

Cetina, O. (1986), Derecho Integral de Seguridad Social, Bogota: Universidad Externado de Colombia, 625.

Colombia, CAJA Nacional de Prevision Social (1987), Servicios Medicos, Bogota: CAJANAL.

Colombia, Departamento Nacional de Estadistica (DANE), (1985), Censo de Poblacion de Colombia, Bogota: DANE.

_____ (1984), Situacion y Perspectivas de la Seguridad Social en Colombia, Bogota: Ministerio de Trabajo.

Colombia, Ministerios de Salud. Instituto Colombiano de Bienestar Familiar (1987), Que es el ICBF: Asistencia Legal, Nutricion y Proteccion, Bogota: ICBF.

_____ (1986), Informes de Actividades 1982/1986, Bogota: ICBF.

Colombia, Ministerio de Salud, OPS and OMS (1984), Colombia: Diagnosticos de Salud: Politicas y Estrategias, Bogota: Editorial Trazo Ltda.

Colombia, Ministerio de Trabajo y Seguridad Social. CAJA Nacional de Prevision Social (1983), El Pensionado un Potencial Desconocido: Investigacion sobre los Pensionados de CAJANAL, Bogota: CAJANAL.

_____ (1983), Estructura Organica Interna del ISS: Niveles Nacional y Seccional, 2nd Edition, Bogota: ISS.

Colombia

Cortes, C.A., 'Cobertura real del ISS: territorios, sistemas de atencion y poblacion amparada', Revista Actualidad Laboral, 19, 20-7.

Cristancho, J.L. (1986), Colombia y los Modelos de Seguridad Social en el Mundo, Bogota: Ediciones Tercer Mundo.

Gaviria, M.J. (1985), 'El seguro de vida frente a la proteccion del seguro social', Revista Actualidad Laboral, 11, 24-8.

Giraldo, H. (1984), 'Reflexiones sobre la seguridad social en Colombia', Revista Actualidad Laboral, 1, 3-6.

Gonzalez, G. (1979), Derecho del Trabajo, Bogota: Editorial Temis.

_____ (1984), 'Sintesis historica del movimiento sindical Colombiano', Revista Actualidad Laboral, 5, 15-22.

_____ (1985), 'Los origenes de la estabilidad laboral en Colombia', Revista Actualidad Laboral, 11, 29-32.

Instituto de Seguros Sociales (1986), Codigo de los Seguros Sociales en Colombia, Bogota: Imprenta Nacional, vi.

Lopez, L. (1986), 'La retencion en la fuente sobre salarios', Revista Actualidad Laboral, 20, 15-21.

_____ (1987), 'La reforma tributaria y los trabajadores', Revista Actualidad Laboral, 20, 15-21.

Madrid-Malo, M. (1984), 'El derecho al trabajo', Revista Actualidad Laboral, 2, 4-7.

Morales, I. (1986), Ensayo sobre Seguridad Social en Colombia, Bogota: Editorial Temis.

Raso, J. (1984), 'Seguridad social para trabajadores independientes', Revista Actualidad Laboral, 3, 27-32.

Colombia

Rengifo, J. (1982), La Seguridad Social en Colombia
    y Legislacion Colombiana de los Seguros
    Sociales, Bogota: Editorial Temis.

_____ (1984) 'Etapas de los seguros sociales en
    Colombia', in Revista Actualidad Laboral,
    LEGIS No.5 (September-October), Bogota, 9-14.

_____ (1985), 'El acto administrativo de
    afiliacion al ISS', Revista Actualidad
    Laboral, LEGIS No.9, Bogota, 4-6.

_____ (1987) 'Prestaciones de la seguridad social
    para trabajadores independientes', in Revista
    Actualidad Laboral, LEGIS No.19
    (January-February), Bogota, 4-25.

Satizaball, C. (1981), Manual para el Cobro de
    Prestaciones Sociales Oficiales, Bogota:
    Editorial Temis.

CUBA
Carmelo Mesa-Lago & Sergio G. Roca

THE WELFARE SYSTEM ENVIRONMENT

<u>Ideological Environment</u>

Within a short time-span almost three decades ago, Cuba's ideological position and socio-economic organisation experienced a drastic reorientation turning away from capitalism and pointing toward socialism, obviously resulting in significant changes in the fabric of the social welfare system. Since 1959, revolutionary Cuba has staunchly advocated an ideological stance broadly characterised by collectivism in the ownership of the means of production, centralism in the decision-making process, egalitarianism in the distribution of goods and services, moralism in the use of work incentives, and internationalism in the conduct of foreign policy.

In large measure, over time and across features, Cuba has successfully implemented her ideological agenda, virtually transforming the island into a radical-mobilisational society (Mesa-Lago 1981 & 1988; Perez-Lopez 1986; Roca 1983). Indeed, even among socialist countries, Cuba exhibits one of the highest ratios of state ownership of economic resources (including over 81 per cent of agricultural lands). In addition, Cuba's commitment to social justice has produced a distributive equality with few parallels, a condition lately reaffirmed by the resurgence of moral incentives and the demotion of material rewards. Internationalist service, by both military and civilian personnel, is upheld as a collective moral responsibility and is deemed to be a mark of individual political maturity.

Cuba has declared the building of socialism and the eventual striving toward communism to be the central political task facing the country and its citizens. At the First Congress of the Cuban Communist Party in 1975, it was agreed that

> the fundamental objective of ideological work is to convert Marxism-Leninism into the real guide to thought, behavior and daily life of millions of people (Partido Comunista de Cuba, 1978)

Among the key tasks to be undertaken was the formation of a Communist attitude with respect to work and social property, which required constant struggle against selfishness, individualism, personal ambition, ostentation and other remnants of the past. In contrast, the new socialist values to be affirmed and fostered included cooperation, sacrifice, modesty and, above all, conciencia. The model citizen was to be patterned after Ernesto 'Che' Guevara, whose life of voluntary work, ascetic habits, and internationalist activity is eulogized in the political education of students and workers in Cuba.

From this ideological foundation, the basic outline of Cuba's social welfare system may be succinctly described. In socialist Cuba, the social security programme and the provision of personal social services feature: universal coverage of the population; extensive range of covered contingencies; generous distribution of benefits, and relative egalitarianism. In Cuba, perhaps more so than in most countries, the social welfare system truly reflects the dominant ideological values.

While such consistency may be properly viewed as an achievement of social policy, it could also evolve into a major economic burden in the years ahead. In this chapter, we endeavour to outline the development, structure, financing and programmes of the social welfare system in Cuba and attempt to indicate what limits and problems it may confront in the immediate future.

Historical Origins

Cuba was one of Latin America's pioneer countries in social security and, even though it attained a significant level of development prior to the

Revolution, the system was stratified and suffered
from extreme inequalities and grave financial
imbalance (Grupo Cubano de Investigaciones
Economicas 1963 & 1964; Mesa-Lago 1960). Between
1913 and 1958, 52 autonomous pension funds were
created: 21 covered salaried workers in the
private sector (white and blue collar), 20 covered
professionals, and 11 covered white and blue
collar workers in the public sector (see Table
1). Each fund covered a group of insured from one
profession, trade or sector (for example, lawyers,
barbers, sugar), and each had its own legislation,
administration, financial sources and benefits.
No coordination existed among the funds, much less
a transfer of resources among them. The state, by
means of special taxes, or general revenue,
substantially contributed to the richer funds
(congressional members, governors and mayors) but
contributed only marginally or after long delay or
did not contribute at all to the poorer funds
(drivers, barbers).

Health insurance (for common illness) did not
exist, even though, as in other Latin American
countries (such as Argentina and Uruguay) an
important urban network of mutualist clinics and
non-profit cooperatives had been developed,
supplemented by public hospitals and private
clinics. As in the case of pensions, the lowest
income strata - especially in rural zones - either
received no health care at all or very low quality
care. All employed female workers were covered by
maternity insurance established in 1934 which
provided paid leave and health-care benefits,
while the wives of the insured were entitled to
medical-hospital care. Even though Cuba did not
initially have health insurance - in contrast to
Chile, Peru, Mexico and Costa Rica - its general
level of health care was among the highest in the
region. Nevertheless, differences between urban
and rural sectors were very marked.

Between 1944 and 1957 not less than eight
studies on social security in Cuba were carried
out and practically all of them recommended a
reform of the system along the lines of
unification (International Bank 1951; Comision de
Aportes Estatales 1957). But the powerful
pressure groups systematically opposed reform, and
the state was unable to correct the
stratification, inequalities and financial crisis
of the system.

TABLE 1: APPEARANCE OF SOCIAL SECURITY LEGISLATION IN CUBA BY RISK AND OCCUPATIONAL GROUPS COVERED: 1913-1983

Years[1]	Social Security Risks Protected	Groups Covered
1913, 1934	ODS	Armed forces
1915	ODS	Communications
1916, 1933	OR	Salaried workers from the public and private sector
1917, 1927	ODS	Judicial power
1919	ODS	Public employees, public school[2]
1920, 1936	ODS	Police
1921, 1923	ODS	Railroads, telephone[2]
1927	ODS	Maritime
1929	ODS	Notaries, recording of deeds, transportation[2]
1934, 1937	M	Salaried workers from the public and private sectors
1935	ODS	Journalists
1938	ODS	Banking
1939	ODS	Commercial registers
1943	ODS	Doctors, sugar workers[2]
1945	ODS	Lawyers, textile workers[2]
1946	ODS	Legal clerks, graphic artists, state workers, barbers and hairdressers, tobacco workers[2]
1947	ODS	Pharmacists[2]
1948	ODS	Customs officials, electricity[2]
1949	ODS	Dentists, veterinarians, architects, commercial, flour[2]
1950	ODS	Congress members, restaurateurs[2]
1951	ODS	Petroleum, radio[2]
1952	ODS	Insurance and finance, nurses[2]
1953	ODS	Brewers
1954	ODS	Civil engineers, stenographers, health sector, construction, cattle[2]

Cuba

1955	ODS	Agronomists, school teachers (private), educators, comptroller office, agricultural instructors[2]
1956	ODS	Governors, mayors, councilmen
1957	ODS	Drivers
1959	ODS	Unifies institutions of salaried workers in private sector
1960-61	ODS	Unifies and regulates public sector institutions
1962	ODS	Unifies professional institutions
1963	ODS,TB,H	Unifies entire social security system: regulates and expands monetary benefits to all salaried workers, creates health insurance for entire population, integrates social welfare
1964	ODS,TB	Special system for self-employed workers
1974	M	New unified maternity system
1976	ODS,TB	Special system for armed forces
1977	OR	Regulates occupational risk prevention and labour hygiene
1979	ODS,TB	New social security system
1983	ODS,TB	Special system for agricultural cooperative members

---

Notation:

ODS = Old-age, Disability and Survivors' Pensions; M = Maternity; H = Health; TB = Temporary Benefits; OR = Occupational Risks.

Notes:

1 The first date refers to the original law and the following dates refer to modifications of the original law.
2 Established by separate laws.

SOURCE: Legislation.

The 1959 Revolution reinforced the power of the state and weakened the pressure groups, thus permitting a gradual process of unification and standardisation of the system. The state gradually seized all funds and programmes: in 1959 the pension funds of private salaried workers; in 1960 the pension funds of the public sector and maternity insurance; and in 1962 the pension funds of professionals and occupational risk insurance. These funds and programmes ceased to be autonomous and became administered by the Ministry of Labor (MINTRAB). The latter standardised contributions and established a general minimum for all pensions (40 pesos in 1960 and 60 pesos in 1969), which represented a substantial increase for the large low-income strata of the population. A constitutional reform gave power to the Executive to borrow from the reserve pension funds and provide monies for national socio-economic development programmes, such as agrarian reform and housing. In the 1960s, all private hospitals, mutualist clinics and cooperatives were nationalised and unified under the Ministry of Public Health (MINSAP). In addition the incipient pharmaceutical industry was nationalised and, from 1965 on, all doctors had to swear an oath at graduation renouncing private practice in their profession.

The standardisation and expansion of coverage of the social security system was accomplished through a 1963 law, which universalised pension coverage to all the salaried labour force and introduced a national health care programme to cover the entire population; which established the exclusive responsibility of the state to finance social security; and which standardised both entitlement conditions for benefits and the method of calculating them. Subsequent laws regulated conditions for pensions and other monetary benefits for special groups: in 1964 independent professionals, self-employed workers, small businessmen and fishing and charcoal cooperative members; in 1966 private farmers who, due to old age or disability, had sold their lands to the state; in 1976 the armed forces, and in 1983 members of agricultural production cooperatives. In addition, in 1974 and 1977 unified norms for maternity and occupational risks were introduced. Finally, a 1979 law - currently in force - integrated all of the social security system and placed it under the administration of the State

Committee of Labor and Social Security (CETSS) which replaced the MINTRAB (CTC 1980a, 1980b; CETSS 1977 & 1983).

In summary, social security developed early in Cuba as in other pioneer nations but in a fragmented manner, responding to pressure groups with diverse powers which created a relatively advanced system for the era yet one that was very stratified, unequal and lacked coordination. The Revolution, reinforcing the power of the state, attained the unification and standardisation of the system (with some exceptions) as well as universal coverage.

Political and Socio-economic Environment

Political power on the island is firmly entrenched in the Cuban Communist Party, under the overpowering figure of Fidel Castro (Dominguez 1978). In the pattern of socialist regimes, Cuba's political organisation consists of parallel party-government structures arrayed from the national to the local levels. At the top, the Party's Politburo, Secretariat and Central Committee have their counterparts in the government's Council of Ministers, Council of State and the National Assembly of Popular Power (the nominal legislative body). At lower levels (provinces and municipalities) party and government bodies uneasily share in implementing and supervising policy directives from above, though since 1985 the power of local party units has increased. Another important conduit of social and economic policy decisions, including many directives in the realm of social welfare, is the vast set of mass organisations: the Committees for the Defense of the Revolution (CDR), the Federation of Cuban Women (FMC), and the Cuban Workers Central (CTC), among others.

At present, the economy in Cuba, as in pre-revolutionary times, is heavily concentrated on sugar production and largely dependent upon foreign trade (Mesa-Lago 1981 & 1988; Roca 1978). Sugar exports are estimated to account for about 75 to 80 per cent of total exports. In the last decade, total merchandise trade (exports plus imports) has averaged over 40 per cent of Gross Social Product (GSP), with the Soviet Union as the main partner accounting for about two-thirds of the total merchandise trade. The Soviet Union heavily subsidises (in relation to world market prices) the economy in Cuba in several ways (for example, paying high prices for sugar and charging low prices for oil). In 1985, the Soviet economic subsidy, excluding military assistance, reached about 20 per cent of the GSP of Cuba.

The record of economic growth in socialist Cuba has been very uneven, with sharp fluctuations ranging from negative rates in the second half of the 1960s and very low rates in the mid-1980s, interspersed with a strong performance in the first half of the 1970s and the first half of the 1980s. Among key factors influencing such erratic records are the volatile behaviour of world sugar prices, natural calamities (hurricanes and drought), intrinsic shortcomings of the planning model, and recurrent changes in Cuba's economic policies and organisational structure. In 1981, the sectoral distribution of the labour force in Cuba was as follows: 22 per cent in agriculture, 19 per cent in industry, 9 per cent in construction, 16 per cent in trade and transportation and 31 per cent in services (mostly education and health). In 1979, 93.6 per cent of the labour force were employed, and 4.9 per cent were private farmers, 0.8 per cent were self-employed and 0.7 per cent were private wage earners and unpaid family workers. In 1979 the unemployment rate was 5.4 per cent of the labour force and declined to 3.4 per cent in 1981, but low productivity (expressed in terms of excessive payrolls and violations of the work schedule) continues to plague the economy in Cuba and its welfare system.

Traditionally, Cuba has been a country with low inflation and in the revolutionary period this phenomenon has been strongly controlled, at least up until the 1980s. Although no official statistics on inflation exist, it has been estimated that inflation increased markedly in the early 1980s (see Mesa-Lago 1986, pp.295-6).

In 1986, Cuba's total population was estimated to be 10.2 million people, with 70 per cent residing in urban centres and 30 per cent in rural areas. The capital city of Havana encompassed 20 per cent of the country's population, a ratio virtually unchanged since the 1950s. In the last decade, the rate of population growth has been quite low (under 1.5 per cent) continuing a secular decline from the higher rates (over 2.5 per cent) of the early 1960s. In 1985 about 25 per cent of the population were under 15 years of age and about 8.5 per cent were over 65 years of age. By the year 2010 these ratios are estimated to register 21 and 11 per cent respectively, while the median age will have increased by 10 years to 35.

THE WELFARE SYSTEM: AN OVERVIEW

Structure, Coverage and Administration of Social Welfare

The present social security system in Cuba, as is typical in centrally planned economies, is run completely by the state, has a high degree of unity and standardisation and is incorporated in national planning. Nevertheless, it is officially reported that gaps still exist in the planning process which must be filled to achieve greater rationality and quality in the plans, and a better evaluation of administrative efficiency (CETSS 1977 & 1983). The system integrates social insurance, social welfare and health care, although these programmes are the responsibility of different state agencies.

The principal agency is the CETSS, which is responsible for all aspects of labour and social security, such as execution, control and inspection. CETSS administers the old age, disability and survivors' pension programme financed by the state social security budget, and also formulates policy for the social welfare programmes and controls its execution.

The national health system is administered by MINSAP, financed by the state health budget, which relies on an extensive national network of hospitals, polyclinics and health posts organised in pyramidal form with various levels: national, provincial, and local. The system provides medical-hospital, rehabilitation and orthodontical care and medicines for common or occupational accidents and diseases and maternity care; MINSAP is responsible for curative and preventive medicine (both are well integrated), operates welfare institutions (such as homes for the elderly and disabled) and administers all pharmaceutical enterprises (which satisfies most of the national demand). Outside of MINSAP there are rehabilitation centres with their own administration and budget.

Monetary benefits, such as subsidies in lieu of salary for common illness, maternity and occupational risks, as well as partial-disability and provisional pensions, and funeral aid, are administered by state enterprises and financed by the state social security budget.

The local Organs of Peoples Power (OPP), municipal and provincial agencies with popular participation, administer provisional pensions for the families of retired workers, some partial disability pensions and funeral aid financed by the state social security budget. The OPPs are also responsible for the concession of social welfare monetary benefits as well as some benefits in kind.

The Ministries of the Armed Forces (MINFAR) and of the Interior (MININ) administer all pensions and monetary benefits for these two groups, with their own autonomous budgets. These two groups are only integrated with the rest of the population in the national health system.

The insured does not have direct participation in the administration of social security programmes except within the OPPs. In addition, there are Labour Councils that initially resolve claims against the decisions of state enterprises concerning short-term benefits. However, when the enterprise is not in agreement with the labour council its decision is annulled and the issue passed to regular courts. Finally, various mass organisations, such as the CDRs, the FMC, the CTC and the National Association of Small Farmers (ANAP), participate in vaccination campaigns, health education, contagious-disease control, blood donations and community activities.

According to the law, the entire population is covered by the health-maternity programme for non-monetary benefits in kind and services, but Cuba does not publish statistics on the population coverage of welfare programmes. In addition, all salaried workers (in the state, cooperative and private sectors) are entitled to monetary benefits, such as pensions and short-term benefits including subsidies in lieu of salary for sickness or accident (occupational or non-occupational) and maternity. Finally, the insured's dependents are entitled to survivors' pensions and funeral aid. The scope of family coverage in pensions is relatively generous and includes: widows (although only entitled to a pension for two years if younger than 40, without children, and capable of working), widowers (if older than 60 or disabled), minor unmarried (or disabled) children and parents. There is neither unemployment insurance nor a programme of family allowances.

Table 2 gives a rough estimate of population coverage, based upon the law, the composition of the labour force in the 1970 and the 1981 census and a 1979 national demographic survey. It is assumed that the total population is completely covered for health-maternity benefits, although with differences in access and quality of medical and hospital services to be discussed below. In accordance with the rough estimates of Table 2, Cuba increased health maternity coverage of the population from 4.2 per cent in 1958 (zero if only health coverage is considered) to 100 per cent in 1970. This accounts for the most rapid and universal expansion in the whole region. Coverage of the economically active population rose from almost 63 per cent in 1958 to 93 per cent in 1981, taking second place for the region, after Brazil, and if the social welfare programme is taken into account, reaching almost universal coverage. Cuba is one of the few Latin American countries where the extreme poverty group is covered by the social security system (Centro de Investigaciones 1983; Mesa-Lago 1980).

Members of agricultural-livestock, fishing and charcoal cooperatives who sell their products to the state, have compulsory coverage and, even though they are not salaried workers, are entitled to the same monetary benefits that salaried workers receive. Members of the armed forces also have compulsory coverage and are entitled to all monetary benefits but under a subsystem that is separate from the general system.

Three population groups are entitled to none or only part of the monetary benefits: owners of small private farms, independent workers, self-employed workers, small entrepreneurs in the service sector, the unemployed, unpaid family workers and domestic servants in the private sector. Those not covered by insured monetary benefits can, if without means, receive social welfare benefits; included are the elderly, the disabled, single mothers with children, and all those whose essential needs are not insured.

TABLE 2: SOCIAL SECURITY COVERAGE OF POPULATION IN CUBA: 1958-1981

| Years | Insured Population | | | | Percentage of Coverage[3] | | Average Annual Growth Rates (log) | | | | Quotient of Demographic Burden[4] |
	Actives[1] ('000)	Passives ('000)	Remaining Insured in health[2] ('000)	Total ('000)	Total Population	Economically Active Population	Total Population	Economically Active Population	Insured Active	Insured Total	
1958	1,388	154	...	290[5]	4.2	62.6	...	...	...	...	0.111
1970	2,337	363	5,869	8,569	100.0	88.7	1.9	1.4	4.4	32.6	0.155
1979	3,100	671[6]	6,040	9,811	100.0	89.6	1.5	3.1	3.2	1.5	0.216
1981	3,364	710[6]	5,650	9,724	100.0	93.0	-0.4	2.3	4.2	-0.4	0.211

NOTES:

1 Excludes private farmers not integrated into cooperatives, unemployed and unpaid family workers.
2 Coverage according to the law; coverage statistics are not published.
3 Total population coverage refers to health (maternity in 1958) and coverage of the economic active population refers to old-age, disability and survivors' pensions.
4 Number of passives divided by active insured.
5 Women employed and covered by maternity insurance.
6 The 1979 survey showed 505,054 retirees and pensioners plus those who received housing payments or welfare assistance from the state whereas the 1981 census showed 607,700, both figures are much lower than those in the table. The number of recipients in 1982 rose to 769,800 according to CETSS (figures provided in March 1984).

SOURCE: Total population and EAP: 1958 from Mesa-Lago, 1970 from population census; 1979 from National Demographic Survey; and 1981 from population census. Actives: 1958 from Social Security in Cuba (University of Miami, 1963); 1970 to 1981 estimates of the author based on legislation, population census figures and the 1979 survey. Passives from Mesa-Lago 1970, p.171 and estimates based on 24 años revolución en la seguridad social cubana (La Habana: CETSS 1983). Percentages, rates and quotients calculated by the authors.

Financing Social Welfare

Prior to the Revolution, a wide diversity in wage contributions existed among the 52 pension funds. In 1962, the contribution of the salaried workers fund (for both the public and private sectors) was standardised at 10 per cent and was paid exclusively by the employer. Table 3 shows the present situation of wage contributions of employees and employers. There are no wage contributions for financing medical-hospital benefits as their total cost is paid for by the state budget assigned to MINSAP. A separate programme for occupational risks does not exist but is, instead, incorporated as part of the two basic types of benefits; there is no contribution payable for this either.

Apart from the wage contribution (or income distribution) social security in Cuba has no other source of funding. There are no reserves and hence no investments. There are no special taxes, lottery revenues nor loans from the exterior directly assigned to the system. Nevertheless, Cuba receives a large amount of economic aid at generous terms from the Soviet Union and part of this aid may have been used to finance the social security system (Mesa-Lago 1981, pp.102-7).

TABLE 3: LEGAL CONTRIBUTIONS TO SOCIAL SECURITY BY PROGRAMME AND SOURCE IN CUBA IN 1986 (as a percentage of salary income)

	Insured Persons			Employer[4]
Programmes	Salaried[1]	Self-employed[2]	Cooperative Member[3]	
Monetary Benefits[5]	-	10	3	10
Medical-Hospital Benefits[5]	-	-	-	-
Total	-	10	3	10

Cuba

Notes:

1   From the private, state and cooperative sectors.
2   Upon the conventional monthly salary selected, and voluntary affiliation.
3   Members of agricultural and livestock cooperatives (in the fishing and charcoal cooperatives that sell to the state, the same system as for salaried workers is applied). The percentage is on an average daily income.
4   For state as well as private: the latter pays 25 per cent for income tax and social security contributions. Contribution of the state employer for the armed forces and internal security is unknown.
5   Monetary benefits for pensions (old age, disability and survivors'), temporary aid (for disease, maternity and accident) and social welfare; covers common risks as well as occupational risks.

SOURCE: Legislation.

All social security contributions enter the state budget as one among other sources of income and, in turn, the budget assigns expenditure lines to CETSS, MINSAP, the OPPs, rehabilitation centres and state enterprises. CETSS confirms that the financing of social security in Cuba is based on a method that approximates what we call pure assessment, under the state budget (CETSS 1977b, pp.106). But note that this is a sui generis pure assessment method, as the state absorbs all revenue and covers any deficit in the system, and that in more than two decades, the contribution percentage has not been raised. Hence, financial equilibrium is not established within the social security system (as it has no independent accounting) but within the macroeconomic framework.

Cuba regularly publishes figures on the partial cost of monetary benefits (at least since the 1980s) and sporadic data on health care expenditures, but there is no recent information on revenue generated by contributions. Table 4 is a reconstruction of the balance of revenues and expenditures for social security monetary benefits. This is based on official statistics in the period 1962-74, but only on official expenditures for 1978 to 1985. Revenue in 1978-85 was estimated by the authors at 10 per cent of the

113

total wage fund (the latter based on official figures). Table 4 shows that the social security balance generated a decreasing surplus in the first half of the 1960s and a growing deficit in the second half of the 1970s. In 1980, the deficit was almost equivalent to half of revenues: 224 million pesos, representing 1.3 per cent of the GSP, one of the highest percentages in Latin America.

Although an official in Cuba has roughly estimated that the cost of monetary benefits takes about 20 per cent of the total wage fund (that is twice the current 10 per cent charged), the position of Cuba's social security administration is that there is no deficit in their system. They argue that the state controls all the economy and guarantees to cover any resulting deficit, hence there is not strict dependency on contributions but whatever funds are annually needed are taken from the GSP and earmarked in the state budget. However, they acknowledge that there is a limit, the economic capacity of the country (Penate Rivero & Lugo Machado 1985, pp.58-75). At this point, the discussion on this issue may appear as a semantic one but the crucial facts are: first, the social security system in Cuba does not have a clear accounting method of revenues and expenditures needed to estimate whether the country can economically afford such a burden; and, second, current social security expenditures amount to twice the current contribution of state enterprises.

TABLE 4: SOCIAL SECURITY BALANCE OF REVENUES AND EXPENDITURES IN CUBA: 1962-1985 (in millions of pesos at 1989 prices)

Year	Revenues[1]	Expenditures[2]		Balance as a percentage of revenues
1962	322.4	151.9	170.5	52.9
1965	344.5	249.8	94.7	27.5
1974	422.7	553.4	-130.7	-30.9
1978	459.1	648.0	-188.9	-41.1
1980	485.1	709.3	-224.2	-46.2
1982	608.9	809.0	-200.1	-32.9
1985	713.9	965.2	-251.3	-35.2

Cuba

Notes:

1　Excludes revenues of the health system.
2　Expenditures for pensions, temporary benefits (both excluding the armed forces) and social welfare; excludes expenditures for health, prevention of and rehabilitation for occupational risks, and administrative expenditures.

SOURCES: Revenues for 1962-65 from the national budget published in the Gaceta Official; 1974 from Seminarut Latinoamericanode Cuentas Nacionales y Balances de la Economia, Cuba: conversion de los principales indicadores macroeconomicos del sistema de balances de la economia nacional (SBEN) al sistema de cuentas nacionales (SCN) 1974 (La Habana, March 1982); 1978 to 1985 estimated by the authors as 10 per cent of total wage bill (based on Anuario Estadistiade Cuba 1985). Expenditures from the same sources as Table 7. Pensions and numbers of pensioners from CETSS, La seguridad social en Cuba, pp.33, 50 and 24 anos de revolucion en la seguridad social cubana, pp.48-49, 66; and Anuario Estadistico de Cuba, 1982, p.126. Inflation index developed by Mesa-Lago. Average pension and indices calculated by the authors.

As Table 5 shows, the cost of social security in Cuba, as a percentage of the gross domestic product (GDP), doubled between 1958 and 1971 from 6 to 12 per cent), but declined in the following years to that in 1980 which was below 9 per cent. (Social security expenditures as a percentage of fiscal expenditures is extremely low in Cuba, as compared to the rest of Latin America, due to the enormous magnitude of the state expenditures in Cuba which encompass the entire national economy.) In spite of this reduction, the percentage of social security expenditures to GDP for Cuba in 1980 was surpassed in the region only by that of three countries (Uruguay, Argentina and Chile), all with older social security systems. It must be taken into account that if the costs of occupational risks prevention and rehabilitation, funeral aid, armed forces' subsidies and administrative costs were included, the cost of social security programmes in Cuba would be greater than it appears in Table 5.

TABLE 5: COST OF SOCIAL SECURITY IN CUBA: 1958-1980

| | Social Security Expenditures | | |
| | | As a per cent of: | |
	(Millions of Pesos)[1]	Government GDP	Expenditures
1958	157	6.0	40.7
1962	241	6.5	13.0
1965	406	8.3	16.0
1971	779	12.2	-
1975	985	9.7	-
1978	1,120	9.2	12.2
1980	1,229	8.6	12.9

Notes:

1   In 1962 and 1965 GDP was roughly estimated using the GSP for those years and the relationship GDP/GSP in 1971-1981.
2   Includes expenditures for pensions, temporary benefits, health care and social welfare; in 1958 private sector expenditures are excluded and, in the remainder, expenditures for prevention and rehabilitation for occupational risks, funeral aid, armed forces' subsidies and administrative costs are excluded.

SOURCES: 1958 GDP from Revista del Banco Nacional de Cuba, 5:5 (May 1959): 756; 1962-65 estimates by the author; 1971-80 from the Banco Nacional de Cuba, Informe Economico (La Habana, August 1982), p.30. Central Government Expenditures: 1958 from Grupo Cubano de Investigaciones Economicas, Un estudio sobre Cuba (University of Miami Press, 1963, p.871); the rest from the state budget published in the Gaceta Oficial and in Granma. Social Security Expenditures: 1958 from Social Security in Cuba, pp.135, 149; the rest from CETSS, La seguridad social en Cuba (La

Habana, August 1977), pp.33, 50, and <u>24</u>
<u>anos de revolucion en la seguridad social</u>
<u>cubana</u>, pp.48-49, <u>Anuario Estadistico de</u>
<u>Cuba, 1982</u>, p.126 and health care figures
from various sources.

Table 6 shows that the two fundamental
components of social security expenditures are
pensions and health benefits. Although the former
takes a higher percentage of funding than the
latter, no clear funding tendency appears to exist
in either, especially in the last decade.
(Information received from CETSS in 1984
indicates, however, that the percent allocated for
pensions in 1983 was over 50 per cent (Penate
Rivero 1984). On the other hand, monetary
benefits show a declining tendency and social
welfare appears to be stagnant.

TABLE 6: PERCENTAGE DISTRIBUTION OF SOCIAL
SECURITY EXPENDITURES BY PROGRAMME IN
CUBA: 1965-1980

Expenditures[1]	1965	1971	1975	1980
Pension[2]	51.4	39.9	45.5	44.4
Health/Maternity[3]	38.4	37.7	40.6	42.3
Temporary Benefits[4]	10.2	15.9	7.2	7.9
Social Welfare & Others	-	6.5	6.7	5.4
TOTAL	100.0	100.0	100.0	100.0

Notes:

1 Excludes expenditures on occupational risks
   prevention and rehabilitation, funeral aid,
   and administrative costs.
2 Old age, disability and survivors' pensions
   including those from occupational risks.
3 Total costs of the national health system,
   including preventive medicine and
   administrative costs.
4 Subsidies for health/maternity and accidents
   with the exception of those paid to members of
   the armed forces.

SOURCE: See Table 4.

THE AGED

In 1985 the estimated population over age 65 was
867,000 or 8.9 per cent of the population. By the
year 2010 the estimate is 1,122,000. In contrast
to most Latin American countries, the population
of Cuba is ageing.

Social Security

Within the Latin American context, the pension
benefits in Cuba are among the most generous
entitlement conditions and among the most
flexible. Although seniority retirement does not
exist in Cuba (except for the armed forces)
retirement ages for old age are similar to the
legal averages for the region (60 years for men
and 55 years for women, both required to have
completed 25 years of employment including
employment prior to entering covered employment).
These ages are very low when one takes into
account the fact that Cuba has the highest life
expectancy in Latin America and that women live an
average of three years more than men (even more
significant in view of the differences in
retirement age). Furthermore, Cuba requires five
years less of employment for retirement than other
countries that have a similar population age
structure and equal retirement ages (Argentina and
Uruguay). It is also possible, in cases of
arduous labour, to retire at 55 if male, and 50 if
female, also with 25 years of employment.
Finally, the system establishes a pension minimum
that is relatively high in relation to the minimum
wage, and grants other benefits, such as the
exemption of rent payments for housing (normally
fixed between 6 per cent and 10 per cent of family
salary or income) to retirees with a monthly
family income under 25 pesos.

There are several legal differences in
entitlement conditions for monetary benefits. The
legislation of the general system regulates
monetary benefits in a uniform manner, but
proportionally to salary in accordance with the
socialist principle of to each according to his
work. In the 1963 law, a fixed ceiling for
pensions (250 pesos) was established which, along
with the fixed minimum (60 pesos) made pensions
fairly equal in amount. The 1979 law, presently
in force, replaced pensions based on a fixed

ceiling with pensions based on 90 per cent of salary (with the goal of favouring highly qualified workers) and established a scale for the minimum amount, also in accordance with salary (from 60 to 36 pesos and less according to a decrease in annual salary from 800 to 540 pesos or less) (CETSS 1983, pp.82, 106). These changes have increased the differences in pension amounts. Thus, while prior to 1979 the ratio between the lowest and the highest pension was four to one, it now can be as high as 20 to one.

The pension laws also established differences in benefits and entitlement conditions among groups. Members of the armed forces and internal security have a special system, a difference justified by 'service conditions, made unique by constant sacrifice'. This system provides conditions superior to those of the general system, including seniority pensions, and higher benefits. Disability pensions resulting from heroic acts in defence of the work place, or internationalist missions are increased 20 per cent over the normal percentage calculation (CTC 1980a; CETSS 1977b). On the other hand, independent workers are subject to the special system (under the old law of 1963) whose conditions are inferior to those of the present law.

Personal Social Services

It is only recently that Cuba has started to face what will probably become a major social policy concern, namely the inadequacy of the personal social services available to the aged. In 1985 there were 93 retirement homes (including 10 private units administered by the Roman Catholic Church) with 9,802 beds and 16 day-care centres for the aged. The ratio of social assistance beds per 1,000 population over 65 has decreased from 16.4 in 1970 to 11.6 in 1985, having remained at that level for the last decade. In May 1987, Castro admitted that in the coming years the government will have to build more institutions for senior citizens and outlined a service-delivery system composed of _circulos_ (community centres without meals), _casas_ (day-care units with meals) and _hogares_ (full-time retirement homes) (_Bohemia_, Dec 26, 1986; _Granma_, Feb 6, 1986 & May 20, 1987; and CEE 1970 to 1986).

119

Evaluation

In the future, the cost of the pension programme in Cuba should increase due to three factors: an ageing population, increasing life expectancy, and relatively low retirement ages. Even though the new pension programme was introduced in 1963, and is thus one of the most recent in the region, approximately two-thirds of the population had previous coverage and a good part of this in mature programmes with very flexible conditions.

On the basis of inflation estimates (see Mesa-Lago 1986) real pensions declined during the period 1963 to 1968 but then rose somewhat in 1970 due to the 1969 increase in the minimum pension. Since then, the real pension has gradually fallen (with the exception of a period of stagnation in 1978-80) and in 1981 it was approximately half the 1963 level. The greatest fall in the real value of pensions occurred in 1981 when, due to an increase in wholesale prices, an inflation rate of 10 per cent was registered, the highest of the revolutionary period. At that time an increase in pensions was considered to at least compensate for the higher cost of living. In any case, one method of controlling pension costs in 1971-81 was apparently to avoid full adjustment of pensions to the cost of living.

In December 1986, in response to a shortage of foreign exchange and domestic budget deficits, a programme of 18 austerity measures was imposed by the government of Cuba. The negative impact of several measures (for example, doubling of urban bus fares, raise of 50 per cent in electricity rates, elimination of subsidised meals for many workers) upon real personal income was probably substantial. In order to partly offset such price increases all monthly pensions under 100 pesos were increased by a maximum of five pesos, a directive which stood to benefit 725,264 retirees (about 75 per cent of the total number) (CETSS Resolution No. 1 of 1987) (Granma, Dec 26, 1986 & Jan 5, 1987).

The current five-year plan stipulates that 87 new 'facilities for the aged' will be built in 1990, an increase of 80 per cent over the 1985 stock. Even so, it is highly likely that much more will remain to be done in this area.

THE DISABLED AND HANDICAPPED

There is very little information available about
the characteristics (size, composition, location)
of the disabled and handicapped population of
Cuba. It is equally difficult to obtain detailed
data concerning government policies and programmes
designed to render assistance to these groups. In
our many years of research on Cuba, we have only
come across a few very general references in
official documents and the press about the
presence and treatment of the physically and
mentally impaired. Thus only a limited discussion
of selected issues is offered.

Social Security

A full pension is granted for total physical or
mental incapacity to work: 40 per cent of average
earnings (50 per cent if work-related) during
highest five of last 10 years of employment, plus
an additional 1 per cent per year of employment
beyond 15 years, with a maximum of 90 per cent of
average earnings. A partial pension is granted if
the ability to perform work has been reduced
(partial disability): up to 50 per cent of lost
earnings; 70 per cent during rehabilitation.
Medical-hospital benefits are provided under the
national health system. Work injury cases cover
appliances and medicines when hospitalisation is
not required.

In 1985, the health system in Cuba
administered 18 centres for the physically and
mentally impaired with a total of 1,175 beds
(Granma, 26 December 1986, p.44). The largest
unit, dating to pre-revolutionary times, was the
Havana Psychiatric Hospital, located in the
outskirts of the capital. The pressing need still
to be addressed in this area is reflected in the
planned construction of 26 new 'homes for the
handicapped' in 1986-1990 (Granma, 6 February
1986, p.2). The official document did not specify
the size or type of these additional facilities.

Personal Social Services

In Cuba, special education programmes are
available to children and youth with mental
deficiencies, physical handicaps, or educational

and social maladjustments. From 1965 to 1985, the number of schools increased almost sevenfold, the number of teachers increased from under 600 to over 7,000 (plus about 5,000 teachers' aides) and enrolment expanded more than 10 times (CEE 1986, pp.484-7). In comparison with regular schools, Cuba's special education centres are amply staffed: in 1985-86 there were 29 teachers per school and six students per teacher in the special system, as against eight teachers and 14 students, respectively, in regular primary schools. In 1987, 12 special education schools with a capacity of 200 students each, were under construction in the city of Havana alone (Granma, 17 March 1987, p.1).

Since 1985 the Ministry of Education has conducted an experimental programme of individualised home instruction for primary and secondary students whose 'grave impairments' prevent them from attending regular classes (Bohemia, 13 February 1987, p.24). At the end of 1986 there were 46 teachers serving 59 children in the programme and plans were under way to extend the service to long-term hospital patients.

Evaluation

The little factual information available suggests that the treatment of the disabled and handicapped in Cuba is quite adequate by regional standards.

CHILDREN AND YOUTH

In 1985 there were about 2.5 million individuals under age 15. By the year 2010 this figure is expected to be about 2.1 million due to the ageing of the population.

Social Security

Social security programmes in Cuba do not include a formal programme of family allowances in terms of monetary benefits for children. However maternity care is provided for the mothers.

Maternity leave, equal to 100 per cent of salary (slightly above the regional average) is payable for 18 weeks, six before and twelve after confinement (the highest in the region) to currently employed females with 11 weeks of employment in the year preceding the leave. Medical-hospital benefits are provided under the national health system.

Personal Social Services

A national programme of day-care centres (<u>circulos infantiles</u>) provides food and education to children (from 45 days to five years of age) of working mothers. From a modest start in the early 1960s (166 centres with 17,161 children in 1965) the system grew significantly to 658 units serving 60,424 children in 1975 (CEE 1986, p.482). However, the rate of expansion slowed markedly in the following decade, especially after 1980. In fact, whereas the 1976-1980 plan envisioned 400 new units with an additional 120,000 enrolment, only 174 centres accommodating 31,000 children were actually built (<u>Partido Comunista de Cuba</u> 1978, p.145). Between 1980 and 1985, just 12 centres and 12,000 children were added to the system.

Early in 1987, Castro announced that 50 day-care centres (each with a capacity of 210 children) would be built during the year in the city of Havana alone (<u>Granma</u>, 17 March 1987, p.1). However, it must be pointed out that only eight centres were constructed in the entire country in the first nine months of 1986 (<u>Bohemia</u>, 26 December 1986, p.49). As it is, in 1985 the city of Havana encompassed 25 per cent of the country's day-care centres and accounted for 36 per cent of total enrolment. Yet in December 1986 over 19,000 children were placed on waiting lists in the city (<u>Bohemia</u>, 30 January 1987, pp.24-5). From this state of affairs, it may be surmised that in provincial capitals and smaller towns, day-care services are also likely to be insufficient.

At first, day-care was provided free of charge but now parents partially contribute to its financing. Monthly fees are determined by a sliding scale based on family income and range from three to 40 pesos for the first child, with a 50 per cent discount for the second enrollee (<u>Granma</u>, 28 January 1987, p.3). The average family cost is 20 pesos monthly, which covers about 25 per cent of total expenses with the government subsidising the rest. For instance, based on two children being enrolled, a family with a monthly income of 280 pesos would pay 30 pesos or 11 per cent of its income, while one earning 100 pesos would outlay only 7 per cent of its income.

Children and youth in Cuba are strongly encouraged to join and participate in the activities of several government-sponsored organisations which promote official values and seek to develop individual involvement in social tasks. The main groups are the Jose Marti Pioneers Organisation, the Federation of Secondary School Students, and the Society for Politico-Military Education. However, when social problems arise (truancy, petty crime, vagrancy and other kinds of social deviance) personal assistance or treatment is rendered by any number of institutions from among government agencies (Ministries of Education, Health and Interior) and mass organisations (Federation of Cuban Women (FMC) and Committee for the Defense of the Revolution (CDR)). In fact, the bulk of social work services in Cuba is provided by the FMC.

In the mid-1980s, the extent and severity of social deviance among young people forced the creation in 1986 of the National Commission for Prevention and Social Care, composed of representatives from 21 state agencies, mass organisations and professional societies under the leadership of Vilma Espin, Politburo member and wife of Raul Castro (Granma, 1 October 1986, p.1). The Commission was charged with the elaboration of policy regarding anti-social behaviour and the coordination of its implementation. To carry out its tasks, the Commission organised 14 provincial and 169 municipal branches throughout the country. In terms of its work among youth between the ages of 16 and 24, the Commission will attempt to facilitate the reintegration into society of maladjusted youth or those who neither work nor study, in part by means of involuntary assignment to special behaviour-modification centres (Granma, 12 May 1987, p.2).

Evaluation

Maternity leave and medical-hospital care in Cuba are among the best in the region as the very low rates of deaths during delivery and infant mortality indicate. Government day-care centres

124

expanded rapidly in the 1960s and early 1970s but their growth slowed down thereafter, particularly in the 1980s, and current services are insufficient although probably more abundant than in other countries in the region. Social deviance appears to be on the rise in the 1980s and has become a major preoccupation of the government.

NEEDY FAMILIES

It is generally agreed among scholars of socialist Cuba that revolutionary policies and programmes have resulted in the establishment of considerable equality in income distribution and in the enjoyment of social services, especially education and health (Brundenius 1984, Ch.4-5; Mesa-Lago 1981, Ch.7; Roca 1984, pp.225-44). There is also a broad consensus that detailed information - income classes, regional differences and other disaggregated data - on distributional issues is virtually inaccessible to most foreign researchers. According to Mesa-Lago (1981, p.143)

In light of the obvious elimination by the Revolution of extreme income inequalities, it is surprising that no hard data are available to substantiate it.

Knowledge of government programmes designed to help needy families is also very limited. Government agencies, including the Central Planning Board and the State Committee on Statistics, have conducted several income studies but their findings were not disclosed. In October 1986, a national survey on earned income of the workforce and social security/assistance benefits of pensioners was undertaken but to date no results have been made available (Granma, 1 October 1986, p.5). In sum, it is impossible to ascertain how many needy families exist in the island, under what conditions they subsist, what government programmes attempt to meet their needs and how effectively such programmes operate.

Social Security

Although Cuba's monetary income distribution is probably the most egalitarian in Latin America and the provision of free-of-charge social services is

very extensive, moderate income differences still
persist. In 1973, according to Brundenius, the top
quintile was earning almost five times the income
of the lowest quintile. In the late 1970s,
according to Mesa-Lago, the monthly wage/salary
range in the state civilian sector went from 80-
100 pesos (farm workers) to 700-1,000 pesos (high-
skilled industrial technicians). In 1987, Castro
estimated that 150,000 workers were earning less
than 100 pesos a month and referred to them as
'low-income workers' (Granma 17 January 1987, p.4).

In early 1987, partly to offset price
increases in many basic goods and services
stemming from the austerity measures of December
1986, Castro directed the CETSS to implement wage
and salary raises in several 'low-wage' economic
sectors. About 186,000 education and service
workers from the lowest wage-scales (85-97 pesos)
were granted raises to a range from 100 to 106
pesos. In addition, salary increments to the
level of 118.17 pesos (or 10.7 per cent) were
given to 283,205 administration and construction
workers. Altogether, wage and salary increases
were approved for about 16 per cent of Cuba's
workforce.

Survivors' pensions are payable when the
deceased was employed or a pensioner at death, or
employed within six months thereof and for
three-quarters of adult life. Eligible dependents
are widow, needy widower age 60 or invalid,
orphans under age 17 or invalid and needy
parents. Welfare assistance is available to the
needy uninsured

Personal Social Services

From scattered information, it is possible to
assemble a broad picture of how the government of
Cuba assists needy families. In terms of housing,
whereas monthly rent payments are generally fixed
at 10 per cent of head of household income,
exemptions are made for: (1) the retired and the
handicapped who pay a flat charge of eight pesos
and (2) families with per capita income under 25
pesos, who pay nothing. Food service (lunch
and/or dinner) is provided at no cost to workers
and students who meet the above income test. Fees
for children's day-care programmes, as explained
in the previous section, are based on a sliding
scale progressively related to income.

Evaluation

Very limited information is available on needy families in Cuba. However, their situation should be relatively good by regional standards because of considerable income equality, combined with almost universal coverage of survivors' pensions and supplementary welfare pensions, as well as free or low-rental housing for the poor or low income families. Very low inflation until the 1980s also helped the needy; increases in prices during the current decade have been partly compensated by wage increases among the lowest wage brackets. However, the increasing use of market prices (at least until the mid-1980s) has reduced the access of the needy to a wide variety of consumer goods.

THE UNEMPLOYED

Until the 1980s there were no monetary benefits for unemployment (but the jobless were always entitled to medical-hospital benefits) as it was ideologically assumed that there was full employment in Cuba (CETSS 1983, p.28; Mesa-Lago 1981; pp.121-32). According to official data, unemployment was reduced from 13.6 per cent in 1959 to 1.3 per cent in 1970 (one of the most positive achievements of the Revolution), but later the rate increased to 5.4 per cent in 1979 before falling to 3.4 per cent in 1981. By 1985 the rate probably edged upward to about 5 per cent. Though these are very low rates it is clear that open unemployment has persisted in socialist Cuba. In addition, underemployment and disguised unemployment have plagued economic policy-makers to the present.

Social Security

At different times, depending on the tilt of ideological postures and on the thrust of economic strategies, Cuba has confronted unemployment in several ways. Sometimes the unemployed have been temporarily kept on the enterprise payroll or subsidised by special funds while being retrained or relocated. With greater unemployment pressure in the 1970s, pressure that is expected to continue throughout the current decade, the

127

problem was officially acknowledged and some measures were introduced to ameliorate its impact, e.g. paying 70 per cent of the unemployed's salary in certain cases. During the period of pro-market economic reform from 1975 to 1985, small private undertakings (mostly in personal services, such as beauty parlours and auto-repair shops) were legalised and state enterprises were granted limited powers to hire workers as needed. Thus, in part, the struggle against unemployment was privatised and decentralised.

Personal Social Services

After 1985, during the 'Rectification Process' which reimposed centralisation (and also stressed moral incentives and ideological primacy), the increasing levels of open and disguised unemployment were widely discussed and new government-run measures were proposed. In early 1987 Castro estimated that the withdrawal of 50,000 workers from industrial plants would not affect production at all and concluded that 'in this country we are underutilising resources, hundreds of thousands of compatriots in the city and the countryside ...' (Granma, 12 February 1987, pp.2-3). Youth were especially over-represented in the labour reserve; for example, in one municipality 67 per cent of the 9,400 unemployed were young people (Granma, 2 April 1987, p.2).

According to Castro, 'the guarantee of employment is one of the obligations of socialism' and it is his belief that 'we do not suffer unemployment ... because we can rationally use our human resources and give employment to everybody' (Granma, 2 February 1987, p.3; 3 April 1987, p.4). To implement this policy, provincial and municipal 'labour relocation commissions' charged with the placement of excess workers (interruptos) were created in the spring of 1987 (Granma, 12 March 1987, p.3). In order of priorities, the commissions will attempt: to find alternative productive jobs for excess workers in the same enterprise or ministry; to retrain interruptos for similar or even different occupations; and to relocate reserves to the agricultural and construction sectors. One of the basic goals is to eliminate the widespread practice of interruptos collecting the 70 per cent wage subsidy without doing any work.

Evaluation

The objective of reducing malingering and of
providing full employment at adequate
productivity, appears to be overly ambitious and
thus of doubtful attainment. For instance, in one
western region, despite great efforts, only 50 per
cent of the unemployed could be found jobs and in
a major eastern city just 10 per cent of the
jobless youth (party militants no less) were
initially enticed to join construction brigades.
More generally, how is the overall unemployment
rate to be lowered and productivity raised by
simply relocating and transferring the unemployed
back and forth among enterprises and sectors?

THE SICK AND INJURED

Medical-hospital benefits in Cuba are organised
under a uniform system although there are
differences in accessibility and quality of
services. Within the general system, monetary
benefits are standardised but special systems
(such as the armed forces) exist with different
entitlement conditions.

Social Security

Medical-hospital benefits, to which the total
population is entitled with the exception of those
resulting from occupational risks, include:
preventive and curative medical care, as well as
odontology, surgery, hospitalisation, medicines
(only during hospitalisation in the case of common
accident or disease, but at any time for
occupational risks, the elderly in nursing homes
and the poor), rehabilitation and orthopedics and
prosthesis (these last three only in occupational
risks cases).

Monetary benefits, to which the active insured
are entitled, include a subsidy in lieu of salary
for sickness, maternity or accident (with a
greater per cent of salary if due to occupational
risks). No qualification period or time limit on
receiving medical-hospital benefits exists; there
is a three-day waiting period for receiving
sickness subsidy but not if caused by occupational
risks. In addition, the per cent of salary paid
as subsidy surpasses the regional average: in Cuba

the average is 60 per cent of earnings (50 per cent if hospitalised) for common sickness or accident, and 80 per cent (70 per cent if hospitalised) if due to occupational risks.

As there is no private sector in medicine, Table 7 reports the totality of services available in the country. The indicators show notable and systematic progress with three exceptions: a slight relative reduction in hospital beds since 1970 (which is not of great consequence as the installed capacity is not fully used); a fall in the index of doctors per 10,000 inhabitants in 1960-1970 induced by the exodus of one-third of the doctors after the Revolution; and an increase in the infant mortality rate in 1960-1970 (less in general mortality) that was, possibly, the result of a decrease in medical personnel, and several infant epidemics, both combined with better statistical coverage. In any case, the deterioration of the indices in the first decade of the Revolution was corrected in the second decade, greatly surpassing the pre-revolutionary levels. At the beginning of the 1980s, Cuba led the region in life expectancy, had the lowest infant mortality rate (similar to that of Costa Rica) and the ratio of doctors and hospitals per inhabitant were among the highest in Latin America. It should be noted that the status of health care in Cuba at the end of the 1950s was also among the highest in the region.

Due to the high degree of universality, unity and standardisation in the health system of Cuba differences in coverage among occupational sectors and geographic areas are probably small. Unfortunately, this cannot be confirmed due to the lack of coverage statistics in Cuba. As a proxy, Table 7 offers an estimation of the differences in monetary benefits and health services among the 15 provinces of Cuba in 1982. The table shows that the province city of La Habana (the most developed and urbanised province where the bulk of industry and services are concentrated) receives twice the amount of benefits per capita, has almost six times the number of physicians per 10,000 inhabitants and has almost three times the number of hospital beds per 1,000 inhabitants than the privince of Granma (one of the most rural and underdeveloped provinces). Other rural and agricultural provinces, such as Las Tunas, Holguin and Guantanamo have indices lower than those of La Habana and other more urban and industrial

TABLE 7: DIFFERENCES IN HEALTH BENEFITS AMONG
PROVINCES IN CUBA: 1982

Provinces	Per Capita Monetary Benefit Expenditures[1] (pesos)	Physicians per 10,000 inhabitants	Hospital and Welfare Beds per 1,000 inhabitants
Pinar del Rio	66.81	11.8	4.6
La Habana	99.85	14.0	2.6
City de La Habana	120.48	41.2	11.2
Matanzas	95.47	16.9	5.4
Villa Clara	93.05	11.7	4.2
Cienfuegos	86.09	12.5	4.8
Sancti Spiritus	85.62	10.1	4.5
Ciego de Avila	79.78	11.4	3.5
Camaguey	79.35	13.5	6.3
Las Tunas	65.30	8.9	4.6
Holguin	58.02	8.6	3.9
Granma	50.34	7.2	4.1
Santiago de Cuba	58.74	12.8	5.5
Guantanamo	52.83	8.9	5.1
Isla de la Juventud	47.69	16.4	7.2
TOTAL	82.20	17.3	5.9

Note:

1   Includes monetary benefits (pensions as well
     as temporary benefits), and social welfare;
     excludes medical-hospital benefits and
     administrative costs.

SOURCE: Estimates based on Anuario Estadistico de
          Cuba, 1982, pp.127, 465, 472-3.

provinces. Nevertheless, in the 1960s, Cuba succeeded in carrying out a programme to develop medical and hospital services in rural zones which notably reduced these differences. In 1978, there were 57 rural hospitals and the concentration of beds and doctors in La Habana (21 per cent of the population) had been reduced from 60 per cent (in 1958) to, respectively, 39 per cent and 36 per cent in 1982.

The health budget increased 25 times between 1959 and 1983. But, as in other aspects, the lack of detailed statistical information makes the evaluation of the cost of health care difficult as there are no figures on the distribution of costs among preventive and curative medicine, costs of salaries, medicines, and so forth.

During the revolutionary period, Cuba has dedicated substantial attention to preventive medicine and, through massive vaccination campaigns, has succeeded in eradicating certain contagious diseases, such as poliomyelitis and diphtheria, as well as substantially reducing the rates of other diseases, such as tuberculosis, typhoid, and malaria. Conversely, the rate of other diseases not controllable by vaccination, such as hepatitis, diarrhoea, syphilis and gonorrhoea have increased, apparently due to inadequate hygiene control and a greater freedom in sexual relations (Mesa-Lago 1981, p.167). In addition, Cuba has experienced a significant change in the pathological profile since in 1982; 70 per cent of the causes of death were diseases of development, such as cardiovascular and cerebrovascular diseases and malignant tumors.

Evaluation

Cuba has eradicated or significantly reduced the diseases most easily controlled and of low cost treatment and now faces the diseases most difficult to eradicate and costly to treat such as chronic and terminal illnesses, and cancer. In this respect, Cuba is similar to the industralised countries.

ASSESSMENT OF THE CUBAN WELFARE SYSTEM

By the end of the 1950s Cuba, as one of the pioneer countries, had one of the most developed social security systems in Latin America and was among the top countries in health levels. But the system suffered from extreme stratification, significant inequalities and severe financial imbalance and, equally important, it left unprotected the most needy sector of the population.

The advances in social security in Cuba in the last quarter century constitute one of the most relevant achievements of the socialist revolutionary process. Among the most notable improvements are: the creation of a national health system of universal scope which protects the entire resident population; the expansion of coverage in the pension programme from 63 per cent to 93 per cent; the unification and standardisation of the pension programme which eliminated its extreme inequalities; the integration of the health system; the reduction in administrative costs and the simplification of the system; and the substantial, steady support of the state. In terms of health services and levels, Cuba ranks second in Latin America in the availability of doctors and hospital beds for the population, first in life expectancy and in having the lowest infant mortality rate.

Nevertheless, Cuba shares two of the typical problems of the pioneer countries: the extremely high cost of social security and its financial disequilibrium. Social security expenditures as a percentage of GDP doubled in 1958-71 from 6 per cent to 12 per cent and, although they declined later, in 1980 the percentage was the fourth highest in the region. Since the mid-1970s, social security has registered a growing deficit which, in 1980, equalled almost half of social security revenues (the second highest ratio in the region) and represented 1.6 per cent of GNP. This financial imbalance has resulted from the universalisation of population coverage, generous benefits and flexible entitlement conditions, the maturation of the pension programme, and a health care system which, even when emphasising preventive medicine more than most countries in the area, still leans heavily on highly capital-intensive, curative approaches.

Social security is financed by a percentage of the wages paid by enterprises, this contribution being insufficient to finance the system. The possibility of re-establishing equilibrium through an increase in revenues appears remote and the limited measures undertaken in the immediate past have been aimed at reducing the cost of monetary benefits through the temporary postponement of pensions, the elimination of benefit payments equivalent to 100 per cent of base salary, and the erosion of the real value of pensions. These measures have not eliminated the deficit and, therefore, other more drastic measures must be considered, such as the establishment of stricter entitlement conditions for monetary benefits and the refocussing of the health system toward greater efficiency and lower costs.

Paradoxically, though Cuba has one of the best social security systems in Latin America, statistical information and technical studies on the subject are extremely scarce. This state of affairs should be overcome not only for a greater understanding of a unique model in the region, but also to enable officials in Cuba to elaborate more effective policies to confront the remaining shortcomings of the system.

REFERENCES AND FURTHER READING

Banco Nacional de Cuba (1982), Informe Economico, La Habana.

Brundenius, C. (1984), Revolutionary Cuba: The Challenge of Economic Growth with Equity, Boulder & London: Westview Press.

Central de Trabajadores de Cuba (CTC) (1980a), Sistema de Seguridad Social, Regimen de Asistencia Social, Regimen de Seguridad Social, La Habana.

_____ (1980b), Sistema de Seguridad Social: Anexo, La Habana.

Centro de Investigaciones de la Economia Mundial (1983), Estudio acerca de la Erradicacion de la Pobreza en Cuba, La Habana.

CETSS (1977a), La Seguridad Social en Cuba, La Habana.

_____ (1977b), 'Investigacion sobre evolucion y tendencias de la seguridad social en el trienio 1974-1976', Seguridad Social, 26, 105-6.

Cuba

_____ (1983), 24 anos de Revolucion en la Seguridad Social Cubano, La Habana.

Comile Estalal de Estadisticos (CEE) (nd), Anuario Estadistico de Cuba, 1982, La Habana.

_____ (1986), Anuario Estadistico de Cuba, 1985, La Habana.

Comision de Aportes Estatales a la Seguridad Social (1957), Bases Tecnicas Para la Reforma de los Seguros Sociales, La Habana: Editorial Lex.

Dominguez, J.I. (1978), Cuba: Order and Revolution, Cambridge, Mass.: Harvard University Press.

Gaceta Oficial (1982), Cuba: Conversion de los Principales Indicadores Macroeconomicos del Sistema de Balances de la Economia Nacional (SBEN) al Sistema se Cuentas Nacionales (SCN) 1974, La Habana.

Grupo Cubano de Investigaciones Economicas (1963), Un Estudio sobre Cuba, Coral Gables: University of Miami Press.

_____ (1964), Social Security in Cuba, University of Miami.

International Bank for Reconstruction & Development (1951), Report on Cuba, Baltimore: The Johns Hopkins Press.

Mathews-Smith, H. (1983), 'Cuban Medicine: An Eyewitness Report', MD.

Mesa-Lago, C. (1960), Planificacion de la Seguridad Social: Analisis Especial de la Problematica Cubana, La Habana: Editorial Libreria Marti.

_____ (1980), 'Seguridad social y pobreza', in Molina, S. (ed.), Se Puede Superar la Pobreza?, Santiago: CEPAL/ILPES, 163-89.

_____ (1981), The Economy of Socialist Cuba, Albuquerque: University of New Mexico Press.

Cuba

_____ (1986), 'Cuba's Centrally Planned Economy: An Equity Trade-Off for Growth', in Hartlyn, J. & Morley, S. (eds), <u>Latin American Political Economy</u>, Boulder: Westview Press, 292-318.

_____ (1988), 'The Cuban Economy in the 1980s: The Return of Ideology', in Roca, S. G. (ed.), <u>Socialist Cuba: Past Interpretations and Future Challenges</u>, Boulder: Westview Press.

Ministerio del Trabajo (nd), <u>Principales Disposiciones Vigentes de la Seguridad Social Cubana</u>, La Habana.

Partido Comunista de Cuba (1978), 'Tesis sobre la lucha ideologica', in <u>Tesis Y Resoluciones: Primer Congreso del Partido Comunista de Cuba</u>, La Habana: Editorial de Ciencias Sociales, 232.

Perez-Lopez, J. (1986), 'The Cuban Economy in the 1980s', <u>Problems of Communism</u>, 35(5), 16-34.

Penate Rivero, O. (1984), <u>Informacion sobre el Sistema de Seguridad Social Cubano</u>, La Habana: CETSS, pp.2-4.

_____ & Lugo Machado, I. (1985), 'Acerca del financiamiento de la seguridad social en Cuba', in <u>Modelos y Estrategias Financieras: Conferencias</u>, Mexico DF: CIESS.

Roca, S.G. (1978), 'Cuba's International Economic Relations', in Roca, S. (ed.), <u>Socialist Cuba</u>, Boulder: Westview Press.

_____ (1983), 'Cuba Confronts the 1980s', <u>Current History</u>, Feb, 74-8.

_____ (1984), 'Rural Public Services in Socialist Cuba', in Lonsdale, R. & Enyedi, G. (eds), <u>Rural Public Services: International Comparisons</u>, Boulder & London: Westview Press.

Rodriguez, B. (1966), 'La seguridad social en Cuba', <u>Cuba Socialista</u>, Dec, 14-30.

Cuba

Seminario Latinoamericano de Cuentas Nacionales y
Balance de la Economia (1982), <u>Cuba:
Conversion de los Principales Indicadores del
Sistema de Balances de la Economia Nacional
(SBEN) al Sistema de Cuentas Nacionales (SCN)
1974</u>, La Habana.

GUATEMALA
Grace Keyes

THE WELFARE SYSTEM ENVIRONMENT

Ideological Environment

The pre-Columbian era of Mesoamerica forms part of
Guatemala's historical roots. Today nearly half
of the population is of Maya Indian descent. The
long colonial period following the Spanish
Conquest also had a tremendous impact on the
history of Guatemala. In recent times, the brutal
injustices of the colonial era have been replaced
by years of political and economic instability and
oppression. A small ruling elite and the military
continue to dominate political and economic
affairs, often aided by United States interests
and foreign policy. Currently, Guatemala is
plagued by political violence and violations of
human rights along with severe economic and basic
social problems. In such a climate social welfare
is pressingly necessary but scarcely achieved.
  The beliefs and values that have moulded the
welfare system in Guatemala are themselves a
product of Guatemala's past and present
condition. Broadly speaking, Guatemala is an
agrarian, predominantly Catholic, socially plural,
underdeveloped, capitalist society trying to
promote economic and technological growth.

Agrarian Society. As an agrarian society, the
majority of the people in Guatemala have a long
and close attachment to the land. However, the
skewed distribution of land tenure in favour of a
small percentage of landowners has been one of the
gravest social problems in Guatemala since

138

colonial times (Adams 1970; Brown 1981; Fletcher
et al. 1970; Handy 1984). By and large, social
welfare programmes have failed to address this
problem.

Catholicism. Almost as important as making a
living on the land are religious beliefs and
practices. The religious syncretism that occurred
after the Spanish conquest in which pre-Columbian
polytheistic beliefs were blended with Catholic
Christianity has formed the basis of an
ideological system that penetrates into most
aspects of life. Through various historical
periods the Church has been both a hindrance and
an aid in the development of social welfare in
Guatemala. The religious belief that suffering
was to be endured because it was the 'will of God'
only encouraged fatalism and Christian resignation
amongst the peasants and urban poor (Handy 1984).
This, in turn, only delayed actions to bring about
a social welfare system on a national level. On
the other hand, the Church's early contribution to
alleviating social problems was due largely to its
belief in the idea of charity. Besides the
Church's direct charitable contributions (shelter,
food, orphanages, and so forth) it tried to
develop a feeling of Christian charity amongst the
rich. It has only been in recent years, since
about the 1960s, that religious organisations in
Guatemala have taken a reformist approach in their
ministries thereby encouraging social welfare
programmes and promoting general social reforms.

Social Pluralism. The high percentage of
indigenous peoples in Guatemala makes it unique
among the Central American republics.
Socio-cultural diversity and pluralism are readily
apparent. There is a pronounced difference
between the Indian culture and world view and that
of the Ladino (those of mixed descent and
primarily Western culture). The Indian-Ladino
distinction has led to a racial ideology which
ascribes negative connotations to Indian culture
(Anthony 1981). Indians are seen as
superstitious, suspicious of outsiders and
backward. From colonial times Indian peasants
have responded to oppression and exploitation by
remaining somewhat isolated in what
anthropologists call 'closed corporate
communities' (Wolf 1957). The dominant values in
these communities revolve around the corporate

139

group and the family. It should also be noted here that the importance of the family and kin group is strong not only amongst the Indians but also amongst the Ladinos.

Underdevelopment. Guatemala considers itself a 'developing' country and as such urbanisation and industrialisation are the guiding values. Most social welfare programmes have been directed at the urban and industrial sectors. Although the rate of urbanisation has steadily increased since the 1950s and industry has become one of the most dynamic economic sectors especially since 1980, Guatemala remains largely an agricultural peasant society (Handy 1984; United Nations 1982b).

Capitalism. Not least amongst the dominant ideologies surrounding the social welfare system is that of capitalism. Under a laissez-faire economy and given its historical and socio-economic background, Guatemala has experienced the multitude of social and economic problems common throughout much of Latin America. The majority of peasants and urban poor lead a bare and meagre existence under what Sol Tax aptly calls 'penny capitalism' (1953). On the other hand, members of the elite continue to provide handsomely for themselves and their families under the current system. Guatemala, as a whole, however, has developed a dependent economy reliant on foreign capital and markets and thereby easily affected by external economic factors (United Nations 1982b; Inforpress 1985). The consequence of the capitalist ideology for health care and social welfare is that welfare services, resources and personnel are skewed, maldistributed and often lacking. As Vicente Navarro (1976) points out, the skewed and maldistribution of health resources in Latin America is a symptom of broader structural problems, specifically the economic and cultural dependency created by capitalism.

Historical Origins

Early Phase. Latin America saw the birth of social welfare with the creation of the first school for social work in Chile in 1925 (Ander-Egg 1971). But as Lally (1970) notes, social welfare did not become a major legislative concern in most Latin American countries until the 1930s and

Guatemala

1940s. The trends experienced by most Latin American countries can also be seen in Guatemala. (Table 1 outlines some of the major events and legislative actions affecting the development of public welfare in Guatemala.)

TABLE 1: MAJOR DEVELOPMENTS IN SOCIAL WELFARE IN GUATEMALA

Year	Events	Significance
1932	Health Code	For disease prevention and health regulation
1945	Constitution of 1945	Established welfare provisions
1945	Ministry of Public Health and Social Assistance	Creation of first secretariat for social welfare
1946	Social Security Law	Established the IGSS
1947	Labour Code	For protection/ rights of workers
1948	Inauguration of IGSS	Began extending benefits
1949	School of Social Service	IGSS; first school for social work
1949	Law of Forced Rental	Allowed peasants to use/rent unused lands near plantations
1956	National Health Planning Unit	To coordinate health and social welfare programmes
1965	Ministry of Labour and Social Welfare	To direct and plan labour and social legislation; to improve social security
1965	National Housing Institute	To promote and improve low-cost housing
1972	National Training Inst. for Public Health	To train rural health technicians
1975	School of Social Work	Affiliated with the University of San Carlos

During the 1920s a few social health services were initiated to improve basic sanitation and hospital facilities and to control diseases, especially malaria (Dombrowski 1970). Foreign agencies were involved in various health projects. For instance, the Rockefeller Foundation participated in a campaign to eradicate malaria-bearing mosquitos. Religious missions carried out most other social services for the needy. During Jorge Ubico's presidency in the early 1930s a Health Code was enacted in the attempt to regulate health practices, create preventive health programmes and to carry out various sanitation projects.

Active Phase. It was not until the 1940s that the government became an active promoter of social welfare. Much was accomplished during what Handy (1984) calls 'the ten years of spring' comprised of the administrations of Juan Jose Arevalo (1945-51) and Jacobo Arbenz (1951-54). For Guatemala this was a period of numerous social reforms and the beginnings of progressive political democracy.

With the Revolution of 1944, Dr Juan Jose Arevalo became the republic's first freely elected president. Influenced by Franklin D. Roosevelt, Arevalo developed the concept of 'spiritual socialism' to initiate his social reforms. For Arevalo, 'spiritual socialism' meant a concern for humanitarian ideals, political democracy and public welfare. Three major legislative accomplishments of the Arevalo administration were the passage of the first Social Security Law, enactment of the Labour Code and initiation of agrarian reforms (Handy 1984; Jonas & Tobis 1981; Schlesinger & Kinzer 1982).

In 1945 Arevalo embarked on a series of social reforms aimed at improving the general standard of life in Guatemala. Rural health clinics were established, projects to provide potable water were initiated, sanitation and vaccination projects were stepped up, drains and sewers were constructed in cities, and the education system was reorganised.

Arevalo made public welfare the primary responsibility of the government by writing these responsibilities into the Constitution of 1945. The Ministry of Public Health and Social Assistance was created in 1945 and the following year the law creating the Guatemalan Institute of

Social Security (Instituto Guatemalteco de
Seguridad Social (IGSS)) was passed. Also in
1947, the Labour Code gave workers the right to
form unions and to strike. It also set minimum
wages, regulated child and female labour and
extended a measure of protection to some rural
workers and employers (Handy 1984; Schlesinger &
Kinzer 1982). Through the National Production
Institute (1948) and the Law of Forced Rental
(1949) Arevalo began to address the age-old
problem of land tenure. These controversial
reforms were designed to help provide credit, land
and other forms of aid to small farmers.

The Arbenz administration steadfastly followed
Arevalo's social reform initiatives. Arbenz's
main concerns were economic modernisation,
agrarian reforms, and increasing production.
Reforms that threatened land holdings of the
American-owned United Fruit Company were seen in
the United States as Communist-inspired. With the
Agrarian Reform Law of 1952 the United States
became convinced that the revolutionary government
of Guatemala had to be ousted. In 1954 the United
States with the aid of its Central Intelligence
Agency was successful in helping overthrow
Arbenz. With the fall of Arbenz social reforms
took a step backwards and progress toward an
efficacious social welfare system since than has
been slow and sporadic.

In 1956 the National Health Planning Unit was
created for the purpose of coordinating all health
and social welfare programmes carried out by
various government agencies. Under a new
Constitution in 1965, the Ministry of Labour and
Social Welfare was established. Part of its
responsibility is to direct and plan labour and
social welfare programmes and, in conjunction with
the IGSS, to improve social security for workers.

The Guatemalan Institute of Social Security
(IGSS). This was created in 1946 but was not
formally inaugurated until January 1948. That
same year the IGSS obtained the services of Walter
Pettit, an internationally known specialist in
social work, to begin a school of social services
(Suslow 1949).

The founders of the IGSS were familiar with
American and European social security systems and
methods but chose not to apply these methods
directly to Guatemala. Rather, they tried to
develop a system more suitable to an under-

143

developed area and to the particular conditions of Guatemala. The orientation of the IGSS was not toward a 'social insurance programme' such as existed in the United States but rather as a 'social budgeting' programme with the aim of improving the standard of living and to provide a minimum measure of protection to the entire population (Suslow 1949; 1955).

By the end of 1948, the IGSS had spent Q498,382 for its programmes and had extended protection to about 80,000 workers and 2,225 employers (Suslow 1949). At its inception only the urban working class in Guatemala City derived benefits, which included hospitalisation and compensation for industrial accidents, and general illness. Since then, the IGSS has expanded its coverage and extended some of its programmes to all of the departments of the republic. A major change since 1948 is that at least some services now extend to rural areas (Annis 1981).

Political and Socio-economic Environment

Political Climate. Guatemala has an elected president with strong executive powers and a 61-member Congress. Locally the republic is divided into 22 departments which are subdivided into about 320 municipios (cities and townships). Each department is headed by a governor appointed by the president while the municipios are run by an elected mayor and council.

The political climate in Guatemala since 1954 has not been one of stability. In recent, years, since about 1980, conditions have greatly worsened (Handy 1984; United Nations 1984 & 1985). Political unrest, violence and violations of human rights have only magnified existing socio-economic problems. Large numbers of Guatemalans have fled the country into Mexico and the United States as a result of these conditions. Progress in social welfare has suffered greatly for, as a United Nations Commission on Human Rights points out, the political climate in Guatemala has created an

> extremely grave economic and social situation which violates the elementary rights of the population to life, nutrition, health, education, work and housing. (United Nations 1984, p.2)

TABLE 2: DEMOGRAPHIC CHARACTERISTICS OF GUATEMALA

Population, 1980[1]   6,054,227

    1985 Estimate[2]   7,963,000
    Urban (1980 Census)[1]   1,980,533
    Rural (1980 Census)[1]   4,073,694

Age Distribution [1] (in percentages)

Ages 0 - 14	45
Ages 15 - 59	50
Ages 60 and over	5

Ethnic Distribution [1] (in percentages)

Ladino (mestizos)	54
Indian	41
Other	5

Illiteracy Rate [3] (in percentages)

Indian	90	Republic	50
Ladino	51	Urban	30
Rural	70		

Birth & Mortality Rates, 1983 [2] (Per 1,000)

Birth rate	38.3
Death rate	7.2
Infant death	71.2

SOURCES: 1.   Guatemala 1981a
          2.   United Nations 1987
          3.   World Bank 1978

Socio-demographic   Elements.   Guatemala   is
characterised by numerous contrasts (see   Table
2).   About 66 per cent of the nearly eight million
people live in rural areas.   The northern Peten
Plains   and   Lowlands,   a   region   of   tropical
rainforests and some grass lands, is the least
populated and developed region. Most of the rural
and Indian population lives in   the   Central
Highlands, a rugged mountainous region marked by
deep canyons, volcanic peaks, and Lakes Atitlan
and Amatitlan.   The majority of the Indians live
in about three departments in the   western portion

145

of these highlands just northwest of Guatemala
City. The Pacific Lowlands is thinly populated
but is the country's most productive agricultural
region producing cotton, sugar and bananas as its
major crops.

Guatemala City, with a population of about 1.5
million people is the largest urban centre not
only in Guatemala but in all of Central America.
During the last decade the capital has experienced
urbanisation at the rate of about 6 per cent per
year.

According to the 1980 government statistics,
the Indian population accounts for about 41 per
cent of the total inhabitants. The remaining 59
per cent is made up of Ladinos and other white
ethnic groups. Foreigners (American, Germans,
Chinese and a few others) comprise a small part of
the population but have considerable influence on
the economy.

Population growth varies but is currently
estimated at about 3 per cent per year. As Table
2 indicates, Guatemala's population is quite young
with approximately 45 per cent of the total
population under the age of 15 (Guatemala 1981a;
Nyrop 1983). The social consequences of such a
youthful population are many including the need
for educational and social services.

Illiteracy is quite high especially in the
rural regions. In 1980, 51 per cent of the
population was illiterate but in rural and Indian
communities this figure is even higher (Calvert
1985). Illiteracy prevents many people from being
able to take advantage of a number of social
services provided by various agencies.

Guatemala has been plagued by numerous health
and social problems, many of which vary according
to socio-economic factors. Life expectancy for
urban Ladinos is about 60 years whereas Indians
and rural inhabitants can expect to live to only
45 or 50 years of age (Nyrop 1983). Similarly,
while the mortality rate for Guatemala as a whole
is about 7 per cent, that of Indians is generally
higher than that of Ladinos. Infant mortality
rates (children under five years of age) are quite
high with about 70 deaths per 1,000 live births.

Extensive malnutrition and the high incidence
of infectious diseases have been two major health
concerns. The most common diseases are
intestinal-tract and respiratory ailments.
Malnutrition and poor sanitation are often
implicated in these illnesses. Some researchers

estimate that one-third of the population is undernourished with a much higher rate among children under five years (Nyrop 1983; World Bank 1978). Although numerous projects have helped to alleviate some health problems, social and health services are still largely inadequate. According to one World Bank report (1978) health services in Guatemala are among the worst in Central America in terms of health personnel, such as physicians and nurses.

Economic factors. Social welfare is also affected by the economy within which it exists. Since 1980 the economy in Guatemala has grown only slowly and at certain times economic activity was almost stagnant. Economic problems are largely attributable to the internal political instability and unrest of the country as well as to external economic factors (United Nations 1982b; Inforpress 1985). For instance, the recession that began in 1979 in the industrial countries had immediate repercussions on Guatemala's economy since it is heavily dependent on foreign capital and trade (Inforpress 1985).

The rate of economic growth in terms of Gross Domestic Product (GDP), which in 1978 was 4.9 per cent, began falling in 1979 and continued a downward spiral until 1983 when the rate of growth of the GDP became a negative 2.7 per cent. In 1984 it rose slightly (Inforpress 1985). During this period there was a deceleration of exports and a deterioration in terms of trade. The fiscal deficit has also put stress on the economy; the budget deficit went from Q39 million in 1978 to Q638 million in 1981. After the coup in 1982 this high deficit was brought down to Q300 million but it still remains a major problem. Inflation was held at a fairly low rate until 1985 when it reached 33 per cent.

Unemployment is also an important economic factor. Unemployment grew from 2.2 per cent of the working population in 1980 to 10.5 per cent in 1984 (Inforpress 1985). This is magnified by the high rate of underemployment which was about 33 per cent in 1984. Underemployment in Guatemala is a structural problem since the minifundia system that still prevails in the rural areas does not provide peasant families with a decent living (Inforpress 1985). Peasants, therefore, must seek wage labour elsewhere. Middle class professions, technicians and other salaried workers have also

147

been affected by unemployment and/or a decrease in incomes.

THE WELFARE SYSTEM: AN OVERVIEW

The welfare system in Guatemala can hardly be called a system since its various parts often do not form an integrated whole and its protection does not embrace the entire population. Social welfare in Guatemala is decentralised, lacks effective mechanisms for integrating its various programmes, and suffers from limited and unevenly distributed services as well as limited funds (Lemus-Pivaral 1975; Pan American Health Organisation 1977; United Nations 1982a).

Structure and Administration of the Welfare System

At the state level of government there exists a Secretary of Social Welfare within the President's Executive Cabinet. Of the 10 governmental ministries several provide a variety of services and programmes for the well-being of various target groups in the country. The two ministries most directly involved in providing social welfare are the Ministry of Public Health and Social Assistance and the Ministry of Labour and Social Welfare (see Figure 1). Besides state agencies there are numerous private, international and religious organisations that provide services to various target groups.

The Ministry of Public Health and Social Assistance (MOH). This ministry was created by the Constitution of 1945 to define and deal with the health problems of the country. It plans and directs activities aimed at improving and protecting the health of the people. A major concern has been the implementation of sanitation projects and to improve the health status of the population by attacking major diseases (Guatemala 1981b). Some specific functions include: providing protection against communicable diseases, providing health care to infants and families, conducting health education programmes, coordinating activities with international health agencies, and making improvements in rural health (e.g. constructing water works to make potable water more accessible).

148

FIGURE 1:   STRUCTURE OF THE NATIONAL SOCIAL WELFARE SYSTEM

President

President's Cabinet

Major Ministries providing social welfare services

Agriculture	Education	Communication & Public Works	Labour & Social Welfare	Public Health & Social Assistance
			General Directorate of Labour	General Directorate of Health Services
			General Directorate of Social Security	
		National Housing Institute	IGSS	
	University of San Carlos			

..... Decentralised agencies with varying degrees of autonomy

SOURCES: Guatemala 1981b; Lujan 1969; Nyrop 1983.

The MOH has a number of dependencies serving specific functions. These include the Department of Social Services which handles requests from needy families and prepares social welfare programmes. The MOH also operates a Neuropsychiatric Hospital, a Mental Health Centre, a Home for the Aged, several general hospitals, a national blood bank, a nursing school, and a Polio Rehabilitation Institute (Dombrowski 1970). Over 600 health centres (<u>Centros de Salud</u>) and Health Units (<u>Unidades Sanitarias</u>) scattered throughout the country are also operated by the MOH. The National Health Planning Unit, created in 1956, coordinates health programmes within the Ministry and maintains a liaison with other ministries and agencies.

<u>The Ministry of Labour and Social Welfare</u> (MOL). This ministry was created in 1965 to oversee labour policy for the republic. Responsibilities include the study and application of laws dealing with labour, such as minimum wage regulation, employer-employee relationships, and labour disputes. It is also in charge of improving the social security system and coordinating its activities with the Guatemalan Institute of Social Security. The MOL also directs and plans recreational programmes for workers. The MOL oversees programmes for the prevention of accidents, for developing social security and for industrial hygiene. It regulates labour practices involving women and minors, as well as industrial, commercial and agricultural workers. It is also involved in the formulation of international labour policies. The MOL is composed of several departments including the National Employment Service, Civil Service, Department of Labour Statistics and Department of Labour Welfare.

<u>The Guatemalan Institute of Social Security</u> (IGSS, Instituto Guatemalteco de Seguridad Social). The IGSS was created in 1945 as a decentralised and autonomous agency. Although the MOL has general supervisory authority, the IGSS remains largely autonomous.

The internal organisation of the IGSS consists of a Board of Directors and a Managing Council. Authority is vested in the Board which is made up of six members appointed by the following institutions: the President of the Republic, the Bank of Guatemala, the University of San Carlos, the College of Medical Doctors and Surgeons, the registered Employers Association and the registered labour unions (Guatemala 1981b; Suslow 1949).

The principal function of the IGSS is to administer the social security programmes established by the Constitution of 1945 and 1965. Its functions include the planning and development of a national hospital system, and the provision of social security services and protection to the population as a whole. As Suslow (1949; 1955), points out, the original intention of the IGSS was not as a social insurance programme but as a more general programme aimed at preventing risks and accidents, providing a minimum measure of protection to the entire population and to help lift the general standard of living. The IGSS includes protection for industrial accidents, occupational diseases, maternity, general illness, invalidism, orphanhood, widowhood, old age and burial expenses (Hernandez Reyna 1965; Suslow 1949). It also coordinates activities with the MOH and MOL to provide hospital and medical services and resources. It also helps carry out sanitation and preventive health programmes. It operates various hospitals, clinics, transportation services, and other auxiliary services.

Other Government Agencies. The Ministry of Education plays a role in providing some social services for various target groups. The Ministry of Education has cooperated with UNICEF and other Ministries in promoting educational programmes that extend beyond academic training. Some of these programmes are designed to improve and solve basic community problems, such as health, hygiene, nutrition, and housing (United Nations 1978a; 1978b). A National Out-of-School Education Board was created to coordinate programmes to provide children, adolescents and adults better educational opportunities and vocational training.

The autonomous University of San Carlos carried out programmes and studies in coordination with various ministries and with the IGSS. The IGSS operated its own school for social work from 1949 until 1975 when the University of San Carlos opened the present School for Social Work. The IGSS and the University of San Carlos, therefore, maintain a close relationship (IGSS 1976).

The National Housing Institute has programmes designed to improve housing, provide housing for low-income families, and conduct studies on housing needs (Dombrowski 1970).

The Ministry of Agriculture also provides social and technical assistance to specific groups. For instance, low-income families may receive milk from the Ministry of Agriculture. Another programme provides farm supplies, technical assistance and credit to farmers (O'Sullivan-Ryan 1977).

By providing some jobs to unemployed and underemployed workers, the Ministry of Communications and Public Works also contributes to social welfare.

Financing Social Welfare

Welfare systems in developing countries are hampered by woefully inadequate financing (Lally 1970; United Nations 1982a). Guatemala is no exception. With limited resources, a low per capita income and a meagre public purse, Guatemala cannot make major plans or investments in social welfare developments (United Nations 1963). Funding for social welfare has increased, especially since the mid-1960s but has not kept pace with actual needs (Lally 1970).

During President Arevalo's administration, when many of the current social welfare programmes were initiated, one-third of the national budget went to social welfare expenditures (Jonas & Tobis 1981; Nyrop 1983). These included expenditures for education, immunisations, literacy campaigns, and other health and social programmes (Nyrop 1983). Had this commitment continued, perhaps social welfare in Guatemala would be far more advanced today. Changes in political philosophy, in administrations, and in economic affairs have affected the course of social welfare as we saw in a previous section.

Funding for social welfare comes from various sectors including the government, industry and commerce, private agencies, philanthropic organisations, foreign governments, and international organisations. The government allocates a certain amount of the budget for social welfare and provides subsidies and assistance to autonomous agencies, private institutions and organisations (United Nations

1963). Foreign governments and organisations (primarily from the United States) also help fund numerous health and social programmes. Religious and charitable institutions often have a limited purse and generally rely on contributions and public donations to support their work and social programmes.

The problem in financing the welfare system has been that all too often funds are unevenly distributed creating an imbalance of services and coverage. As Nyrop (1983) points out the budgets of the MOH and MOL show that per capita expenditures in the Department of Guatemala were nearly three times higher than in the rest of the country. As a result Guatemala City enjoys far greater and better services than most other departments and municipalities. Furthermore, about 80 per cent of government spending in public health goes to curative services and expensive public hospitals leaving few funds for other essential public welfare projects (Nyrop 1983). The ministries most directly responsible for providing social welfare are also the ones which receive the smallest amount of the national budget. In the past the ministries of health, labour and agriculture received not more than about 15 to 20 per cent of the budget combined (Dombrowski 1970).

Financing the IGSS. The IGSS began its operation in 1948 with a sum from the state. At the end of its first year the IGSS had spent Q498,392 for its programmes (Suslow 1949). Of course, this sum has increased considerably since then but limited revenues are still a cause of limited services and protection. The IGSS receives funds from three major sources: the employers' contribution, payroll deductions of workers, and a government contribution. Employers contribute approximately one-half of the funds, workers and the government contribute one quarter each. These amounts vary, however, depending on various circumstaces (Suslow 1949). The state's portion is financed by taxes expressly created for this purpose. Table 3 shows the amount of revenue received by IGSS for Accident, Illness and Maternity programmes for the year of 1976, the last year for which detailed IGSS information was available.

Not all businesses and employers in Guatemala participate in the IGSS system. In 1976, there were 18,350 active employers registered, many of

Guatemala

them located in the Department of Guatemala where employers with three or more employees are required to register. In the remainder of the country employers with fewer than five workers are not required to register. Numerous such employers exist, especially in rural, agricultural regions. Many small employers also fail to register because of illiteracy. The necessary paper work makes it difficult if not impossible for many small employers to comply (Whetten 1961). Thus it is the bigger, urban enterprises and the larger plantations that remain the active participants in and major contributors to the IGSS system.

TABLE 3: IGSS REVENUE FOR ACCIDENT, ILLNESS AND MATERNITY PROGRAMMES, 1976

Source	Amount (in Quetzules)	Percentage
Employers	24,185,312.86	55.6
Workers	13,040,829.05	29.9
State	5,753,979.38	13.2
Other (various)	577,806.44	1.3
TOTAL	43,557,927.73	100.0

SOURCE: IGSS 1976.

THE AGED

In a country where the elderly, those 60 years and over, constitute only a small percentage of the population (5 per cent) (see Table 2) social welfare services for the aged are not highly developed.

Social Security

Under the IGSS old age programmes for workers began in 1971 providing old age pensions at retirement of 40 per cent of the worker's average monthly income during the previous five years of work (IGSS 1976). Persons have to be over 65

154

years of age and must have contributed at least 180 months into the system. If the individual's contribution was less than that, a lump sum is provided. Persons 60 years old may also receive full benefits if they have been unemployed for the previous 12 months or have a health disability. Widow's or invalid widower's pensions provide 50 per cent of the pension paid to the insured. The extent of this coverage is extremely limited. As of 1976, only workers of the IGSS itself were eligible for this coverage (IGSS 1976). Extension of benefits is to be carried out gradually to industrial and other workers.

Personal Social Services

The MOH provides some assistance to the aged who are homeless. For instance, the Ministry operates Hogar de Ancianos Fray Rodrigo, a home for the aged in Antigua, which provides housing, food and medical care for those without families or financial means (Dombrowski 1970; Lujan 1969).

Most elderly people in Guatemala depend on their families to provide assistance when in need. Indeed, it is not uncommon for the elderly to live with sons or daughters and their families. If living alone, the aged can still rely on family members to make contributions of food, clothing, medicines and so forth as needed. In Indian villages the role of family, neighbours, and the community as a whole is important in providing for the elderly. The greater respect accorded the older generation combined with the Indian's sense of community and kinship gives the individual a sense of security in later years.

Evaluation

On the whole, the aged must rely principally on their families for support. In a country where extended families are common and family ties tend to be fairly strong, caring for the aged is accepted as one's duty. Social security and personal social services provided by the government are minimal at best, although the IGSS plans eventually to extend its benefits to a much wider sector of the aged population than currently receives protection.

THE DISABLED AND HANDICAPPED

The incidence and extent of disabilities in Guatemala is not well documented. Persons handicapped because of congenital, mental or debilitating diseases are often cared for by the family. Welfare measures tend to focus on work-related disabilities in urban areas leaving the bulk of agrarian workers outside its scope.

Social Security

Disability, whether due to work injuries or not, has some degree of coverage under the IGSS. Older workers who become unable to work due to illness or injury are eligible for invalidity pension equal to 40 per cent of their average monthly earnings during the previous five years. Accident insurance for workers who have sustained a work-related injury is provided to employees of firms with five or more workers (three or more if within the Department of Guatemala). Cash benefits of about 66 per cent of earnings are provided to workers who become incapacitated due to accidents. These benefits usually last for the duration of incapacity or are converted to a lump sum if the disability becomes permanent. Permanent disability grants vary according to region (those with higher living costs receiving the most) and according to the degree of incapacity.
Medical benefits for the disabled and handicapped are also provided through IGSS. Workers needing constant care or attendance may receive a certain sum to supplement their pension.
Medical benefits also include hospitalisation, specialist care, surgery, laboratory work, medications, and medical appliances. These are provided through a number of hospitals and clinics operated by the IGSS.

Personal Social Services

Rehabilitation and job retraining is also available to workers to some degree.
Individuals with mental disabilities may seek assistance from the Centre for Mental Health (Centro de Salud Mental) which is operated by the MOH. The MOH also operates a psychiatric hospital

in the capital as well as a Polio Rehabilitation Centre.

Evaluation

Workers who become disabled have some measure of protection under the IGSS. Nevertheless, the total number of persons receiving such protection is still limited (IGSS 1976). Disabled and handicapped persons may also seek services from various public institutions, such as medical facilities and rehabilitation centres operated by the MOH and/or the IGSS. Such services are concentrated in Guatemala City, cosequently the handicapped in rural regions more often rely on family and local community services which tend to be scarce in the countryside.

CHILDREN AND YOUTH

Unlike the aged, children and young people comprise a large percentage of the population in Guatemala (45 per cent under age 14). Policies and programmes geared towards the needs of children and youth are quite pressing with education and health being the two major concerns.

Under the MOL minors have some protection from labour abuse, such as forced labour and other unfair labour practices. A large number of children are economically active in Guatemala. Official labour statistics define the labour force as anyone over seven years of age who is working (Dombrowski 1970). Indeed, thousands of children between the ages of seven and nine are counted as economically active, most of them engaged in agriculture. About half of the labour force is under 29 years of age. Youths working on plantations, in commerce and industry have protection under the Inspectorate General of Labour of the MOL.

Social Security

The IGSS provides an orphan's pension to children of deceased covered workers. It also protects covered working children in the event of occupational accidents or illness. The majority of working children, however, work in agriculture, on small family farms which are not covered by social security.

Personal Social Services

The MOH has programmes to place orphaned children in homes or institutions and to educate them. The National Orphanage and Reformatory is located on the outskirts of Guatemala City (Dombrowski 1970). Institutionalised children receive services through state agencies as well as outside organisations such as United Nations agencies and private organisations (United Nations 1963). Besides academic training most institutionalised children also receive some sort of vocational training in areas such as carpentry, tailoring, shoemaking, office skills, printing, bookbinding, and so forth (United Nations 1963). While under institutional care children may receive social counselling and psychological examinations. Social and psychiatric services are available to these children and social workers provide counselling and assistance during the child's stay and upon leaving the institution.

While these services exist for some orphaned and needy children, the role of the family is far more important in meeting their needs. Orphans are frequently adopted by extended family members (Dombrowski 1970). In Indian communities that tend to be self-contained and have little contact with outside agencies, the family is especially important. In these closed corporate communities it is the duty of family and kin to look after the welfare of orphaned children just as it is to take care of the aged.

The institution of compadrazgo (god-parenthood) also plays an important role in providing assistance to children. The godparents of a child often provide a measure of personal security especially in times of need. Compadrazgo extends the ties of kinship forming a wider network of social relationships. Not only is a relationship established between the child and godparents, but a relationship of mutual aid is established between the child's parents and the godparents. Godparents may fill the role of the natural parents when a child is orphaned or left homeless (Mintz & Wolf 1950). Godparents often bestow small gifts or other privileges on the child even under normal circumstances. The importance of <u>compadrazgo</u> is seen in the method of choosing godparents. A child's parents will select godparents that are preferably in a better socio-economic position than themselves since this will ensure a more secure future for the child. Some Indian parents may choose a Ladino godparent for this reason (Whetten 1961).

Providing for the educational needs of children and youth is a task of the Ministry of Education, as well as a number of private and international organisations. For instance, some of the programmes of the Ministry of Education have been funded by UNICEF and other organisations. One such programme attempted to bring educational reforms to isolated highland regions (United Nations 1978a). In another joint venture, Chicazango, a small highland Indian village, was selected for a programme designed to improve not just education but general community living standards (United Nations 1978b). A voluntary organisation, the <u>Servicio Auxiliar de Bienestar Social</u> (Auxiliary Service for Social Welfare) provides services to children in a variety of ways (United Nations 1963). They assist in training young girls in domestic arts, provide recreational activities for boys and girls, and provide books, school supplies and other materials to institutionalised children. This organisation also provides counselling and assistance in seeking and maintaining employment for youth.

Private, religious and philanthropic organisations also provide some services for children and youth. The American-based agency, CARE, for example, has funded various projects and has supplied materials for educational and health programmes (Wilgus 1965). Catholic and Protestant organisations often attempt to provide some of the basic living and educational needs of children. The World Health Organisation (WHO), Pan American Health Organisation (PAHO), and INCAP (<u>Instituto de Nutricion de Centro America y Panama</u>) are other international organisations providing some social welfare services to children. Their role has been primarily in sponsoring or funding programmes for improving the educational and health status of children.

Guatemala

Evaluation

The welfare and education of children has been a
major national concern and has received much
support from international agencies. A number of
educational, health and recreational programmes
exist for children and young people, especially in
the Department of Guatemala. As with other social
welfare programmes, Guatemala's rural children
receive fewer benefits. Among many Indians the
child's education and welfare is the complete
responsibility of the family. Today a large
percentage of Indian children are attending
schools but many drop out at an early age to help
the family economically. This also is true of
numerous rural Ladino children. Even in the
capital, services are still insufficient to meet
all the needs. The number of young children one
sees roaming and living on the streets of
Guatemala City (abandoned, semi-abandoned,
homeless, begging, etc.) is an immediate
indication of the short comings of the welfare
system.

NEEDY FAMILIES

Poverty in Guatemala is pervasive. Income levels
and agricultural production are insufficient to
meet the needs of large numbers of families for
nutritional, medical and housing necessities.

Social Security

Through the Department of Social Services of the
MOH families in need may receive some aid, but as
with most other government services, some families
must be rejected because of insufficient funds
(Dombrowski 1970; Roberts 1970).

The IGSS provides maternity coverage for
insured workers and their wives. This includes
cash benefits for 30 days prior and 45 days after
confinement. Hospitalisation and other medical
expenses are also covered. The newborn is
provided with milk and/or other dietary
supplements, some clothing and pediatric care for
two years. The family receives compensation if
the mother dies while giving birth (IGSS 1976).
The maternity programme of the IGSS, however, only
provides coverage to a few thousand women and

160

money spent on maternity represents about 12 per cent of the total IGSS budget.

The IGSS also provides survivors' pensions to dependents of deceased covered workers.

Personal Social Services

Food provisions are supplied to needy families through various agencies. The Ministry of Agriculture provides some food supplies, such as milk, to low-income families. INCAP has been instrumental in fighting malnutrition amongst children and low-income families. Incaparina, a dietary supplement rich in protein and vitamin A, is made available through INCAP at a nominal cost. INCAP also cooperates with other organisations, such as PAHO, WHO and the UN Children's Fund on various nutritional campaigns.

Low-cost housing is available to some low-income families through the National Housing Institute which has supervised the building and improvement of thousands of dwelling units. Assistance from the National Housing Institute comes in the form of direct loans, direct construction of housing, aid for self-help projects, and assistance on joint employer-employee ventures (Dombrowski 1970). Some landless rural families have received assistance from the Guatemalan Rural Development Programme, funded in part with financial aid from the United States. These programmes have attempted to resettle landless families in underdeveloped and unused lands mainly in the Peten and Pacific Lowland regions. Families are generally given family-size plots of about 50 acres. Government agencies, such as the Institute of Agrarian Reform assist these resettled families with credit and technical expertise (Acedo Mendoza 1974; Dombrowski 1970).

Families needing emergency assistance because of catastrophic events may seek relief from a variety of agencies and organisations. For instance, the thousands of families left destitute and homeless after the 1976 earthquake were aided by government agencies, private, religious and international organisations.

Most women in the country rely on the family for various forms of assistance during pregnancy and delivery. Traditional midwives are still important in maternity care. Ladino women use hospitals more than Indian women, many of them now preferring to deliver their first-born in a hospital. Many rural Ladino and most Indian women give birth at home aided by a midwife and/or kinswomen. As Greenberg (1982) points out, the MOH has recognised the importance of midwives and has developed midwife-training programmes to upgrade their standards and practices. Unfortunately many of these programmes have not been as effective as had been hoped by the MOH because of cultural differences and misunderstandings.

Evaluation

The number of families needing social assistance is greater than the services or money available for such families (Roberts 1970). Needy families, therefore, must use whatever resources are at hand. Many rely on informal networks of friends and family. Some of the children seen in the streets begging and peddling various goods help support their families. The lack of housing for low-income families is evident in the large quantity of make-shift housing in the squatters' shanty towns in Guatemala City. Relatively few families receive the assistance they require although some government agencies and private organisations attempt to provide some assistance.

THE UNEMPLOYED

Since 1980 unemployment has been increasing in Guatemala. Urban unemployment is aggravated by the increase in rural to urban migration of workers and families. In the country underemployment is extremely high and is, indeed, a major reason for many people migrating to cities in search of work. Some statistics indicate that over 10 per cent of the working population is unemployed and underemployment affects over a third of the population (Inforpress 1985). These figures are probably somewhat conservative so that in reality unemployment is a graver problem.

Social Security

Unemployment insurance in Guatemala has received little attention and does not constitute a

programme of benefits under the national social
security system. Schottland (1970) points out
that unemployment insurance has been more common
in industrialised countries because it is designed
primarily for an industrial wage economy. In an
agricultural economy, such as Guatemala's
unemployment insurance has not been easily
adopted. Most of the economically active workers
in Guatemala are farmers working for themselves on
small plots of land or working for a small
employer who may not even be enrolled in the IGSS
system.

Personal Social Services

Government employment offices do exist in urban
areas where unemployed workers may register for
work (Dombrowski 1970). The Ministry of
Communication and Public Works provides work for
some of the work force but this falls short of
alleviating the problem. Private and charitable
institutions may provide some assistance by giving
food or other necessities to the families of the
unemployed.
Augmenting urban unemployment is the high rate
of underemployment in Guatemala. It is estimated
that between 30 and 50 per cent of the
agricultural work force is underemployed
(Dombrowski 1970; Inforpress 1985). Many of these
workers seek to supplement their incomes through
wage labour either on larger farms, plantations or
in the city.
Government workers and some urban wage earners
receive a one month's severance pay in case of
lay-offs. Benefits provided by industrial and
commercial enterprises, however, are not uniform
nor sufficient.

Evaluation

Unemployment insurance is largely undeveloped in
Guatemala, despite the fact that unemployment is
at about 10 per cent and underemployment is very
high. Unemployment programmes such as those found
in industrial nations have not been applied to
Guatemala because of significantly different
economies. To address this problem through
national unemployment insurance would require
funds beyond the reach of current resources.

Thus, unemployed workers have few options beyond the family, community and private charitable organisations.

THE SICK AND INJURED

The high incidence of malnutrition and communicable diseases that has plagued its population has led Guatemala to make some strong efforts to improve the health status of its people. Because of its concern with primary health care, measures dealing with the sick and injured have often been infrastructural (building of hospitals and clinics, disease eradication campaigns, sanitation projects, etc.).

Social Security

IGSS coverage for the sick and injured is similar to that applying to the disabled. Under accident insurance, the sick and injured receive cash benefits as well as medical treatment, hospitalisation, rehabilitation, and other medical expenses. The insured worker's family also receives protection from the IGSS in the form of survivors' pensions in case of death. The family receives a monthly sum plus a funeral grant for burial expenses.

A worker who becomes permanently disabled as a result of a work injury receives a permanent disability grant which is usually a lump-sum that varies according to the degree of incapacity.

Outside the IGSS system, the sick and injured in Guatemala have a fairly broad spectrum of services from which they can receive medical attention. The cost of these services ranges from free medical treatment to nominal fees to expensive private care. The MOH operates a number of hospitals, clinics, health dispensaries and health posts to serve the sick and injured throughout the country.

The IGSS also operates a number of hospitals and clinics which serve not only insured workers but non-affiliated persons as well (IGSS 1976). In 1976, the IGSS provided emergency medical care to over 23,000 non-insured individuals.

Besides general and specialised hospitals, the MOH manages a network of health facilities throughout the country.

164

Personal Social Services

To alleviate health problems in rural ares, the MOH has encouraged the training of auxiliary health workers known as health promoters (**promotores**) and Rural Health Technicians (**Tecnicos en salud rural**) (Bossert 1984; Nyrop 1983; Viau 1980). Rural Health Technicians are middle-level paid health workers trained in disease prevention and curative skills. Dr Alberto Viau began the programme in 1971 and it was funded by USAID. Shortly after, UNICEF funded a separate programme to train lower-level promoters of health who are volunteers from rural villages (Bossert 1984). The main focus of these efforts is to provide primary health care.

As with all previous groups, the sick and injured rely on the support and aid of the family. Among the more traditional Ladino and Indian sectors, there is also a reliance on folk medical practices to alleviate certain ailments. Folk medicine is discouraged by government health personnel and the medical community but many still utilise folk practitioners or healers (**curanderos**) such as herbalists, masseurs and shamans.

Evaluation

For the sick and injured a fairly adequate infrastructure of health and medical facilities and legislation exists to protect and serve them. Good medical care can be found, especially in Guatemala City. In the rural areas the MOH has attempted to establish adequate medical coverage but many individuals go unattended or poorly attended for numerous reasons. Uneven distribution of resources, poor equipment, lack of effective planning, manpower shortages, and problems due to cultural barriers between Ladinos and Indians contribute to uneven protection of the population. For instance, Guatemala City has 20 per cent of the population but 80 per cent of the republic's doctors and major medical facilities, such as hospitals (Nyrop 1983; PAHO 1982). Even in the capital some of the sick go under-served because of inaccessibility of facilities. Mulvihill's (1979) locational study of health services in the capital points out that the spatial distribution of health dispensaries often reflects local and national political factors rather than actual needs.

AN ASSESSMENT OF THE GUATEMALAN WELFARE SYSTEM

The shortcomings of an underdeveloped welfare system, such as exists in Guatemala, are often easier to point out than its accomplishments, especially when one compares it to the social welfare systems of industrialised nations. Many of the failures seen in the welfare system are reflections of the broader problems of the society at large and its socio-economic conditions.

There are several important elements that characterise the social welfare system in Guatemala. The first is the lack of centralisation in the administration and planning of services and programmes. The second is the shortage of services, facilities and manpower, so coverage applies only to a relatively low percentage of the population. Moreover, there is an urban-rural dichotomy in services. Finally, there is a severe lack of funds for programmes and innovations.

The lack of centralisation can be seen in the numerous government ministries and agencies that are involved in social welfare programmes along with the variety of private, religious and international organisations. The National Health Planning Unit was created to coordinate health and social welfare programmes at the national level. Yet this has not been a sufficient mechanism for centralisation. Mulvihill, for instance, demonstrates how some services are hampered by the rivalry and political differences between agencies. He states: 'Not only does a central authority not exist, but ... these services often act as competitors through their association with different levels of government ...' (Mulvihill 1979, p.304).

The shortage of welfare services, facilities and personnel is tied closely to the urban-rural dichotomy of services. While adequate resources, such as hospitals, physicians, etc., exist in the capital city, rural areas are often lacking even in basic services and facilities. Health facilities have increased in number (for example health posts, clinics) but these often lack the trained personnel and adequate equipment to be effective (Annis 1981). Another factor is the fact that many social welfare personnel come from the Ladino and urban sectors (with the notable exception of the promotores). Many health and social workers are trained with Western conceptions of health and welfare which often conflict with Indian and rural cultural beliefs. Conflicts and misunderstandings arising from such cultural differences make the implementation of social and health programmes more difficult to achieve (e.g. Greenberg 1982; Paul & Demarest 1984).

Social security coverage for workers in Guatemala is still limited both in types of coverage and the number of people protected under the system. Estimates of the number of people covered by the IGSS varies from about 20 per cent of the economically active population (Borelli 1971) to almost 33 per cent (IGSS 1976). According to the IGSS, 586,552 workers out of the 1,810,522 economically active were covered by social security in 1976. Of these almost equal numbers came from the urban and agricultural sectors. This actually means that only about 5 to 8 per cent of the total population has some measure of protection under the IGSS. The social security programmes most developed under the IGSS are those for Accidents, Illness and Maternity with those for Disability and Old Age forming a minor part of the system. In terms of the money spent on each of these programmes, almost 78 per cent went to Accidents while Old Age received slightly less than 1 per cent (IGSS 1976). The MOH provides assistance to another percentage of the population but it is difficult without enough data to determine what percentage of the population receives how much assistance.

Within the urban-rural imbalance, it is also important to note that governments usually respond most readily to groups that are fairly well organised and urbanised and that rural communities (and the urban poor) often have a weak political voice (Adams 1970; United Nations 1982).

Improving social security and welfare has been slow and limited for the many ideological, economic, political, and social reasons cited earlier. The fairly low priority given to social welfare results in limited funding. Some see this lack of funds as probably 'the single most intractable problem facing social welfare reform' (United Nations 1982a, p.31).

Given these conditions, the welfare system of Guatemala operates as a decentralised network of agencies and organisations. Individuals and families rely on informal networks of family, friends and acquaintances. Roberts (1970) notes how common it is for workers to seek financial help (e.g. a loan) from working friends or from the employers. Others may use the relationships established through compadrazgo to ask favours or aid. The family remains the first and most important source of assistance for most people.

Due to the limitations of the welfare system self-help projects have been encouraged both by the government and non-governmental agencies. Many of the United Nations sponsored programmes have been efforts to improve aspects of health and nutrition by encouraging and teaching communities to take an active role in bettering aspects of their communities. For example, the municipal authorities of Guatemala City have sponsored 'betterment committees' in the shanty towns and poor neighbourhoods. These self-help committees act as informal mechanisms by which the community can establish contact with city authorities in the effort to improve living standards (Roberts 1970).

Setting aside the many problems and weaknesses, the social welfare system in Guatemala also has some strengths and accomplishments upon which a stronger system could be built. First of all, social welfare has a laudable philosophical foundation. The 'spiritual socialism' of Arevalo initiated a long-term commitment to public welfare. Many legislative acts and programmes have been created to improve and protect the health and social life of the citizens of Guatemala. Although not yet fully achieved, the goals of the IGSS are very broad, envisaging protection for the entire population.

Secondly, by focussing on primary health care Guatemala has taken a first and important step toward building a solid public welfare system. The main concern of most programmes from Arevalo's time onward has been the improvement of health: improving nutrition, eradicating communicable diseases, improving sanitation, preventing illness, reducing health risks, etc. The WHO, PAHO, INCAP, United Nations organisations, and American foundations have joined with Guatemalan agencies to combat such things as malnutrition, tuberculosis, and a host of other health problems. These efforts have been successful in controlling some diseases to varying degrees. Smallpox was eradicated and malaria, which was the major cause of death in 1950, has been greatly controlled.

Efforts to improve the health status of its people has led to the creation of a fairly broad network of health facilities in the form of hospitals, clinics, health centres and health posts. The infrastructure for a potentially effective health care system has, therefore, been set in place. The use of auxiliary personnel (e.g. Rural Health Technicians, promotores, trained midwives) is an innovative step toward making the system more effective and accessible.

To resolve the problems seen in the social welfare system of Guatemala requires extensive changes that would reach to the roots of the problems, changes that are not easily achieved. Somewhat more specifically, a couple of proposals can be made for solving, at least in part, two major problems of the system: lack of funds and lack of centralisation.

As was noted earlier, the public purse in Guatemala is meagre, making it difficult for the government to allocate large sums to social welfare. One problem is that the government relies heavily on indirect taxes for a large portion of its revenue. Three-quarters of the government's income comes from taxes, and over 80 per cent of this is derived from indirect taxation. Direct taxation on income and wealth (both corporate and personal) accounts for less than one-fifth of the tax revenue, while in other countries this is closer to 80 per cent (Inforpress 1985). What is needed, therefore is a restructuring of the tax system so that direct taxation of corporate and personal income provides greater revenue to the state. The business community has been resistant to changes in the tax system but such changes would provide the state with some income and thereby permit it to spend more on social welfare.

The problem of decentralisation is another thorny problem. Centralisation is needed if the existing programmes are to be coordinated into an efficient system. One possible way to achieve centralisation would be to give greater authority to an existing structure or agency that would act as the unifying entity. This could be one of the government ministries or the National Health Planning Unit which already has coordinating and liaison functions.

Another interesting solution to the problem of centralisation has been proposed by Kenneth Borelli (1971). He suggests that the five Central

American republics could consolidate their social
security systems into a regional one. The
consolidation would be under the auspices of an
international agency, such as the Organisation of
American States and its structure would be based
on a semi-private insurance model. Borelli
suggests that already there is a close
relationship between the five republics, each
sharing similar histories, economies, interests
and problems. He further suggests that
integrating the individual social security systems
would lessen the financial burden of each
country. Whether such a system would be feasible
is difficult to determine but it is an interesting
proposal worthy of being explored.

REFERENCES AND FURTHER READING

Acedo Mendoza, C. (1974), Social Welfare in Latin
America, Caracas: XVII International
Conference of Social Welfare.

Adams, R. (1970), Crucifixion by Power, Austin:
University of Texas Press.

Ander-Egg, E. (1971), Apuntes para una Historia del
Servicio Social, Quito: Editorial Casa de la
Cultura Ecuatoriana.

Annis, S. (1981), 'Physical Access and Utilization
of Health Services in Rural Guatemala', Social
Science and Medicine, 15D, 515-23.

Anthony, A. (1981), 'The Minority that is a
Majority: Guatemala's Indians', in Jonas, S. &
Tobis, D. (eds), Guatemala, Berkeley: North
American Congress on Latin America.

Borelli, K. (1971), 'Social Security in Central
America: A Developmental Model', International
Social Work, 14(1), 4-15.

Bossert, T. (1984), 'Health-Policy Innovation and
International Assistance in Central America',
Political Science Quarterly, 99(3), 441-55.

Brown, A. (1981), 'Land of the Few: Rural Land
Ownership in Guatemala', in Jonas, S. & Tobis,
D. (eds), Guatemala, Berkeley: North American
Congress on Latin America.

Guatemala

Calvert, P. (1985), Guatemala: A Nation in Turmoil, Boulder: Westview Press.

Dombrowski, J. (1970), Area Handbook for Guatemala, Washington D.C.: Government Printing Office.

Fletcher, L. et al. (1970), Guatemala's Economic Development: The Role of Agriculture, Ames: Iowa State University.

Greenberg, L. (1982), 'Midwife Training Programs in Highland Guatemala', Social Science & Medicine, 16, 1599-1609.

Guatemala (1981a), Censos Nacionales de 1981, Guatemala: Instituto Nacional de Estadistica.

_____ (1981b), Manual de Organizacion de la Administracion Publica, 2ª ed., Guatemala: Oficina Nacional de Servicio Civil.

Handy, J. (1984), Gift of the Devil: A History of Guatemala, Boston: South End Press.

Hernandez Reyna, L. (1965), La Seguridad Social a Traves del Seguro Social y los Seguros Facultativos, Tesis, Guatemala: Universidad de San Carlos.

Inforpress (1985), Guatemala: Elections 1985, Guatemala: Inforpress Centroamericana.

IGSS (1976), Detalle de Labores, Guatemala: Instituto Guatemalteco de Seguridad Social.

Jonas, S. & Tobis, D. (1981), Guatemala, Berkeley: North American Congress on Latin America.

Lally, D. (1970), National Social Service Systems, Washington: U.S. Department of Health, Education and Welfare.

Lemus-Pivaral, D. (1975), La Prevision Social en el Derecho Guatemalteco, Guatemala: Universidad de San Carlos.

Lujan, H. (ed.) (1969), Estudios sobre Administracion Publica en Guatemala, Guatemala: Instituto Nacional de Administracion para el Desarrollo.

Mintz, S. & Wolf, E. (1950), 'An Analysis of Ritual Co-Parenthood (Compadrazgo)', Southwestern Journal of Anthropology, 6, 341-68.

Mulvihill, J. (1979), 'A Locational Study of Primary Health Services in Guatemala City', Professional Geographer, 3(13), 299-305.

Navarro, V. (1976), Medicine Under Capitalism, New York: Prodist Press.

Nyrop, R. (ed.) (1983), Guatemala: A Country Study, Washington: U.S. Government Printing Office.

O'Sullivan-Ryan, J. (1977), 'Information and Rural Services: Marginality in the Guatemalan Highlands', (mimeograph), Houston: Institute of Latin American Studies.

Pan American Health Organisation (1977), Extension of Health Service Coverage Based on the Strategies of Primary Care & Community Participation, Washington: PAHO.

_____ (1982), Health Conditions in the Americas, 1977-1980, Scientific Publ. No. 427, Washington: PAHO.

Paul, B. & Demarest, W. (1984), 'Citizen Participation Overplanned: Health Project in the Guatemalan Community of San Pedro la Laguan', Social Science & Medicine, 19(3), 185-92.

Roberts, B. (1970), 'The Social Organisation of Low-Income Urban Families', in Adams, R., Crucifixion by Power, Austin: University of Texas Press.

Schlesinger, S. & Kinzer, S. (1982), Bitter Fruit: The Untold Story of the American Coup in Guatemala, Garden City: Doubleday & Co.

Schottland, C. (1970), The Social Security Program in the United States, 2nd ed., Englewood Cliffs: Prentice-Hall.

Suslow, L. (1949), Aspects of Social Reforms in Guatemala, 1944-1949, Hamilton, NY: Colgate University.

Guatemala

_____ (1955), *Social Security in Guatemala*, Unpublished Ph.D. Dissertation, Storrs, CN: University of Connecticut.

Tax, S. (1953), *Penny Capitalism: A Guatemalan Indian Economy*, Washington: Smithsonian Institution.

United Nations (1963), *Asistencia a los Ninos en Instituciones*, ST/SOA/31, Buenos Aires: Editorial Humanitas.

_____ (1978a), 'An Attempt to Reach the Isolated and Under-served', *Basic Services for Children I*, Paris: UNESCO.

_____ (1978b), 'An Effort to Identify Educational Responses at the Village Level', *Basic Services for Children II*, Paris: UNESCO.

_____ (1982a), *Administration of Social Welfare*, ST/ESA/147, New York: United Nations.

_____ (1982b), *Economic Survey of Latin America, 1980*, E/CEPAL/G1191, Santiago: United Nations.

_____ (1984), *Question of the Violation of Human Rights*, E/CN.4/1984/NGO/16, New York: Commission on Human Rights.

_____ (1985), *Report on the Situation of Human Rights in Guatemala*, E/CN.4/1985/19, New York: United Nations.

_____ (1987), *Population and Vital Statistics Report*, ST/ESA/STAT/Ser.A/160, New York: United Nations.

Viau, A. (1980), 'Guatemala's Rural Health Technicans', *World Hospitals*, 16(1), 31-4.

Whetten, N. (1961), *Guatemala: The Land and the People*, New Haven: Yale University Press.

Wilgus, A. (1965), *The Caribbean: Its Health Problems*, Gainsville: University of Florida Press.

Guatemala

Wolf, E. (1957), 'Closed Corporate Peasant Communities in Mesoamerica and Central Java', <u>Southwestern Journal of Anthropology</u>, 13, 1-18.

World Bank (1978), <u>Guatemala: Economic and Social Position and Prospects</u>, Washington: The World Bank.

MEXICO
Marian Angela Aguilar

THE WELFARE SYSTEM ENVIRONMENT

Ideological Environment

Mexico is both similar and dissimilar to most
Latin American countries. It is similar in that
the universal language is Spanish, the dominant
religion is Roman Catholic and a two-class system
exists in which the majority of the population is
poor. Mexico is dissimilar in that it has not
been governed by military rule in over 60 years;
has not had a civil war or a serious uprising
since 1910; has not in the past defaulted on its
public debt and borders one of the most developed
countries in the world. These factors are
important in preserving Mexico's ideological
environment that has moulded the fabric of its
welfare system.

The Constitutional Welfare Legacy. Ideologically,
the guarantee of social security is found in
section 123 of the 1917 Mexican Constitution,
which pre-dates recruitment to social security in
the United States. Under the Mexican Constitution
citizens have the right to improve their social
condition through the promotion of just systems,
reasonable opportunity for advancement, and the
means to become a productive worker. Social
scientists in Mexico write about social security
as being synonymous with well-being in terms of
health, job security and insurance against
accident and misfortune. It is an instrument with
which to battle poverty and unemployment. It is
the document that elevates the dignity of the
person in every respect. The difference between
social provision and social security is that

175

social provision is a conglomerate of ideas and institutions which act passively and reactively (residual social welfare), while social security is a pro-active idea that focusses on prevention and the maintenance of human dignity (institutional social welfare).

The Work Ethic and Industrial Control. Tannenbaum (1950) aptly expressed that the

> improvement of labour conditions, the increase in workers' dignity and self-respect, the creating of a feeling of power, and participation of unions in national affairs were all to the good, but the greater by-product was the increase in the power of the government against foreign influence.

The principle upon which social welfare was based related, not to the work ethic, but to the giving of privileges to workers, who, in turn, would subordinate their individual needs to the good of the state.

Social Justice and Human Rights. The basis of social justice and human rights was established in the 1917 Constitution under which Mexican citizens were guaranteed human rights and the legal basis for the provision of social security was established. In the years after 1917 public finances were limited and little development could take place because of social and political instability. Consequently even though much was said about the desirability of social development in terms of the development of social security, little was done until the 1940s. The recurrent theme emerging from the social welfare debates reflected the need to introduce social welfare programmes to prevent public unrest.

The Virtues of Resilience and Survival. The Mexican worker has long been confronted with a harsh social, political and economic working environment, characterised by poor working conditions, extensive underemployment, and a feeling of helplessness. In this environment resilience and survival have become a virtue.

Mutual Aid and the Collective Spirit. Though Mexican workers are guaranteed more rights than other Mexican citizens, they have been accorded these rights in order to strengthen the political power of the state. The unions are tools of the state. The collective spirit captured in the unions is far more important to the welfare of the worker. Indeed the worker must forfeit individualism to gain improved labour conditions. However, this does increase the workers' dignity and self-respect and provide them with a sense of power and participation in national affairs.

<u>Industriousness</u>. Mexicans are industrious people. Given the high level of unemployment and underemployment, individuals have developed creative skills that allow them to supplement their incomes. This industriousness has been fostered by a social system that values hardship, endurance and survival.

<u>Class Distinctions</u>. The gap between rich and poor continues to be a major social problem in Mexico. The welfare system focusses on the urban worker almost exclusively leaving those outside the formal urban sector receiving very few services and benefits. Some efforts are being made to bring welfare programmes to the isolated areas of Mexico.

<u>Elitist Leadership and Decision-making Processes</u>. The idea of popular participation in decision making has not gained any currency in Mexico. The President, his delegates and their spouses determine the level and type of welfare services and programmes to be provided. Only unionised workers have any involvement in effective decision-making processes.

Historical Origins

Mexico became a nation on the eve of the adoption of its 1917 Constitution, which provided the foundation for the subsequent development of social security and the present social services in Mexico. The first public agency with welfare responsibilities was the Department of Health, which was established in 1917.

Personal Social Services

It was not until 1937 that the Secretariat of
Public Assistance was created by President
Cardenas. In 1942 President Camacho created the
first Secretariat of Labour and Social Welfare.
President Aleman in 1948 reorganised the various
departments to combine public assistance and
health care into the Secretariat of Health and
Public Assistance. At the same time he
established an office to investigate the working
conditions of women and children. He also
established the Institute of Infant Nutrition.
President Cortines subsequently promoted the
nutrition programme and held the First National
Congress for the Protection of Infancy which led
to the establishment of the Institute for the
Protection of Infancy. Between 1958 and 1964
President Mateos expanded the National Institute
for the Protection of Infancy to include school
age children. President Mateos also inaugurated a
public health programme for potable water and
drainage systems.

During the Presidency of Diaz Ordaz (1964-70),
the first public hospital for the mentally ill and
the first children's psychiatric facility were
founded. Through the National Institute for the
Protection of Children the first day-care centres
were established and the Mexican Institute for the
Assistance of Children was formed. During the
Presidency of Luis Echeverria in the 1970s Mexico
was able to formulate long-term goals for the
first time in its history. President Echeverria
introduced an urban development plan and created
the Secretariat for Human Settlement Public Works
and the National Urban Development Commission
(Montgomery 1982). At this time the General Law
on Population was enacted in an attempt to reduce
population growth (Alba 1982). The Institute for
Protection of Infancy became the Mexican Institute
for Family and Infancy. In the mid-1970s, during
the Presidency of Hosea Lopez Portello which began
in the mid-1970s and ended in the early 1980s, a
myriad of child-related institutes were
consolidated under what is now the National System
for the Integral Development of the Family (DIF).
During this period the National Council for the
Concerns of Youth was formed, as well as the
National Programme for Family Alimentation and a
range of other rural development programmes
(Street 1983).

Mexico

Social Security Programmes

The 1917 Constitution afforded social security
rights to two classes of the Mexican population:
agrarian communities and trade unions (Tannenbaum
1950, pp.114-6). Article 123 regulated hours of
work, wages, labour, the protection of women and
children, profit making and dismissal from work.
It was not until 1939 however that social security
became obligatory in the form of a workers'
compensation programme which provided workers with
protection against disability, unemployment,
sickness and accidents, and which required large
industries to make provision for housing, schools,
infirmaries and public services. The 1939 social
security law established the Board of Conciliation
and Arbitration, which comprised representatives
of labour, employers and the state, with the state
having the greatest number of votes. All disputes
between labour and employers were settled by this
Board. It was not until 1943 that the first
social insurance bill was passed. In the same
year the Secretariat of Labour was established.
Over the years numerous amendments have been made
to the 1943 legislation, most recently to extend
coverage to include rural labourers.

Trade unions also administer a subsidy
programme for workers who are destitute.

Although the 1917 Constitution targeted the
rural worker for specific social security
protection, it has taken many years for the social
security programmes' coverage to be extended to
this group. Even now coverage is far from
complete.

In summary, although many welfare programmes
exist to promote the social and economic
development of the Mexican people, the major ones
are the social security programme for workers, the
social security programme for state and federal
employees, the health and social assistance
programme, the national system for the development
of the family, and the national council of
recourse for attention to youth.

Table 1 provides an historical chronology of
these programmes.

TABLE 1: A CHRONOLOGICAL HISTORY OF MEXICO'S MAJOR
SOCIAL WELFARE PROGRAMMES

Programme	Year	Target Population
Mexican Social Security Institute (IMSS)	1943	Workers and their families
Ministry of Health and Welfare (SSA) (modified in 1982)	1917	Those in need
Institute for Social Security and Services for Government Workers (ISSTE) (modified in 1968)	1960	Civil servants and their families
National System for the Integral Development of the Family (DIF) (modified in 1982)	1946	Family
National Council for the Concerns of Youth (IMJUEE) (modified in 1982)	1976	Youth

Political Environment

Mexico is a federal republic comprising 31 states
and a federal district. Under the 1917
Constitution legislative power is vested in the
bi-cameral National Congress, elected by universal
adult suffrage. The Senate has 64 members (two
from each state and a federal district), who serve
a six-year term. The Chamber of Deputies,
directly elected for three years, has 400 seats,
of which 300 are filled from single-member
constituencies. The remaining 100 seats allocated
by proportional representation are filled from
political party lists. The executive power is
held by the President directly elected for six
years at the same time as the Senate. He governs
with the Cabinet he appoints. Each state has its
own constitution and is administered by a governor
who is elected for six years, and an elected
Chamber of Deputies.

Mexico

Although Mexico is a multi-party state, its form of government is essentially authoritarian as the Institutional Revolutionary Party (PRI) is dominant. The PRI has long served as the mechanism for social control, recruitment and electoral activities. The only other party which has any influence in Mexico in recent years is the Partido de Accion Nacional (PAN). The key to understanding politics in Mexico is to appreciate that the elite ruling class uses a form of bargaining and mutual accommodation to gain support. As the 'patron' or elite boss rises in power his constituents also gain access to political and economic rewards. Corruption has been crucial to the effective functioning of Mexico over the years.

It is important to distinguish between the electoral strength and social force when discussing Mexico's political system. Social forces or pressure groups are often organised around specific issues or programmes and are thus more important than electoral strength in creating an environment for social change (Aguayo 1986).

Socio-Economic Environment

Mexico is the third largest country in Latin America with a land area of 1,978 million square kilometres, bordering the United States on one side and Belize and Guatemala to the south. Mexico has a pronounced regional and socio-economic diversity with highly prosperous industrial and agricultural areas co-existing with extremely impoverished areas. Even in the rural areas there is a wide gulf between the rich and those in dire poverty.

Mexico's population in 1986 was estimated at 80 million (Broyles 1986), of which approximately 43 per cent were under the age of 15. The crude birth rate is 34.3 per 1,000, while population growth is about 25 per 1,000. The infant mortality rate is 35 per 1,000. A little over 62 per cent of the population lives in urban areas.

Anthropologists have divided the Mexican population into two ethnic groups: Indian and Mestizo (Spanish-Indians). The latter group constitutes 88 per cent of the population. A very small percentage of the Mexican population is of European extraction.

181

Mexico

Mexico is predominantly a Roman Catholic country with over 90 per cent of the population adhering to that religion.

Mexico has been on the edge of bankruptcy for several years. Its inflation rate has run over 200 per cent and it has a foreign debt of US$100 billion.

With the discovery of oil in the 1970s Mexico sacrificed its social development for technological and industrial development, hoping that this would create economic stability. Furthermore, despite the efforts of the government to encourage and subsidise farmers engaged in food production, population growth exceeds the growth in food production.

Mexico has an unemployment rate estimated to be between 12 and 25 per cent of the workforce, whilst the underemployment rate is almost 40 per cent (Anderson et al. 1986). Underemployment and unemployment is worst in the rural areas, therefore serving as an incentive for rural-urban migration. Mexico is currently attempting to shift its industrial base to areas where the population density is lower (Street 1983).

In summary, Mexico exhibits a picture of a country with the potential for economic growth, for it is rich in minerals and hydrocarbons, but plagued with very high inflation, unemployment and underemployemnt and depletion of the treasury, also its extremely high budgetary deficit places it in danger of bankruptcy.

THE WELFARE SYSTEM: AN OVERVIEW

The Mexican welfare system has five significant features. First, it is centralised with most important programmes administered directly by the central government. Each social security system has its own regulations governing coverage, financing, and benefits scales. There is no single agency planning or coordinating this conglomeration. Second, several programmes are administered jointly by the public and private sectors. Third, organisations (including the Secretariats of National Defence, Navy and Finance, and the oil company PEMEX) operate extensive social security and welfare programmes. Fourth, voluntary religious-based agencies are regulated by the government, although they are self-financing. Finally, because the system is centralised in each state or city, the benefits highly vary.

Public welfare programmes administered by the state are those that come under the Secretariat of Health and Public Assistance; those jointly administered by the Mexican Social Security Institute (IMSS) and National Plan for the General Coordination of Depressed Areas and Marginal Groups (COPLAMAR); those sponsored by the IMSS and the Social Security Institute for Government Workers (ISSTE); and those offered by the National System for the Integral Development of the Family (DIF).

Social Security Administration

Mexican Social Securiy Institute (IMSS). Programmes administered by this agency cover all non-government employees and their dependents and provide social insurance protection against disability, old-age and death, as well as medical and maternity care and day-care for children of working mothers.

It governing body is the General Assembly comprising 30 members, 10 of whom are appointed by the federal goverment, 10 by employers and 10 by the workers. This body is presided over by a Director-General who is appointed by the President. The General Assembly determines wage scales as well as the contribution rates payable by workers, employers and the government.

The Technical Council is responsible for the administration of the IMSS. This comprises 12 members who represent the workers, employers and state.

The Vigilance Commission, comprising six members, advises the General Assembly and the Technical Council on measures necessary to improve the functioning of the social security programme. This includes investment advice and internal auditing functions.

The IMSS services about 12 per cent of the urban population and 3 per cent of the rural population. In total this constitutes about seven million workers or 28.8 million people (including dependents). This apparently low coverage must be placed within the context that only one-third of the Mexican population is engaged in formal employment (Levy & Szekely 1983), and that the programme covers a significant minority of workers in metropolitan Mexico City (Spalding 1980).

Institute of Social Security and Social Services
for Government Workers (ISSTE). This agency
services civil servants, teachers and their
dependents by providing them with social insurance
protection in the event of illness, disability,
old-age and death. It also provides a range of
personal social services to improve the quality of
life of government workers and their families.
Specifically, it provides programmes for the
well-being and the development of infants and
children, housing assistance (low cost loans for
home purchase and improvement as well as rent
subsidies). It also operates a network of
hospitals and clinics.

The Institute is governed by a Board of
Directors composed of 11 members. Five are
representatives of the government secretariats of
Programme and Budget, Housing and Public Credit,
Health and Assistance, Urban Development, Ecology,
Labour and Social Provision. The Director-General
is the President's representative. The remaining
five members are chosen by the Federation of
Syndicated Workers for the Service of the State.

The President designates the individual who
presides over the Board. The Board members may
not be employed by the Institute with the
exception of the Director-General. The Executive
Committee of the Housing Fund is composed of nine
members, one of whom is appointed by the Board. A
representative from each of the various
Secretariats also serves on this Committee. The
third administrative branch is the Vigilance
Commission composed of seven members, one of whom
represents the Controller-General of the
Federation, the Secretariat of Housing and Public
Credit and one the ISSTE. Three are designated by
the Federation of Syndicated Workers for the
Service of the State.

The ISSTE programme is administered by
federal, state and municipal authorities,
industrial concerns and other institutions.

Personal Social Services Administration

The personal social services are provided by both
the public sector and voluntary agencies.

Secretariat of Health and Public Assistance. Most
public programmes are administered by distinctive
commissions and institutes affiliated with this
Secretariat, most notably the National System for

the Integral Development of the Family (DIF). At the federal level, the President of Mexico has administrative responsibility, but in fact his spouse appoints a Director-General to administer the programme and a Director of Administration. At the state and local levels the Governor and Mayor, respectively, have the administrative authority, although their spouses preside as presidents of the Boards which administer the programmes. At all levels of government the spouses appoint a Director-General and a Director of Administration to manage programmes. Figure 1 clarifies the administrative structures.

Under the auspices of the DIF a number of agencies provide specific services. These include the Centre for Special Therapies and for the Study of Therapy, the Centre for the Integral Assistance of the Elderly, the Centre for Integral Rehabilitation, and the Centre for the Detection, Diagnosis and Control of Epilepsy.

Particular government departments have responsibility for the administration of particular programmes. The Department of Health sponsors a network of health clinics that provide maternal and child health care, as well as other public health programmes. COPLAMAR is the organisation designated to work in the area of rural poverty (Street 1983). Most personal social services are provided by the Department of Public Assistance which has a number of institutions under its auspices. The Department of Community Development, the Department Street Educators and the Department of Recreation provide a range of services to children and youth.

FIGURE 1: ORGANISATIONAL STRUCTURE OF THE OFFICE OF INTEGRAL DEVELOPMENT OF THE FAMILY

PRESIDENT
(President's, Governor's or Mayor's wife)

DIRECTOR GENERAL   DIRECTOR OF ADMINISTRATION

| Director of Assistance | Director of Alimentation | Director of Medical/ Social Assistance | Director of Education | Director of Judicial Assistance |

SOURCE: DIF 1984.

Mexico

Financing Social Security

Social security programmes administered by the
IMSS are financed by contributions from employees
(3.8 per cent of wages), employers (11.2 per cent
of payroll) and federal, state and municipal
government (20 per cent of the employers'
contribution).

Social security programmes administered by the
ISSTE is similarly financed with the contribution
rates being: 8.0 per cent by civil servants, and
any resulting deficit is paid by the government.

Financing the Personal Social Services

The funding of personal social services is at the
discretion of the First Lady, who determines how
general revenues and charitable funds are to be
distributed to particular programmes.

THE AGED

Adults who are aged 60 years and over constitute
about 11 per cent of the Mexican population.
Those covered by the IMSS and the ISSTE receive
social security protection. Those considered to
be economically disadvantaged qualify for a range
of personal social services.

Social Security

IMSS. Covered workers who have contributed for
500 weeks to the IMSS during their working lives
qualify for an old age pension upon reaching the
age of 60. The pension is based on the wages
earned over the last 250 weeks in which
contributions were made.

ISSTE. Civil servants who qualify for a pension
for old age have to be 55 years of age, have
completed 15 years of service, and paid
contributions for that amount of time. The
worker's pension is determined by the number of
years of employment. For example, if an
individual worked 15 years the pension would equal
50 per cent of his salary at the time of
retirement. If the employee had worked for 29
years, the pension would equal 95 per cent of that
person's salary.

186

Mexico

Personal Social Services

<u>DIF</u>. This provides the elderly with a range of
support services as well as health care.
Assistance in the form of food supplements is also
given. The elderly also qualify for social and
legal services. There are a number of artisan
occupational and recreational centres where the
elderly can enjoy recreational activities.
Convalescent homes for the poor elderly provide
medical care, food, shelter and other support
services.

<u>IMSS</u>. Old age pensioners are entitled to receive
health and social services such as medical care,
hospitalisation, allied health services, drugs,
surgical intervention, prosthetics, preventive
health services, transmittable diseases, chronic
degenerative diseases, health education, oral
hygiene, nutrition, and mental health services.

Evaluation

The difficulty in evaluation arises from the
differences in the nation's geographic and
industrial distribution of wealth and application
of the law. The basic structure of the systems is
sound. In essence, if the elderly have worked
under any of the systems, they qualify for a
pension. If the governor of the state, or mayor
of the municipality, supports the DIF programme,
then the personal social services provided for the
aged in the larger cities is adequate but quite
minimal in rural areas. If accessible, it is
estimated that at least 3.5 million peasants earn
$.04 a day. What kind of minimal pension might
one expect if contributions were made? Given the
economic condition of the nation's pensions,
services to the aged are adequate.

THE DISABLED AND HANDICAPPED

Placement of services for the developmentally and
mentally disabled within a social and cultural
context is important. Traditionally, handicapped
individuals were seen as the responsibility of the
family. At times further mental and physical
development have been impaired because the family
maintains a protective attitude toward the

187

maintains a protective attitude toward the disabled family member. Disabled individuals have been kept hidden from the public because of fear of public harassment, shame or guilt. Accessibility to the media by a greater portion of the population has made possible an awareness of the epidemiology of mental illness, mental retardation, and developmental disabilities, and the need to maximise a person's learning and functioning capacity.

Social Security

<u>IMSS</u>. Monetary benefits are provided to workers suffering temporary, partial or permanent disability. The amount of the benefit is determined by the extent of disability, permanency of disability and salary. A worker is also entitled to the amount of wages based upon the group insurance to which contributions are made. An individual receives compensation if an accident or illness occurs within the context of the work situation or environment. An individual can be considered for benefits if the person was en route to work when the accident took palce.

A covered worker who is partially disabled receives compensation in accordance with the degree of incapacity. Unfortunately, an uninsured worker does not qualify for benefits or compensation. An employee who becomes incapacitated temporarily or permanently is eligible for such benefits as: medical, surgical, pharmaceutical, and hospitalisation services as well as for rehabilitation and prosthetic devices. A constant attendance allowance is also payable where necessary. The benefits to which an individual is entitled is determined by IMSS guidelines.

<u>ISSTE</u>. An individual who is mentally or physically disabled as a direct result of employment as a civil servant, has both a minimum of 15 years of employment, and many contributions to the ISSTE system qualifies for consideration for a pension and/or disability payments based on length and percentage of liability. The disabled individual also qualifies for medical and rehabilitative services.

Mexico

Personal Social Services

DIF. People who are mentally, intellectually and physically disabled qualify for a range of personal social services. There are rehabilitation services to help individuals reintegrate into society. There are therapy and orientation and education programmes for parents who have children with hereditary physical or mental disabilities. There is a therapy programme for adults and pre-school age children who have audio and speech communication difficulties. Special programmes exist for children with learning difficulties, including evaluation services to assess the extent of audio, visual, speech, intellectual or any other impairment. Early childhood education programmes are available for children with disabilities.

Religious institutions and other voluntary agencies provide rehabilitation centres for the deaf, blind and disabled. There are also a number of institutions for the blind, deaf, disabled, mentally ill and mentally retarded people.

Evaluation

Because of vast differences in geographic wealth and population density of residents, the services available to residents who are disabled vary from state to state. For those who qualify for benefits, services are adequate. Unfortunately the programmes apply mainly to urban workers. An individual who is employed as a civil servant or under a large industrial firm qualifies for compensation and medical care if the accident or illness resulted from carrying out work duty. Citizens not covered under the ISSTE or IMSS system may receive services from DIF if such a service as needed exists in the community and if medical and rehabilitative services are provided. Seventeen to 18 per cent of the citizens needing services are outside the system.

CHILDREN AND YOUTH

Mexico has a high crude birth rate (34.3 per 1,000) and an equally high infant mortality rate (35 per 1,000). Approximately 43 per cent of the population is under the age of 15; that is some 34

million people. In a report published on the
eight leading causes of death in 1975, 17.7 per
cent of registered deaths were due to parasites
and infections and 5 per cent to perinatal
mortality. Of the registered deaths, 36.5 per
cent were children under five. Three years later
(1978) 36.6 per cent of deaths were related to
such illnesses as enteritis, diarrhoea, and
ameobiasis (Oster 1985). Educational institutions
have had a difficult time keeping up with the pace
of growth of the school age population. The
health care system is more centralised and is,
therefore, more accessible to children and youth.

Social Security

IMSS. Children who are orphaned as a result of a
covered worker's death receive a pension equal to
20 per cent of the pension that the deceased
worker would have received had he or she become
permanently disabled. This pension is payable
until the orphan child reaches the age of 16.
Orphans who have lost parents, one of whom was a
covered worker, receive a pension equal to 30 per
cent of their parents' wage for as long as they
remain at school up to the age of 25. Infant
health care and day care services are also
provided by the Institute

ISSTE. Children up to 18 years of age, or 25
years of age and studying, qualify for a pension,
if the deceased worker was employed a minimum of
15 years and was covered by that number of years
or has 10 years of service and expired at age 60
or over.

Personal Social Services

The DIF offers medical, social, juridical,
educational and recreational programmes for
children and youths. Children benefit from
day-care and nutritional programmes. Abandoned
and abused children, including those sold into
prostitution are also provided with assistance.
Assistance is also given to children who wish to
work as street vendors and those who live on the
street. There are limited programmes available
for youths with drug addiction problems. Children
also receive housing assistance, meals and
counselling.

Mexico

Evaluation

Children are a source of pride in most families. Steady efforts have been made to provide for the health, welfare, social and educational development of children. The media has been a major source of education for parents in such areas as health care, teenage pregnancy, nutrition, drugs, AIDS, and family communication. Social programmes continue to improve and provide services to children who are medically or socially at risk.

NEEDY FAMILIES

In 1983, the daily minimum wage in the Federal district was US$3.50. The basic amount needed for sustenance was US$13.45. If 17 to 35 per cent of the population is middle class and most of the wealth is in the hands of 2.9 per cent of the population, then the poverty rate must, indeed, be fairly high (US Government Printing Office 1985). The financial crises which have occurred since 1982 have added many working class families to the poverty rolls. Mexico has not even begun to address the issue of homeless families. The 1985 earthquake left many families homeless. Many of these are still living in makeshift housing. In rural areas needy families have limited access to social services.

Social Security

IMSS. A widow's pension is payable to wives of deceased covered workers provided they have lived with the deceased during the last five years preceding the spouse's death. The widow's pension is equal to 50 per cent of the pension to which the deceased covered worker would have been entitled. In addition, the widow receives a small lump sum equal to two months' minimum established wage to assist with expenses. The amount is dispensed after proof of death is established and a statement of funeral expenses has been furnished.

The law does not clearly distinguish occupational from non-occupational death. In this case what determines a widow's pension is the number of years the spouse was employed and the contributions the deceased made.

A maternity benefit equal to full pay is payable during 84 days' maternity leave.

ISSTE. A widow is eligible for a spouse's pension whether the cause of death was occupational or non-occupational. The criteria used is whether the employee had worked and had been covered by the system for at least 10 years. Secondly, if the deceased spouse had reached the age of 60, then the widow is entitled to 100 per cent of the pension to which the spouse would have been entitled. The children are entitled to benefits until the age of 18 or 25, if still in school. The Institute pays the individual designated by a deceased worker the sum of a month's minimum salary to help with funeral costs once a death certificate and statement of funeral expenses have been submitted.

Personal Social Services

The DIF provides a range of health and social services to needy families. Day-care services are provided for working women. Legal services are available to stop the exploitation and abuse of children. Counselling to assist families reconcile their conflicts is provided by the Department of Social Services. The Department of Psychology provides mental health assessment services.

Other services provided to needy families include public dining rooms, public dormitories, boarding homes for working women, boarding homes for children whose mothers work, women's shelters, community information assistance, emergency funds, and dispensaries. Again most of these services are found in large cities. The rural needy families have very limited access to services.

Evaluation

Most social security programmes provide adequate benefits, but only a modest proportion of needy families qualify for them.

The DIF provides a range of programmes to assist families in need. They are generally well organised in the larger metropolitan areas, but the majority of the rural population remains unserviced. This has begun to change as there are now a number of mobile units delivering services in the rural areas.

Unfortunately, an individual has to have been employed and contributed to the system in order for the members of the family to receive social security benefits. If contributions are not being made by an employee, then the family does not qualify for social security benefits.

Religious groups provide a range of services for needy families - shelters, soup kitchens, orphanages, day-care - to name a few.

THE SICK AND INJURED

The country has many industrial, manufacturing, assembly plants and mining enterprises where a large percentage of its citizens are employed. Although there is a labour law which allows the government to regulate occupational hazards, plant safety regulations are not adequately enforced. Accidents and illness result from hazardous conditions and/or polluted environments. In 1978, the government reported that 61.3 per cent of disease cases were attributed to respiratory problems and 36.6 per cent to digestive diseases. The three major diseases were cardiovascular, diabetes, and cancer (US Government Printing Office 1985). Interestingly, the programme which has been most homogeneous in terms of financing is that of insurance against occupational hazards.

The insured and dependents who are injured or ill qualify for a range of services provided for by their respective social security institutions.

Medical care for the non-insured is provided either by institutions set up by the Ministry of Health, states, municipalities, or private institutions. The number of physicians varies according to geographic region, some with as few as 1.5 physicians per 10,000 inhabitants and others with as many as 8.9 physicians per 10,000 inhabitants, and from 0.4 hospital beds per 1,000 inhabitants to 1.4 hospital beds per 1,000 inhabitants (Mesa-Lago 1978, p.253).

Social Security

IMSS. Workers insured under IMSS receive a sickness benefit equal to 60 per cent of wages, for up to 52 weeks of sickness. Moreover, insured

workers; the spouse or individual with whom the
worker has lived for the last five years; children
under 16; children up to 25 years of age if in
school; children over 16, who are at least 50 per
cent disabled; parents of the worker, if they live
in the same household, all qualify for medical
assistance when sick or injured. The
beneficiaries are eligible for medical care,
hospitalisation, medication, diagnostic services,
surgical procedures, ambulance transportation,
orthopedic and prosthetic devices.

Social services to which covered workers are
entitled are dispensed through educational and
other programmes which promote health care and
involve mass communication. These include:
education in hygiene; sanitation; maternal infant
care; nutrition; improvements in living
conditions; development of activities which are
cultural or athletic; courses related to improving
and updating technical skills; and services which
enhance individual or collective functioning.

ISSTE. The insured worker, spouse, or individual
with whom the worker has lived for the last five
years; children under 25, if still in school;
children over 18, if mentally or physically
handicapped, have a right to medical and social
services, if they are injured or become ill.

Medical care to which the worker and
beneficiaries are entitled include: preventive
health care; pharmaceutical, diagnostic, treatment
and surgical services; orthopedic and prosthetic
devices; and rehabilitation.

Social services for which the insured qualify
are education for the prevention of work accidents
or other risks, mental health services, cultural
and recreational services for the promotion of
mental health. These services promote the social
and familial integration of the worker and the
development of colleague cooperation and support.

Covered workers and their families have the
right to use the network of hospitals and clinics
provided by the ISSTE.

Personal Services

Individuals who have limited means qualify for
medical care, speciality care services such as
internal medicine, gynecological, diagnostic,
family therapy and legal services.

Mexico

The Secretariat of Health and Public Assistance served about 18 per cent of the national population in 1984. It provides the sick and injured who have limited means with low-cost or free medical services.

Evaluation

The services and benefits available are adequate for those who are eligible, namely urban workers.

The government of Mexico established the General Coordination of the National Plan for Economically Depressed Zones to reach deprived geographic zones and marginal groups, especially rural groups. Mexico also has a number of social security, social welfare and health care programmes both private and public to meet the social and health needs of its workers and their dependents. Efforts have been made to treat the sick and injured. Institutes for the rehabilitation of such groups as the blind and disabled have been established. Still a large percentage of the population remains under-served when it comes to health and social services. There are fewer than 100,000 physicians to serve a population of 80 million.

THE UNEMPLOYED

The unemployment rate in Mexico is estimated to be between 12 and 25 per cent of the economically active population. A further 40 per cent of the population is under-employed either working only a few hours a week or holding part-time jobs. The problem is as crucial as that of unemployment as the problem tends to be under-valued when simply viewed as an unemployment problem. There is a difference between saying the unemployment rate is 15 per cent, when in reality, the under-employed constitute a much greater number, about 55 per cent of the work-eligible population. Due to the nation's economic problems and the devaluation of the peso, which in 1989 stood at $2,500 pesos to US$1, the workers and their families are being forced to reduce consumption of even some basic food products. The malnutrition rate is on the rise. In 1983, the labour force was estimated at 22.4 million workers, 77 per cent of whom were male and 23 per cent female. Nonetheless, 48.5

million persons participated in the labour force
in 1983. The economically active population is
defined as anyone aged 12 and over. The
participation of females in the labour force is
rising at a faster pace than that of males.
Employment in agriculture continues to decrease
and a gain in the manufacturing arena has been
noted (US Government Printing Office 1985). In
1987, the minimum wage in many large cities was
raised to $3.23 per day, or US$64.40 per month
(Conger 1987).

Social Security

IMSS. Of all programmes available to the worker
under IMSS the unemployment benefit is the least
developed. The only persons eligible for
unemployment benefits are individuals who have
been laid off at 60 years of age and have made the
minimum contribution to retirement funds. This is
more of a retirement pension than unemployment
compensation. A lump sum is given to someone who
has been laid off.

ISSTE. When an insured individual who does not
qualify under any eligibility category is laid off
a lump sum, based on current salary and years of
employment, is paid (Mesa-Lago 1978).

Personal Social Services

The DIF programme provides orientation and
referral services for the unemployed. Medical and
nutrition services are also provided to the family
of someone who is unemployed. Services provided
to youths who are unemployed include information
and referral to jobs related to street corner
vending. Many of the young are employed to sell
such items as gum and candy on street corners.

Evaluation

Programme coverage is limited to unemployed in the
older age citizens, therefore providing only
limited protection. The major cause of this is
the structure and organisation of the social
security system.
    According to Mesa-Lago (1978), Mexico does not

have a single legislative body regulating the
organisation of social security nor even a single
compilation of all the laws, decrees and
regulations in force. Each group or sub-group has
its own laws determining coverage, financing and
benefits. There are, in effect, five recognised
occupational groups protected by five distinct
social social security systems: the civil
servants, blue collar workers, the armed forcs,
railroad employees and petroleum workers. Both
the insured and uninsured are taxed to finance the
social security programmes. The federal
government uses taxes to cover whatever is not
covered by employees or employers, thus creating a
somewhat regressive system. The whole system is
based on labour. The country has many more
labourers than jobs. There is no incentive for
the provision of services to the unemployed when
the jobs do not exist. The government has
encouraged the building of industrial and
manufacturing plants in areas in which the
population density is not as great to encourage
movement away from overpopulated cities and create
jobs in more depressed geographical areas.

It has also encouraged industries in the
United States to establish plants in towns within
Mexico, along the border, to provide for jobs for
the unemployed and to control the flow of
immigration.

In summary, the unemployed qualify to receive
few, if any, benefits. The system is built for
the employed worker. In a country where the
population is growing at an extremely fast rate,
it is difficult to keep up with the needs of the
work force, much less so with the unemployed. The
percentage allowed for health and social services
is greater than for other nations but not enough
given the social economic conditions of the nation.

AN ASSESSMENT OF THE MEXICAN WELFARE SYSTEM

The social welfare system in Mexico is based on
the principle of dignity and respect owed to each
and every citizen, but more particularly to
workers and their families. Mexico believes that
the guarantee of human rights and the improvement
of the social conditions of its workers also
generates its strength as a nation. It is for
this reason that the government has aligned the
workers to its power base and the workers have

received most benefits provided by the social welfare system.

The underlying basis for this welfare philosophy is the idea that if the best interests of workers are served, then social and economic stability will be achievable, despite the nation's serious problems.

On the other hand, Mexico has sacrificed social development for economic and industrial development in the hope that it will achieve social development as a consequence. One result has been the introduction of technology, which has caused a loss of jobs. Moreover, the highly subsidised private sector industries have profited at the expense of the national economy. While the organised working class has benefited from Mexico's social expenditures, those in the informal sector, largely in the rural areas, remain marginal. Whilst the proportion of the published budget allocated to health and social services is impressive (10.4 per cent in 1979), more than a quarter of the population remain without health services. Currently 20 per cent of the health and social services available are provided by religious institutions. Because the majority of the population is Roman Catholic, the church has penetrated the most remote areas of the country.

Most personal social services remain basic, although the proximity of Mexico to the United States has allowed the flow of ideas and research into the needs of the under-served populations (such as the mentally ill, the mentally retarded, battered spouses, battered children, the elderly and the victims of AIDS) and Mexico continues to combat public health problems which have resulted from the lack of sanitation services and public health programmes for a large percentage of the population. Currently over 40 per cent of the population lacks sewage facilities, 22 per cent are without electricity and 28 per cent are without water on tap (Oster 1986).

Income distribution continues to be a problem in Mexico. Mobility has allowed for a growing middle class. Sixty-five per cent of the population is still found in the lower class. Above and beyond all social services, family support and mutual aid ensure survival of the citizens of Mexico. Migration of some of its members to the United States, in order to gain work, has allowed for a degree of upward mobility.

Mexico

Much progress has been made over the last 40
years to improve the quality of life in Mexico.
The indigenous population living in the
mountainous regions, however, has not been touched
by western civilisation. These regions have their
own form of mutual aid to ensure their survival.
There is a paucity of fiscal and other
information regarding the performance of the
Mexican welfare system. It should be stressed
that the people of Mexico have survived because
mutual aid has been supported, encouraged and
fostered by the Roman Catholic church and other
denominational organisations. The progress made
by the organised workers, in terms of social
security, has been phenomenal, although the
benefits have reached only a small percentage of
the workers and their families. Mexico was the
first developing country to implement a social
security programme in rural areas (Nugent &
Gillaspy 1983). The economic problems confronting
Mexico have reduced the capacity for it to
adequately finance its social welfare activities
and thus preclude it from being an effective
welfare system. Population growth has slowed
significantly and, with the progress that Mexico
has made, the redistribution of resources towards
the poor could become a reality. While the
economic costs of such a strategy could be high,
the social and political costs of not doing so may
prove to be even higher. It is these factors
along with the modernisation and economic
development of Mexico that will determine the
extent to which Mexico is able to address its
social welfare problems.

REFERENCES AND FURTHER READING

Aguayo, S. (1986), 'As Mexico Sees Us', The Texas
    Observer, 78(16), 9-11.

Alba, F. (1982), The Population of Mexico,
    translated by Urquidi, M. M., New Brunswick,
    New Jersey: Transaction Books.

Anderson, H. DeFrank, T. M. & Harmes, J. (1986),
    'Bordering on Bankruptcy', Newsweek, 103, 37.

Broyles, W. (1986), 'The Key is Mexico, not
    Nigaragua', U.S. News and World Report, 100,
    10.

Mexico

Conger, L. (1987), 'US, Mexico Try to Work out Trade Tensions', The Light, 106(97), D9.

Correa, F. P. (1982), 'Urban Development in Mexico', in Montgomery, T. S. (ed.), Mexico Today, Philadelphia: Institute for the Study of Human Issues.

Fehrenbach, T. R. (1985), Fire and Blood, New York: Bonanza Books.

Levy, D. & Szekely, G. (1983), Mexico: Paradoxes of Stability and Change, Boulder, Colorado: Westview Press.

Mesa-Lago, C. (1978), Social Security in Latin America, Pennsylvania: University of Pittsburgh Press.

Montgomery, T. S. (ed.) (1982), Mexico Today, Pennysylvania: Institute for the Study of Human Issues, Inc.

Needler, M. C. (1982), Mexican Politics - The Containment of Confict, New York: Hoover Institution Press, Praeger Publishers.

Newell, R. G. & Rubio, L. F. (1984), Mexico's Dilemma: The Political Origins of Economic Crisis, Boulder, Colorado: Westview Press.

Nugent, J. B. & Gillaspy, T. (1983), 'Old Age Pensions and Fertility in Rural Areas of Less Developed Countries: Some Evidence from Mexico', Current History, 31(4).

Oster, P. (1986), '"Intestinal Problems" Kill in Mexico', The Light, 105(96), MI.

Spalding, R. J. (1980), 'Welfare Policy-making: Theoretical Implications of a Mexican Case Study', Comparative Political Studies, 12(4), 419,438.

_____ (1981), 'State Power and its Limits: Corporatism in Mexico', Comparative Political Studies, 14(2), 139-161.

Street, J. H. (1983), 'Mexico's Development Dilemma', Current History, 12, 410-14.

Mexico

Tannenbaum, F. (1950), <u>Mexico</u>, New York: Alfred A.
    Knopf.

Urquidi, V. L. (1982), 'Economic and Social
    Development in Mexico', in Montgomery, T. S.
    (ed.), <u>Mexico Today</u>, Philadelphia: Institute
    for the Study of Human Issues.

U. S. Government Printing Office (1985), <u>Mexico</u>
    <u>A Country Study</u>, 3rd Edition, Washington, D.C.

PUERTO RICO
Raquel M. Seda

THE WELFARE SYSTEM ENVIRONMENT

Ideological Environment

Puerto Rico has been a dependent territory since its discovery in 1493. Puerto Rico was controlled by the Spanish until 1898, and since then the United States.

Political and economic dependency on the United States has had a significant impact on the development of the welfare system. To a great extent social welfare programmes have increased the state of dependency of large sectors of the population.

The fabric of the social welfare system has been determined by diverse and contradictory ideological forces.

The Roman Catholic Legacy. The Roman Catholic Church has emphasised charity as the Christian way of helping the poor. This help has been given through outdoor relief (limosna) and indoor relief (beneficencia) with poverty being viewed as a dignified condition.

The Protestant Work Ethic. Although the obligation to be charitable is a fundamental tenet of all Judeo-Christian religions, the Protestant view is that the virtues of charity might be better enacted through religiously inspired individuals than by organisations. It is an ethical principle that those who work hard deserve to be rewarded, with poverty being viewed as a personal deficiency.

Puerto Rico

Scientific Humanism. The concern for the welfare of humanity is not only based on a personal conviction, but above all, on scientific explanations of social organisation and human needs and problems.

Individualism and the Capitalist Work Ethic. This philosophy stresses the individual's responsibility to make their own way, to stand on their own and support themselves and their families. Work is not only seen as the means for self-support but a way to prosper and accumulate wealth, which represents meritorious achievement. Those unable to behave as such are considered unable to manage their affairs. Subsequently, a residual conception of welfare persists in Puerto Rico as a diagnostic differentiation and means-tested needs system and is mainly used with allocative principles for the provision of benefits.

Equity. This value prescribes that people receive what they deserve, based upon their contributions to society, modified only by considerations for those whose inability to contribute is clearly not of their own making.

Adequacy. It is desirable to provide a decent standard of physical and spiritual well-being, quite apart from concerns for whether benefit allocations are equal or differentiated according to merit. Provisions based on state estimates of the costs of basic needs as occurs with the economic assistance programme, are determined by this value.

Income Redistribution Through State Intervention. The state intervenes to control the free enterprise economy and to guarantee minimum social welfare standards to the population, as a right, not as charity. In Puerto Rico, social welfare provisions are based on horizontal redistribution of income, rather than on the more egalitarian vertical redistribution. Through its intervention, the state also performs the political function of social control, maintaining the existing social order.

Paternalism. The concept of paternalism has permeated the evolution of social welfare in Puerto Rico. The Roman Catholic legacy, colonialism and political loyalty have made paternalism a dominant feature of the social welfare system, particularly the personal social services. Beneficiaries of the programmes are often visualised as passive recipients, not as active deliberating agents.

Centralisation. This value finds expression in financing and administration of programmes. The social welfare programmes in Puerto Rico are highly centralised in both aspects. The share of federal funds (United States Government), particularly of special purpose or categorical grants, to a great extent limits local autonomy. Unemployment compensation and personal social services are heavily financed by the United States Government.

Competitiveness. In a competitive, pluralistic system of formal representative democracy, and informal political processes, social welfare funds are often distributed on the basis of competition among eligible groups for limited pools of social welfare dollars. In Puerto Rico, social welfare interests have to compete with internal and external economic and political interests. A growing tendency has been for agencies to have specialised units to compete for federal funds.

Historical Origins

Before the Nineteenth Century. Early in the sixteenth century the Spanish philosopher Juan Luis Vives had a strong influence in changing the system of outdoor relief for the poor (limosna), into a system of indoor aid. Vives' ideas were quickly exported to Latin America. By the end of the seventeenth century all important cities in the colonies had at least one public-charity hospital that provided free medical care for the poor, mostly Indians and Negroes (Mesa Lago 1978, p.18). In 1667 the Charity Hospital of San German was founded in Puerto Rico. Society assumed responsibility for the institution as it was financed by tithes (Rivera 1985, p.316).

From the sixteenth century the social legislation that applied to Puerto Rico was framed within the Recopilacion de Leyes de los Reynos de las Indias, a legal code established by the Spanish Crown in 1680. Any charitable efforts needed the approval of the King. These efforts were private in nature and the royal disposition regulated and directed the private initiative.

<u>The Nineteenth Century</u>. In the nineteenth century the Spanish government maintained the philosophy that poverty was a dignified condition and with an aura of holiness. The social policy was to recognise the poor category and provide beneficence.

The oldest and most important social welfare institution established in the nineteenth century was The Beneficence House. It was a joint effort of public, private and religious sectors. The Boards of Beneficence had been created in Spain on 6 February 1822. On 20 June 1849 beneficiary institutions were made public agencies. In 1868 the General Regulations of Beneficence were enacted in the Island, replacing the <u>Leyes de Indias</u> excluding those parts pertaining to the <u>Regio Patronato</u> (Rivera 1985, p.111).

During the Spanish-American War, American troops invaded Puerto Rico on 25 July 1898. On 12 August 1899, the Military Governor of the Island appointed an Insular Charity Board. Assistance was given at the municipal level for food, clothing, home construction materials and other basic articles. The government also established a work programme. According to Diaz (1956, p.8), the first to bring the concept of public assistance to Puerto Rico were military men, who emphasised the principles of local responsibility, aid in kind and public work.

<u>The Twentieth Century</u>. The secularisation of welfare has been a dominant feature in this century. The state has assumed the main responsibility for the welfare of the population through incremental adjustments. This incremental approach has created a complex and non-integrated social welfare system, bound to a great extent to the policies and programmes of the United States.

Pratts (1987, pp.41-98) has identified three phases in the development of social welfare policy in Puerto Rico: 1898-1946, 1947-74 and 1975-80. The period 1898-1946 was characterised by change and a structural crisis in the economy, misery, insecurity, hurricanes, political control on the part of the United States, and political instability. The principal strategies used in terms of social welfare policy were birth control and the extension of the New Deal policies to the

island. The direct and massive intervention of
the federal government in the social welfare
system of Puerto Rico had its origins in 1929 when
Governor Theodore Roosevelt, Jr. asked charity
institutions in the United States to send
donations to the island. The main federal
programmes established during the Great Depression
were the Puerto Rico Emergency Relief
Administration in 1933, the Puerto Rico
Reconstruction Administration in 1935, and the
Work Projects Administration in 1939. The only
social security programme established in this
phase was Workmen's Compensation (the first law in
1916 and the current law in 1935). A main
historical event was the enactment of Law No. 3 on
2 April 1941, creating a Commission on Social
Security to study, draft and report to the
Governor on the establishment of a comprehensive
social security system. The affirmative
recommendations for such a system were not
accepted due to the lack of an economic basis. In
1943, through Law No. 95, the Public Welfare
Division was established within the Department of
Health.

From 1947-74 numerous changes in social
welfare policy were related to the relative
success of the dependent economic development
model. Through population policies (birth control
and migration) and provision of services, the
government aspired to improve life conditions and
integrate sectors of the population into the
process of industrialisation and service
activities. Social welfare programmes in the
1950s and 1960s were articulated to a new economic
condition. The public welfare programme was
modified to make possible the extension of titles
of the federal Social Security Act to the island.
In 1950 needy children, aged, blind, totally and
permanently disabled began to benefit from that
Act. In that same year a social security
programme for drivers was established. In 1951
Title II of the Social Security Act (old age and
survivors), was extended to the Island. The same
occurred with disability benefits in 1955. In
1956 unemployment compensation was established
through the Employment Security Act of Puerto
Rico. In 1961 unemployment insurance was extended
to agricultural workers, succeeding the sugar-cane
scheme of 1948. In 1965 titles XVIII and XIX of
the Social Security Act (medicare and medicaid),
were extended to Puerto Rico. The year 1968 was

prolific in social security programmes and personal social services. The Department of Social Services; the non-occupational temporary disability insurance; the no-fault automobile insurance; and the right to work administration were established by law in that year. By 1970 the relative success of the economic model began to decline. The exhaustion of the conditions which made possible economic growth implied a change from innovative social policies to dependency on federal policies.

The decline of investment in the light industry triggered a heavy capital investment in the petro-chemical industry (1966-74) and the establishment of the primary production phase of the chemical and pharmaceutical industry. The oil price escalation and the 1974 recession brought a collapse in that industry that served as a pressure mechanism for the extension to the Island of federal programmes and funds. The 1974 recession signalled the third phase, 1975-80, which was federalisation of programmes. In absolute terms, the level of federal transferences increased from US$513.1 million in 1973 to US$1,463.0 million in 1976 (185 per cent) and US$3,416.1 million in 1980, for an increase of 133.5 per cent. By enactment, the Anti-addiction Department was created in 1973 due to an alarming drug addiction problem. In 1974, the federal Food Stamp Programme was extended to the Island, providing nutritional benefits to 60 per cent of the population. The same occurred in 1973 with the scholarship programme for higher education (BEOG) and in 1975 with the Comprehensive Employment Training Act (CETA). Both programmes required an increase in productivity and an open employment market; however, since these conditions were lacking, both of them became assistance programmes.

The Political and Socio-economic Environment

In 1952 the majority of the people of Puerto Rico approved a constitution and the political status came to be known as Estado Libre Asociado de Puerto Rico, referred to as the Commonwealth of Puerto Rico. The undefined political status is a problem of great significance to Puerto Ricans. The three ideological forces which have struggled for a final definition are autonomy, statehood and independence. Although Puerto Rico is considered a self-governing state, it is a fact that it preserves characteristics of a classic colony. According to the Commerce Department of the United States, 480 aspects of the life of the Puerto Ricans are controlled by the Congress of the United States.

The Puerto Rican society is racially mixed: a blend of Taino indians, Spaniards and negroes. Catholics, Protestants and fundamentalist sects coexist. Spiritualism is common and more recently santeria is being practised by some sectors of the population.

Puerto Rico is 100 miles long and 35 miles wide. The population in 1985 was 3,282,500, 30 per cent of whom were aged 15 or less; 60 per cent aged 16.64; and 10 per cent aged 65 and over. The dependency ratio was 66.6 per cent (Junta de Planificacion 1986a, p.IX-4, IX-5).

In 1986, 2,300,000 people were 16 years of age and over. The labour force was 977,000 of whom 777,000 were employed and 200,000 unemployed, a participation rate of 42.4 per cent and an unemployment rate of 20.5 per cent. The unemployed were mainly young: 54.6 per cent in the 16-19 age bracket, and a further 39.1 per cent in the 20-24 age bracket (Junta de Planificacion 1986b, p.IX-8 to IX-17).

Public administration, services, trade and manufacturing are the major industrial sectors in Puerto Rico. Agriculture, which used to be a main economic sector three decades ago, has declined noticeably. In 1986 only 40,000 persons worked in agriculture (Junta de Planificacion 1986a, p.A-25). The government has assumed major responsibility in the provision of jobs as the economy has been unable to incorporate the available labour force. Economic growth has been declining, in 1985-86 it was 2.6 per cent. The Gross Domestic Product in 1986 amounted to US$15,794.4 million and personal income to US$14,946.5 million (Junta de Planificacion 1986a, p.A-1). The principal components in personal income in 1985-6 were: wages (64.0 per cent); transfers received by persons (30.1 per cent); and production originated in property (17.0 per cent) (Junta de Planificacion 1986a, pp.I-18-19). The per capita income in 1985-6 was US$4,549, reduced to US$4,227 after payment of contributions (Junta de Planificacion 1986a, p.A-1).

Puerto Rico

The economy of Puerto Rico is a dependent one as it rests mainly on foreign investments, principally north American. The dependent economic model has been able to survive due to the federal transfers: US$6,000 million in 1986; the public debt, US$9,119.4 million in 1986; the funds generated by the corporations which benefit from Section 936 of the Federal Internal Revenues Code: US$14 to US$15 billions deposited in the Island; and the emigration of Puerto Ricans: an estimate of 1,358,000 from 1950 to 1985 (Seda 1984, 1987).

THE WELFARE SYSTEM: AN OVERVIEW

The welfare system in Puerto Rico is the product of incremental and adaptative planning. A complex and disintegrated system has resulted from this type of planning. The administration of the welfare components is highly centralised, particularly in the public sector. Dependency on federal policies and funds characterises two of the major social security programmes and personal social services in general. Personal social services are basically the responsibility of the Department of Social Services. Universality and selectivity have been used as allocation principles. Governmental, private and voluntary sectors coexist in the provision of welfare benefits, with the government the major provider.

Social Security Administration and Finance

Puerto Rico does not have an integrated social security system, but a variety of programmes constituting this system.

Old-age, Survivors', Disability and Health Insurance (OASDHI). The federal programme of OASDHI operates on the same basis as in the United States. The programme is administered by the Social Security Administration (SSA) within the United States Department of Health and Human Services. The SSA operates through regions, areas, districts and local branches. Puerto Rico is part of the New York region. Medicare is handled by the Health Care Financing Administration but SSA offices help people apply for that type of benefit.

During working years, employees, their employers, and self-employed people pay social security contributions, used to finance the benefits provided to the insured and for administrative costs. Part of the contributions go for hospital insurance under Medicare so workers and their dependents will have help in paying their hospital bills when eligible for Medicare. The medical insurance part of Medicare is financed by contributors from the federal government grants. The government's share of the cost for medical insurance and certain other social security costs comes from US general revenues.

Employed persons and their employers pay an equal share of contributions. For 1986-7, the total contribution rate for employees and employers was 7.15 per cent of covered earnings. The self-employed pay twice the employee contribution rate.

The United States Treasury Department, through its Internal Revenue Service, handles the collection of contributions, payment of benefits, and management of reserves.

Monthly payments in December 1986 for Puerto Rico totalled US$140 million. Of this amount, US$77 million was paid to retired workers and their dependents; US$26 million to survivors; and US$37 million to disabled workers and their dependents (SSA 1987, p.1).

Unemployment Insurance. Unemployment insurance consists of a meld of United States-Puerto Rican programmes. The insurance is administered by the Bureau of Employment Security, Puerto Rico Department of Labor and Human Resources, and the Manpower Administration of the Federal Department of Labor. In Puerto Rico, this Administration operates through local offices which make the determination of eligibility. Appeals are made in the Appeals Division, then to the Secretary of Labor and Human Resources.

The Unemployment Insurance Division administers 13 different unemployment programmes: industrial; extended benefits; agricultural; agricultural except sugar cane; benefits to ex-federal employees; benefits to ex-servicemen; addition to benefits; addition to agricultural benefits; interstate programme; benefits for training; assistance for readjustment in trade; assistance for unemployment in disasters; programme to combine employment and salary.

Puerto Rico

The industrial and agricultural programmes are
financed by taxes paid by employers. In the
industrial programme the tax rate is 5.4 per cent
of the first US$7,000 of the payroll a year. In
the agricultural programme the rate is 2.95 per
cent. In addition, a Federal-State Benefit
Extension Programme, with 50 per cent cost-sharing
by the federal government, extends the duration of
benefits for ten weeks when national unemployment
exceeds specified rates. For workers who have
exhausted all rights to regular or extended
benefits, these are extended under a Federal
Programme of Emergency Unemployment Compensation,
financed with federal funds on a non-reimbursable
basis. Federal civilian employees and
ex-servicemen are covered under special federal
legislation. A Federal Programme of Special
Unemployment Assistance, financed with federal
funds, provides benefits to uncovered persons in
the regular programmes, when fully or partially
unemployed (notably domestics, Commonwealth and
Municipal employees, agricultural workers other
than sugar cane workers). Besides, Puerto Rico
has received a number of loans from the Federal
Unemployment Account. Excluding loans, federal
funds amounted to US$32,659,652 in 1986 (ELA 1987,
Section 58, p.8). In that same year an estimate
of 175,790 workers claimed unemployment
compensation. Benefits paid amounted to
US$123,887,096.00.

Workmen's Compensation. Workmen's Compensation is
the oldest social security programme in the
island. It is administered by the State Insurance
Fund, an independent government corporation.
Appeals are heard by an independent Industrial
Commission, which has almost judicial power. It
revises the decisions of the State Insurance Fund
related to workers' claims and to premiums imposed
on employers. The Commission's operations are
financed by the Fund. The programme provides
services through eight regional offices.
In the Claims Division, there is a section to
coordinate claims procedures with the Non-
occupational Temporary Disability Insurance, the
No-fault Automobile Insurance, and Social Security
for Drivers, to avoid doubling benefits.
The programme is financed by contributions
paid by employers, which vary according to the
payroll size and occupational risk, which relates
to the type of industry or business. The 1986

budget amounted to US$78,423,986, all of which originated in the General Fund of the State Insurance Fund (ELA 1987, Section 75, p.3).

In fiscal year 1986-7 a total of US$113.4 million was paid in benefits. The cost of medical services was US$45 million and administrative costs totalled US$38.3 million. In that year, 832,000 employees and 83,448 employers were covered by the programme, for a total of 915,448 persons.

Social Security for Drivers

Social Security for Drivers is a Puerto Rican social insurance programme administered by the Secretary of Labor and Human Resources through the Director of the Bureau of Social Security for Drivers, which operates at a central level with six regional offices.

The programme is financed by compulsory contributions of 80 cents per week, with employees paying 50 cents and the employer 30 cents. The self-employed pay the whole contribution. The 1986 budget amounted to US$1,081,711 (ELA 1987, Section 58, p.20).

In fiscal year 1986-7 benefit payments totalled US$945,765 and the administrative costs US$263,210.38, a total of US$1,208,975.38. At present 52,594 persons are covered by the insurance.

Non-occupational Temporary Disability Insurance.
This special Puerto Rican social insurance programme is administered by the Employment Security Bureau of the Department of Labor and Human Resources, through the Division of Non-occupational Disability Insurance. The nine area offices are shared with the Unemployment Insurance and Employment Service programmes.

The employer and the employee contribute to the disability fund with 30 per cent of paid salaries up to US$9,000 per annum. In the case of agricultural employees, contributions are paid from general revenues. The government also pays an extra 25 per cent of that amount for administrative costs.

The law provides that an employer can have the option of self-insurance, provided that plan offers equal or better benefits than the government's plan. Employers who prefer the

private plan are required to pay 0.0015 per cent
of taxable earnings for administrative costs. The
1986 budget amounted to US$2,251,998 (ELA 1987,
Section 58, p.18).

In fiscal year 1986-7 benefit payments in the
public plan totalled US$5,595,668.12 and
US$6,226,405.11 in the private plans. Persons
covered by the public plan were 126,451 and
281,487 by private plans (Castro 1987, pp.1,4).

Automobile Accident Compensation No-fault
Automobile Insurance. This special Puerto Rican
social insurance programme is administered by an
independent organisation: Administration of
Compensation for Automobile Accidents. Its
Executive Director is subject to a Board of
Directors and the Board to the Governor. The
programme operates at the central level with ten
regional offices.

It is financed by a flat-rate annual tax of
US$35.00 to be paid by owners of motor vehicles at
the time in which the vehicles' licence is paid.

In 1986 benefit disbursements totalled
US$41,033,072. The cost of the accident preven-
tion programme was US$422,649. Administrative
costs totalled US$7,724,611. Total costs amounted
to US$49,180,332 (ELA 1987, Section 72, p.2).

Other Public Retirement Programmes. These cover:

. Teachers.

. Employees of the University of Puerto Rico.

. Employees of the Authority of Electrical
Energy of Puerto Rico.

. Employees of the Government of Puerto Rico and
the Judicature.

Personal Social Services Administration and Finance

Department of Social Services (DSS). DSS is
responsible for the provision of personal social
services in Puerto Rico. Other governmental
departments, as well as private and voluntary
organisations, provide such kind of services but
the major responsibility rests with the DSS.

With its creation the DSS incorporated the
Public Welfare Division, the Child's Commission,

the Geriatric Commission, and various programmes and functions of other governmental agencies. The DSS is responsible for implementing the government's programmes to solve or alleviate social problems. Emphasis is given to rehabilitation and the interrelationship between individuals, families and communities. By its own action or in coordination with other governmental, private and voluntary organisations, it carries on programmes of direct economic assistance to needy persons; welfare services to children, youth and handicapped; community action programmes; employment programmes for unemployed; orientation services to individuals and families; and any other activities to promote welfare in individuals, families and communities.

The department is structured at three levels: central, regional and local. The central level includes the areas of direction, administration, planning and administration of resources. The regional level includes ten regional offices. They coordinate the operational phase of the programmes as well as the communication between the central and local levels, and supervise the performance of the local level. Local offices exist in each one of the 78 municipalities of the island.

The operational areas are: services to families; public assistance; social treatment centres; vocational rehabilitation; community and family development; nutritional assistance; children's support; and disability determination programme. Forty-five per cent of the population is served by these programmes.

The services provided and the administration of the programmes are financed by the General Fund of the Government of Puerto Rico, Federal Funds, and Special State Funds. The proposed budget for fiscal year 1987-8 is as follows (DSS 1987a, p.9):

TABLE 1: PERSONAL SOCIAL SERVICES FINDING

Source	Recommended	Per Cent
General Funds (US$)	105,292,258	39.2
Special Funds (US$)	600,000	0.2
Federal Funds (US$)	162,947,286	60.6
Total (US$)	268,839,544	100.0

Puerto Rico

The legislature of Puerto Rico assigns grants
to non-profit private organisations which provide
welfare services to needy children, adolescents,
adults, the aged and disabled. These funds are
channelled through the DSS. In 1986 120
organisations benefited from these grants. The
minimum annual grant was US$2,000 and the maximum
of US$235,000 (DSS 1987a, pp.202-10).

Besides the DSS, other governmental
departments which provide personal social services
are Public Education, Health, Housing,
Anti-Addiction, and Recreation and Sports.
Non-subsidised private and voluntary
organisations, secular and religious, also share
the provision of personal social services in the
Island.

Occupational Social Welfare

The employees of the Government of Puerto Rico
receive the following occupational benefits from
the employer: contributions to the medical plan,
workmen's compensation, social security and
retirement fund; two months' pay for maternity
leave; sickleave; vacations; and a Christmas bonus.

Employees of the University of Puerto Rico
have an additional benefit: six hours a week for
studies.

A private sector fringe benefits survey
carried on by the Puerto Rico Manufacturers'
Association in 1985, which covered 25 industrial
groups, revealed that with varying requirements
and proportions, fringe benefits included paid
holidays, vacations, Christmas bonus and profit
sharing, pension plans, life insurance,
hospitalisation, major medical, and cash
disability benefits (PRMA 1985).

THE AGED

Care for the aged, considered for many years the
private domain of the family, has emerged lately
as a social problem, demanding the intervention of
the state, as well as the private and voluntary
sectors. The increase in life expectancy,
currently 74 years, makes Puerto Rico one of the
33 countries with 10 per cent of the population
(or 350,000 people) over 60 years of age (Sanchez
1987, p.1). Changes in size and proportion of

this cohort of the population are the result of a decline in birth and mortality rates, and the migratory movements to the United States.

Social Security

Old-age, Survivors', Disability and Health Insurance (OASDHI). The objective of this federal programme is income replacement. It does not intend to replace all lost earnings. A worker builds up protection under the programme through covered employment. Coverage is, in general, compulsory.

Almost every kind of employment providing wages, salaries, or earnings from self-employment is covered under the programme. In some occupations, employees and self-employed are covered if certain conditions are met. These conditions mainly involve meeting minimum earnings requirements or choosing elective or optional coverage.

Cash benefits may go to the worker and his dependents when the worker retires, becomes severely disabled, or dies. Medicare helps pay the cost of health care for eligible people who are aged 65 or over, or disabled. Benefits are paid as a matter of earned right to workers who gain insured status and to eligible dependents and survivors of such workers. A lump-sum payment is also payable on the death of a fully or currently insured worker. Certain persons aged 72 and over who do not meet the insured status requirements can qualify for small fixed-rate benefits under special transitional provisions.

The amount of a monthly benefit award is related to past earnings, except for the fixed-rate benefits. Benefits for dependents and survivors are calculated as a percentage of the insured worker's primary insurance amount. The calculated amounts are subject to minimum and maximum limits stated in the law. Benefits payable to workers and their spouses who choose to retire before age 65 and to certain survivors under age 62 are subject to an actuarial reduction.

The two parts of Medicare - hospital insurance and medical insurance - help protect people 65 and over from the high costs of health care.

The benefit rates are based on automatic increases in the cost of living. Cost of living increases apply only after first eligibility effective January 1979.

Up to one-half of the benefits may be subject to federal income tax for any year in which the adjusted gross income for federal tax purposes plus non-taxable interest income and one-half of the retirement benefits exceeds US$25,000 for an individual, US$32,000 for a couple filing jointly, and zero for a couple filing separately, if they lived together any part of the year.

Occupational Retirement Benefits. Besides OASDHI, the retirement systems for teachers; University of Puerto Rico employees; employees of the Electrical Authority; and employees of the Government and Judicature, provide benefits at the age of retirement and to survivors in case of death of the insured person.

Fiscal Welfare. These include:

.   retired ex-employees of the Government of Puerto Rico aged 60 years or over, and having worked ten years of more, may exclude from their gross income the profit received in the sale or interchange of a principal residence, up to the amount of US$50,000 for one time only.

.   the first US$4,000 of all annual pensions granted by retirement systems subsidised by the Government of Puerto Rico, its instrumentalities or political subdivisions, or the United States to persons aged 60 or over, are tax exempt.

Personal Social Services

The Department of Social Services. The programme Services to Adults provides the following services: information and referral, protection, day-care, rehabilitation, home-care, house-keeper, substitute homes, prosthetic and orthopedic services.
Under the Department's Economic Assistance Programme, persons aged 65 and over qualify for regular and emergency cash payments. Beneficiaries also qualify for cash payments under the Nutritional Assistance Programme.
The Support to the Aged Project, created by law in 1984, authorises the Department to initiate administrative and judicial actions to obligate

217

relatives of the aged, served by the agency, to contribute economically for services provided.

The Puerto Rican Geriatric Commission coordinates the activities and services provided to persons aged 60 and over all over the Island. Direct services are provided to 87 geriatric centres through 10 regional committees. Services provided include: transportation, escort, information and referral, nutrition in day-care centres and meals on wheels, recreation, and occupational therapy.

The Housing Department. This provides low-cost subsidised housing for the single aged. To qualify the family of the aged person cannot live with them.

Private and Voluntary Organisations. The government subsidises 60 organisations which provide services to persons aged 62 and over, 40 of which provide day-care and 18 provide residential care. Services include: protected jobs, recreation, nutrition, occupational therapy, medical referrals, orientation, handcrafts workshops, and socio-cultural activities.

Asylums and group-homes operate under religious and secular auspices without government subsidies. Private group-homes have proliferated. Civic groups provide sporadic recreational activities, summer camps, and voluntary services.

Evaluation

Benefits provided to the aged have not had a significant impact on the reduction of poverty. In 1980, 63.3 per cent lived below the poverty line (56 per cent in urban areas and 78.7 per cent in rural areas) (Carnivali & Vazquez 1985). This fact is directly related to health and housing problems.

In general, the social welfare system has not been able to share with the family the responsibility for the aged. The Support to the Aged Project can be seen by relatives of the aged as a punitive measure, resulting in deteriorating family integrity and increasing loneliness, which are real feelings among this section of the population.

THE DISABLED AND HANDICAPPED

Care of the disabled and the handicapped has been considered traditionally a family responsibility. Slowly and increasingly the state has been providing and subsidising services to this sector of the population.

At present, 17.2 per cent of the population of Puerto Rico is severely or moderately handicapped (DSS 1987b, p.29). In the active population (16 to 64 years), 12.2 per cent present some kind of physical or mental disability, which limits their productive capacity (DSS 1987a, p.94).

Social Security

OASDHI. This programme covers the risk of disability. An 'insured in event of disability' status is required to qualify for a disabled-worker benefit or to establish a period of disability. Disabled under 65, who have been entitled to social security disability benefits for 24 or more months are eligible for Medicare. Coverage and benefits provided are identical to those applying to the aged.

Social Security for Drivers. The objectives of this programme are to protect chauffeurs and other persons who operate a motor vehicle in the course of their work, to provide payment for sick and total-permanent disability benefits, and to establish life insurance and funeral expenses for wives and children up to 15 years old.

Benefits provided include a weekly benefit when any physical or mental condition impedes job performance. The payment ranges from US$16.00 to US$60.00 depending on contributions paid, during 30 weeks of disability in any period of 60 consecutive weeks. A lump-sum (US$360-US$3,600) is paid in case of total and permanent disability to operate a motor vehicle. Additional lump-sum benefits are provided in the event of an insured person's spouse dying (US$800), the death of a dependent child (US$300 (if under 6) or US$500 (if 6-15)). These benefits are neither tax exempt nor indexed.

Non-occupational Temporary Disability Insurance. The main objective of this programme is temporary income replacement due to disability caused by

219

sickness or accident not work connected nor as a result of an automobile accident.

Covered are all employees in private or public employment, unless they are receiving temporary disability or sickness benefits from OASDHI, Workmen's Compensation or occupational benefits.

Benefits include temporary disability benefits under which an industrial worker can receive from US$7.00 to US$104.00 a week depending on salaries received in the insured employment. An agricultural worker can receive from US$7.00 to US$50.00 a week depending on their salaries in agricultural employment in a basic year. The benefit is paid up to 26 weeks in any disability period or in any consecutive 52 week period. Dismemberment benefits involve a lump-sum ranging from US$1,000 to US$3,000 depending on the gravity of the injury. Death benefits involve a lump-sum of US$4,000 payable to immediate dependents of the deceased. Maternity benefits are available to female workers on maternity leave, who have the right to receive weekly benefits from the fund of Disability Benefits equal to 75 per cent of their salary. To receive these benefits the worker must be unable to work and under medical treatment, and they must be earning an annual salary of US$150.00 from their covered employment (DTRHb no date, pp.1-4; DTRHc no date, pp.1-4). These benefits are neither tax exempt nor indexed.

Workmen's Compensation. The main objective of the programme is to compensate workers who are disabled as a result of a work injury or illness; and to compensate the dependents of the workers who die as a consequence of such injury or illness.

The law is compulsory and exclusive, as all employers who employ one or more workers are obligated to insure them with the corresponding policy at the State Insurance Fund. The insurance covers all governmental employees, including municipal governments, boards, commissions and public corporations.

Workers do not have to prove their employer's negligence in case of a work accident to benefit from the insurance. The employer cannot claim negligence on the part of the worker. The State Insurance Fund serves a working population of 758,000 (average) and 80,244 employers.

Excluded are those who work at home, in incidental or casual employment not within the trade or industry of the employer. Also excluded are sharecroppers working under a written contract with the owners of the land. The following disability benefits are provided by the State Insurance Fund.

Medical services, includes medical assistance, medicines and hospitalisation when necessary. There is no limit as to time or costs in the provision of services. Services are provided at State Insurance Fund dispensaries and the Industrial Hospital. Contractual relations are maintained with private clinics or hospitals, medical specialists, laboratories, and ambulance firms.

Permanent partial disability compensation is based on the loss of physiological functions in the affected part of the body and the wage received by the worker at the time of the accident. Maximum payment is US$12,000.00. The worker receives an initial maximum payment of US$1,000 and additional monthly payments of US$150.00.

Total and permanent disability benefit is equivalent to two-thirds of the wage or salary of the worker, with a monthly minimum of US$65 and a maximum of US$200, which is paid for life. The worker may choose to take a lump-sum of up to US$18,900 in lieu of a life pension.

Death benefits to dependents range from a minimum of US$65 to a maximum of US$200.00 a month. The widow may choose a partial lump-sum as compensation.

Funeral benefits are provided (US$600).

House keeper services are available to totally and permanently disabled workers who need the service. Maximum monthly payment is US$60.00.

Disfigurement of face, head, neck, hand or arm, determined according to the seriousness of the injury, qualifies for a maximum benefit of US$3,000 for a disfigured face, head or neck; and of US$1,600 for hand or arm.

Lawyer's fees are also paid if the worker decides to hire a lawyer for a better defence in the liquidation or resolution of the case, the Industrial Commission will fix the percentage to be paid as a fee to the lawyer. The State Insurance Fund pays such fees.

Medical care is freely provided.

Per diem and transportation benefits are provided when the injured worker is asked to attend treatment in any facility of the State Insurance Fund.

Medical equipment such as wheelchairs, hospital beds, and house remodelling assistance when needed, are provided to the totally and permanently disabled. The cost of living indexation is not taken into consideration for changes in benefits.

Fiscal Welfare. Physically and mentally disabled who cannot support themselves, blind, and aged over 65 can be considered as dependents of the tax-payer with a credit of US$1,000 for the contributory year.
In the case of the handicapped there is a credit of US$400.00 for non-compensated expenses in the acquisition of orthopedic equipment.

Personal Social Services

Department of Social Services. The Vocational Rehabilitation Programme provides services to the physically and mentally disabled to develop their maximum capacities in order to be able to perform satisfactorily in paid employment. Injured workers, blind, mentally ill, mentally retarded, and deaf are served through the Programme. Services include diagnosis; orientation and counselling; physical restoration; vocational evaluation; rehabilitation equipment; vocational training; support, and transportation; post-placement services; interpreters to deaf; and readers to blind. Disabled beneficiaries of OASDHI, Economic Assistance, and Workmen's Compensation can benefit through coordination with each programme.
Under the programme Services to Families with Children, in-kind benefits are provided to mentally retarded children. Services include orientation for parents; purchase of services to

specialised private organisations; specialised house-keepers; foster homes; group homes; and specialised day-care centres.

The programme Services to Adults aspires to maximise the welfare of blind adults, disabled, and aged through services oriented to a self-sufficient life. The following services are provided: information and referral; protection; medical attention; self-support; home-care; housekeepers; substitute homes; orthopedic equipment; and dental services. At present 12,375 disabled and 165 blind adults benefit from the programme (ELA 1987, Section 53, p.8).

Under Economic Assistance, totally and permanently disabled, totally or partially blind, as well as persons temporarily disabled who cannot work, can benefit from cash payments, emergency aid, and information and referral services.

The programme Disability Determination for Social Security focusses on the medical aspect of each one of the disability applications filed in the DSS district offices. The programme operates through an agreement between the governments of Puerto Rico and the United States since 1954. The objective is that disability applicants may receive economic benefits in the shortest possible period.

An Institute for Blind Children and a Home for Blind Adults operates under the Social Treatment Centers Programme. They provide education, rehabilitation, treatment and services, and residential care for the adults.

Industrial Corporation of Blind, Mentally Retarded and Disabled Persons. Created by law in 1948, the objective of the corporation is the social and economic rehabilitation of the blind, mentally retarded, and disabled adults, to be achieved through direct services. The aspiration is to incorporate the population group into the country's productive process. The Corporation operates industrial facilities in which the beneficiaries manufacture mops, brooms and related articles.

The Secretary of the Department of Social Services is the President of the Corporation. Administration and operational functions are the responsibility of the Executive Director through production and administrative areas and commercial operations. At present only one plant is operating, employing 19 disabled individuals.

Puerto Rico

The Pediatric Center for Handicapped Children and Youth. The goal of the Center is the rehabilitation of the physically or mentally handicapped under the age of 21 to make possible their maximum development. The Center operates under the Administration of Health Facilities and Services of the Department of Health.

Services provided are pediatric evaluation and follow-up by specialised medical doctors and allied professionals, surgery, orthopedic and similar equipment, and others in coordination with related programmes (Rivera 1987, pp.12-21).

Mental Health Programme. The objectives are the improvement of the quality of life of the family in Puerto Rico, to minimise or eliminate daily life stress, to reduce the incidence and severity of emotional disorders and the resulting disability.

In-kind benefits are evaluation, diagnosis, treatment and rehabilitation of the beneficiaries.

Anti-addiction Department. Established by law in 1973, its main objective is to promote the welfare of individuals and families affected by drug addiction or alcoholism.

Special Education Programme. This programme provides benefits to students aged five to 21 years old. Besides special education provided in the classroom, other services include transportation; social work; psychological and psychiatric services; orientation; speech, physical and occupational therapy; hearing and visual tests; and recreation.

Interdisciplinary Evaluation and Treatment Center. The Center was established in 1980, through the initiative of the Department of Public Education and the Medical Sciences Campus of the University of Puerto Rico. It is a model project to evaluate and treat handicapped children up to 21 years of age residing in the educational regions of Bayamon and San Juan.

The programme provides educational services to the medical sciences' students, parents, teachers and other community members, for a better

224

understanding of the handicapped. Evaluation and treatment services are provided to referred students following an interdisciplinary model of intervention (Rivera 1987, pp.26-28).

<u>Division of Adapted Recreation with the Recreation and Sports Department</u>. This recreational programme promotes activities for handicapped children living in public housing such as: the Handicapped Child Festival; play-day for handicapped children; swimming courses for mentally retarded children; and basket-ball tournament in wheel chairs.

<u>Private and Voluntary</u>. The government subsidises 21 organisations that provide services to handicapped persons, of which 18 provide day-care and four residential care. Seventeen serve physically and mentally handicappped children and youth and provide physical, occupational and speech therapy; psychological orientation; evaluation; transportation; nutrition; medical services; rehabilitation; neurological services; pre-vocational education; and recreation. The other four organisations serve handicapped adults under 62 years. They benefit from pre-vocational training and independent life; nutrition; transportation; medical referrals and equipment.

The emergence of non-subsidised private and voluntary organisations to provide services to the handicapped is an indicator of the responsibility being assumed by the community.

<u>Office of the Ombudsman for Handicapped Persons</u>. Created by law in 1985, this office has as its main objective the protection of the rights of the handicapped, so that they might achieve an effective integration within society. The population to be served is estimated at 300,000 physically or mentally handicapped.

Evaluation

In December 1986 OASDHI benefits were paid to 76,000 disabled workers. The average monthly payment was US$393, for a yearly average of US$4,716, which is slightly above the national income per head (US$167), but still lower than any state of the United States (SSA 1987, p.1).

In the case of the Non-occupational Temporary Disability Programme, 407,938 persons were covered in fiscal year 1986-7. This is only 12.35 per cent of the population of Puerto Rico. The average benefit in the public plan was US$69.57 (5.67 per cent of average earnings). In the private plans, the average benefit was US$96.83 (7.89 per cent of average earnings) (Castro 1987, pp.1-6). This indicates that coverage and benefits are very low.

In September 1987, 279 blind and 23,366 disabled adults were served by the Economic Assistance programme. Those 23,645 persons make up 4.16 per cent of the estimated disabled and handicapped population of Puerto Rico. The average monthly payment in the blind category is US$37.20, annual benefit of 9.81 per cent of national income per head, and in the disabled category US$37.10, annual benefit of 9.79 per cent of the national income per head.

The diverse programmes which cover the risk of disability results in a confusing array of programmes and agencies and high administrative costs. A special problem emerges in relation to disability determination. The worker has to fill out a large number of claim forms and repeat medical exams if covered by more than one programme. The result is a waste of resources and time. A problem of coordination exists, in spite of the mechanisms established by the programmes.

The in-kind benefits are greatly affected by low budgets and dependence on federal funds. The Vocational Rehabilitation Programme provides services to 50,000 persons (8.8 per cent of the intended target group), and aspires to rehabilitate 5,029 people. The Anti-Addiction Department aspires to serve 22,432 drug addicts and alcoholics (12.3 per cent of the intended target group).

Most of the private and voluntary organisations that take care of the disabled and handicapped need government subsidies to survive. Needless to say this subsidy is too low given the needs of this section of the population.

CHILDREN AND YOUTH

In 1985, 1,567,413 people (47.45 per cent of the population) were aged under 25 years (JP 1986b, pp.15-6). The family still is the institution mainly responsible for the care of children and youths. The school system is also seen as responsible for their socialisation. Other public and private organisations collaborate in this task.

Social Security

OASDHI. If a worker is receiving retirement or disability benefits, monthly benefits can be received by their unmarried children under 18 (or under 19 if full-time high school students) and unmarried children 18 or over who were severely disabled before 22 and who continue to be disabled.

Monthly payments can be made to a deceased worker's unmarried children under 18 (or under 19 if full-time high school students and unmarried children severely disabled before 22 and who continue to be disabled).

In December 1986, benefits were paid to 121,000 children. Average payments for children were US$220 for children of deceased workers; US$100 for children of retired workers; and US$95 for children of disabled workers.

No-fault Automobile Insurance. In case of the death of a victim of an automobile accident, the dependents can be compensated up to a maximum of US$25,000. This compensation is distributed according to the degree of dependency of the spouse, children, parents or any other person under or over 18 years with physical or mental defects, not able to function independently. The compensation is paid weekly in US$50.00 cheques per family unit.

Social Security for Drivers. A lump sum is paid to persons who were totally or partially dependent on the insured at their death. The payment is distributed among the dependents according to the condition, need or dependency of each one of them. The payment varies from US$800.00 to US$6,000.00.

Non-occupational Temporary Disability Insurance. A lump-sum of US$4,000 payable to immediate dependents of the deceased.

Workmen's Compensation. If death occurs as a result of work-related accidents, and the children of the insured worker are the only beneficiaries, the compensation to be paid will not exceed 60 per cent of the salary of the worker; a minimum of US$50.00 and a maximum of US$100.00 monthly will be paid. If other beneficiaries exist, the compensation will not exceed two-thirds of the salary and will be distributed according to law.

The compensation to children will be paid until they reach 18 years of age or until the age of 25 if they are students. In the case of permanent disability, physical or mental, the compensation will not cease.

Fiscal Welfare

A special deduction of US$400 for one dependent child and of US$800 for two or more is granted to the taxpayer for expenses in payments to a person (who is not a dependent of the taxpayer) who takes care of their children under 14 years old.

Another special deduction of US$200 for elementary school students and US$300 for secondary school students is granted for expenses in payments for registration, school transportation and textbooks. The student should be under 21 years of age.

Personal Social Services

Department of Social Services. The objectives of the Social Services to Families with Children programme are to maintain the family united in a harmonious environment in which each member feels accepted and loved and to provide substitute homes for children who cannot stay with their own families.

Direct services are provided to the families who are beneficiaries of economic assistance. In-kind services are preventive and rehabilitative and are provided by helping professionals, including protection, house-keepers, day-care, foster homes, group homes for mentally retarded and social protection, adoption, youth counselling, family counselling, purchase of services to private organisations, and licensing of public and private establishments which take care of children.

In September 1987, 53,773 families with 118,631 children received benefits from the programme. These families received an average monthly payment of US$102 under the Economic Assistance Programme. Children with tutors, which totalled 951, received an average monthly payment of US$31.98.

Social Services and Shelter in Social Treatment Centers exist to provide care and treatment to children and youth from five to 21 years of age, who are removed from their homes through the Children's Court and those with problems in their social adaptation. The aspiration is to reintegrate them to their families in the shortest possible period.

The programme is structured at two levels: central and operational. The central level formulates policy and norms; coordinates and supervises the treatment and habilitation services of the youngsters under the custody of the Department of Social Services. The operational level includes a clinical centre for evaluation and diagnosis; three detention centres; four group homes; two specialised service units; two industrial homes for law breakers; one residential institute for school drop-outs with behavioural problems; one rural camp for law breakers with interest in agriculture; one social treatment centre for law breakers with moderate behavioural problems; and a juvenile home for multiple use.

Services include shelter; evaluation and diagnosis; treatment and social rehabilitation; formal and individualised education; special education; and medical, pyschological, pyschiatric and social work services.

Economic assistance is provided for clothing and shoes for children of poor families who attend school.

Through the Minor's Support programme parents of abandoned children are obliged to assume their legal and economic responsibility toward them. The objective is to protect the right of the children to receive economic support from their parents. The potential clientele is around 230,000 abandoned children by one or both parents.

Services include localisation of absent parents, legal representation, collection and distribution of alimentary pensions and referrals to the Alimentary Unit of the nearest court.

Public Education Department. The programme Services to Students has as its main objective to achieve the maximum performance and school

229

retention through nutritional and health services, orientation, counselling and economic assistance.

Among the services provided are lunch, medical attention, vocational and personal counselling, social work, scholarships, economic assistance, and community relations.

Recreation and Sports Department. Created in 1980, the Department aspires to contribute to the welfare of individuals, the family, and the community through recreation and sports. Attention is focussed primarily on children and youth.

Services are provided through the following programmes: recreational, sports, and the conservation and operation of 3,612 recreational facilities on the island.

In coordination with the Education Department, recreational programmes for children with behavioural problems are sponsored in various school settings including exercise programmes at the elementary and intermediate levels. A football programme in the three school levels is co-sponsored with other governmental organisations.

The Youth Affairs Office. Located at the Governor's Office, this office is mainly a coordinating body whose main objective is to promote the integral development of youth through participation in activities oriented to the fulfilment of goals and aspirations of this sector of the population. The emphasis is on education and employment programmes, health services and services to the juvenile delinquent.

The statutory programme develops its activities through three sub-programmes: coordination and follow-up of activities and orientation of youngsters; students' trips; and prevention of juvenile delinquency.

Private and Voluntary Organisations. At present 18 subsidised institutions, of which 14 are residential, serve children with the following conditions: learning, social adaptation and behavioural problems; neglected and abandoned; all of whom need social protection services.

Services include shelter; orientation; legal and medical benefits; educational and psychological counselling; nutrition; recreation; pre-vocational workshops; religious education.

Puerto Rico

Secular and religious organisations not
receiving government subsidies provide services to
needy children, orphans, abandoned, sick and from
broken homes. Most of them are affiliated to the
United Funds of Puerto Rico.

Evaluation

Five of the six main social insurance programmes
in Puerto Rico provide benefits to dependent
children of the insured person. In the OASDHI
programme, 121,000 children received benefits in
December 1986. Some 10 per cent of the target
population.
Benefits provided by OASDHI are much higher
than those provided by the specialised systems in
Puerto Rico, but was still lower than in any state
of the United States.
In September 1987, 118,631 children received
economic assistance from the Department of Social
Services. Their families received an average
monthly payment of US$102 or about US$25 for each
child.
The in-kind benefits provided by the diversity
of governmental departments added to the economic
benefits already mentioned do not seem to
contribute to a healthy development of children
and youth in Puerto Rico. Unemployment among
youngsters is associated with qualitative
deficiencies in the public school system with
approximately 20,000 students dropping out of
school each year. Absolute illiteracy is 10.5 per
cent and relative (functional) illiteracy is 30
per cent. Lacking the knowledge and skills to
enter the employment market this population group
joins the ranks of the unemployed (Seda 1987, p.7).
One of the findings of the Project on
Psychiatric Epidemiology in Children is that from
125,000 to 150,000 children have severe mental
disorders that require professional intervention
(Rivera 1987, p.5). Suicide is the third cause of
death in males aged 15 to 34 and fifth cause in
females, in that age cohort. In adolescents aged
13 to 19 it is the fourth cause (Parrilla 1987,
pp.1-2). Addiction to drugs and alcohol has
increased in the young population. One out of two
individuals over 15 years drinks alcohol
frequently.
These indicators tend to show that the
existential situation of thousands of children and

youth in Puerto Rico is not different from that of
adults. State officials have expressed concern
and engage in efforts to share with the family the
socialisation process. These efforts follow the
incremental pattern of adding programmes without
an integral vision and with scarce resources. An
example is the Youth Affairs Office, which seems
to duplicate efforts of agencies more than
coordinate these efforts.

NEEDY FAMILIES

According to the 1980 Census, 439,567 families
lived below the poverty line, which is 58.1 per
cent of the total number of families. The poverty
line was established at US$7,412.00 for a family
of four (JP 1985, p.284). Due to the poverty in
which more than half of the population lives, the
State, with the aid of the United States
government, has established a diversity of
programmes to alleviate that condition.

Social Security

In general, needy families do not benefit from
social insurance programmes due to a lack of work
history, low wages, exclusion from coverage and
illiteracy.

Personal Social Services

Department of Social Services. The Nutritional
Assistance programme whose objective is to
supplement the nutritional needs of low-income
families and improve their socio-economic level.
Economic assistance is provided through bi-monthly
cheques for food. Eligibility is determined by a
combination of income and members in the family.
Nutritional Assistance has as its main
activities the orientation, promotion of the
programme, eligibility certification, quality
control, appeals, cheque sending, analysis and
evaluation. Activities are carried on by a
central office, 10 administrative offices at the
regional levels and 99 local offices for
certification. Approximately 430,000 low-income
families which represent 1,591,000 persons receive
benefit at present.

Puerto Rico

The Economic Assistance Programme has as its
objective the alleviation of the effects of
economic deprivation on children and adults whose
income does not permit them access to the
essential means for subsistence. Its basic
function is to provide regular and emergency
economic assistance to individuals and families
who suffer economic need due to physical, mental
or social conditions which hinder their capacity
for self-support. The programme also provides
individual or family assistance in case of
disasters and other emergency situations, and
refers parents to the Minor's Support Programme.
An annual subsidy for payment of energy
consumption is provided to approximately 86,159
families below the poverty level (DSS 1987a,
p.88). This service is totally financed by the
United States.
Families under this programme can benefit from
surplus food donated by the Agriculture Department
of the United States.

The Work Incentives to Economic Assistance
Beneficiaries (WIN). This programme was created
by the Congress of the United States to help
persons who receive economic assistance in the
category Families with Needy Children, so that
they may become employable and achieve economic
and social independence.
Around 5,200 families on economic assistance
and who cannot compete in the job market could
benefit from the following services: day-care for
children; medical, dental and ophthalmological
attention; payment of expenditures caused by
training or job; social services; and vocational
rehabilitation.

The Community and Family Development. This
programme is to promote family unity and community
life. The aspiration is to strengthen family life
within the context of the community, stimulating
responsible and active citizen participation.
Services are offered through three
sub-programmes: Community Development;
Educational Development; and Volunteers.
Thirty-one local offices which respond to 10
regional offices, are responsible for the
provision of services.
The potential clientele of the programme is
all the families in Puerto Rico. At present only
126 low-income communities are being served.

Housing Development. Created by law in 1972, the Department's main purpose is to centralise into one organisation responsibility for the formulation and implementation of public policy for housing and community development in Puerto Rico.

Health Department. The Economic Assistance to Medically Indigent (Medicaid) programme's objective is to provide health services to the medically indigent population, emphasising preventive medicine and assistance services.

The Division of Mothers and Children promotes health in mothers and children and provides methods to reduce infant and mother's mortality levels; assists and provides advice related to family planning; offers services to rape victims. Supplementary food is provided to needy mothers and children.

Economic Opportunity Office. The Office was created by an Executive Order in 1983. It is localised at the Governor's Office. Its objectives are to detect and minimise the negative effects of the problems which affect persons in deprived socio-economic areas; and to promote the participation of the private sector in training and employment. Services provided include technical, administrative and management advice for innovative projects and activities in areas such as training, employment, housing repair, nutrition, vocational rehabilitation, special education and electric energy supply.

Commission for the Protection and Strengthening of the Family in Puerto Rico. Created by law in 1978, its objective is to develop, coordinate and implement public policy for the preservation and strengthening of the family and the improvement of its living conditions. Activities carried on include studies and research, information gathering and dissemination and statistical analysis. Services are channelled through an Executive Director and a diversity of officials and divisions.

Office for Human Development. Created by Executive Orders in 1983 and 1985, it is localised at the Governor's Office and carries on its functions through three principal programmes: development of Head Start projects, development of special projects, direction and administration. The objective is to reduce poverty through the utilisation of local, central, private and federal resources to enable low-income individuals and families to organise, identify their problems, look for alternatives, establish priorities according to their needs, and become self-sufficient.

The programme aspires to serve 15,000 families under the poverty level. Through Head Start projects it intends to serve 8,745 pre-school children. It also intends to serve 100 drop-outs under 18 years of age through special projects which offer temporary shelter, individual and family counselling, referral and follow-up of run-aways.

Evaluation

Indicators of the personal income (US$4,549 in 1986) show that the economic situation in the Island has improved. In spite of this large numbers of families in Puerto Rico live in poverty. The poverty line established in 1980 in the United States and applicable to Puerto Rico is an annual income of US$7,412. According to the 1980 Census, 62 per cent of the population lived below the poverty line (DSS 1987a, p.3).

The range of support services available to needy families is extensive and reveals a concern by government with family integrity, but it is naive about the structural factors that have contributed to the deterioration of family and community life in Puerto Rico.

THE UNEMPLOYED

Unemployment has been a chronic problem in Puerto Rico. During the fiscal year 1986-7, the unemployment rate was reduced to 20.5 per cent after having increased to 21.4 per cent in 1984-5. The historical data indicate that unemployment has been greater in the younger population. The highest unemployment rate occurred in the 16-19 age group, 53.2 per cent in 1984-5 and 54.6 per cent in 1985-6.

The unemployment rate for males of all ages was 23.8 per cent in fiscal year 1986-7 and for females, 14.5 per cent. In both categories, the highest unemployment occurred in the 16-34 age group. Female unemployment in the 16-19 age group increased to 54.4 per cent in 1985-6. In the case of males the change was not significant (JP 1986a, pp.IX-15-18).

Social Security

Unemployment Insurance. The 1956 Employment Security Law of Puerto Rico established an unemployment fund and provides unemployment compensation to workers who lose their job involuntarily.

In 1961, the programme in Puerto Rico was affiliated with the Federal-State programme of the United States by virtue of laws passed by the United States Congress (1961) and the Legislature of Puerto Rico (1960). At present unemployment insurance consists of a meld of Federal-Commonwealth programmes with a low degree of decentralisation and autonomy.

The objectives are to maintain the economic security of the workers while unemployed, maintain their acquisition power, and stabilise the economy. This insurance requires only compulsory employer contributions.

Protected persons include workers who are involuntarily unemployed but willing to work. To be eligible the covered worker must have worked at least two different quarters in a basic period and have earned a minimum of US$75 in the quarter of greater income and US$280 in both quarters. The law provides for a weekly benefit of US$7.00 to US$95, dependent upon earned income, payable for 20 weeks. In the case of an agricultural worker, they must have earned a minimum of US$400 in the basic period. The weekly benefits fluctuate between US$10.00 and US$35.00 for a maximum period of 20 unemployment weeks.

In special situations of unemployment due to technological changes or the disappearance of an industry or occupation, the workers have the right to benefit from unemployment compensation for a maximum of 52 weeks. Agricultural workers in the sugar-cane industry who are displaced at harvest time, have the right to benefits for 67 weeks. The cost of living indexation is not taken into consideration for changes in benefits. Benefits have to be reported by persons who file the federal income tax form which is not true for those who file the local form.

The affiliation with the federal system implied the extension to Puerto Rico of the federal contribution. The federal law permits employers to reduce the State tax from the federal tax up to a maximum of 2.1 per cent of the payroll. At present the federal tax rate is 3.40 per cent of the first US$6.000 annual paid salaries to each worker.

The coverage of the local law is also affected by the federal law. At present the federal law covers all employers whose payroll in a natural quarter reaches a minimum of US$1,500 or employs one or more persons in each day or portion of day in at least 20 weeks of a natural year. Charity, religious and educational non-profit institutions are exempt of the federal law.

Personal Social Services

The Department of Labour and Human Resources. The Equal Opportunities for Youth Employment programme was created in 1985. Its main objective is the reduction of unemployment in youth between 16 and 29 years of age by providing equal employment opportunities to increase their participation in the labour force. The programme is to serve 147,920 unemployed youngsters. Services include work orientation, referrals and job placement.

The programme Creation and Strengthening of Employment, Training and Re-training Opportunities in the Private Enterprise was created in 1980, and authorises the Secretary of Labor and Human Resources to utilise the interests earned from the investment of the special fund for disability benefits to develop and strengthen employment and training programmes aimed at private enterprise. The main objective of the programme is the creation of employment opportunities in the private sector, providing economic incentives to employers.

The Bureau of Employment Security of the Department of Labor and Human Resources provides employers with information, documents and orientation for the preparation of training proposals, which should be based upon the priorities established by the Advisory Council of the Secretary and which, if approved, result in the provision of subsidised training.

237

Puerto Rico

The Right to Work Administration established in 1968, and ascribed to the Department of Labor and Human Resources in 1977, exists to identify, evaluate and train the unemployed, particularly youngsters.

The sectors of the population served are the unemployed, under-employed, low-income persons, non-skilled family heads, low-schooling persons, disabled veterans, addicts and law breakers, youngsters between 14 and 21 years of age, and public and private employers.

The Administration channels its objectives and goals through four programmes: technical training and incentives to private employers: remedial employment and skill development; services to participants; and direction and administration. Services are directly administered by the Office of the Administrator and Sub-administrator. Advisement and auxiliary services are administered by a diversity of offices.

The Corps of Volunteers at the Service of Puerto Rico. This was created in 1985 and its objective is to organise and develop a broad and innovative programme of activities focussed on character formation, technical-vocational training, and the integral development of the most needy youngsters. Through workshops, camps, farms and other centres they are trained for self-employment in small businesses and cooperatives or for productive work in public and private organisations.

The Corps administratively is attached to the Governor's Office. The functions are carried on through four programmes: formation and training; community action; economic development; and direction and administration. Any unemployed resident of Puerto Rico between the ages of 16 and 29 years can be eligible to participate in the programme.

Department of Social Services. Unemployed persons also qualify for the Nutritional Assistance Programme administered by this Department.

Evaluation

The official unemployment rate does not reveal the real unemployment problem in Puerto Rico, as the government defines the unemployed as those who are

238

not working and are actively looking for paid employment. The rate does not include those voluntarily unemployed nor the disappointed who have abandoned the job-seeking task. Unofficial estimates almost double the government's numbers.

The number of unemployed in 1986 was 977,000, of whom, 737,742 or 75.51 per cent were covered by unemployment insurance. Of those covered, an estimated 175,790 made unemployment claims during that year or 23.83 per cent of the covered labour force. Based on these percentages it could be concluded that coverage of the unemployed is high.

Unemployment benefits are really low for those who receive the maximum compensation and for those who receive the minimum, the situation is worse.

Programmes under the personal social services are mostly oriented toward unemployed youth. It is obvious that the government has a great concern with the most productive population which has the highest unemployment rates. Different studies have shown a direct relationship between unemployment, migration, drug and alcohol addiction, and criminal behaviour. Various policy issues arise from these programmes. Is the economy ready to incorporate the trained and re-trained employee? Is the government subsidising private enterprise more than alleviating the problem? Are the programmes merely an additional assistance programme instead of a real training mechanism? Are they able to make a significant contribution to the unemployment problem? Some of the programmes have been in operation for quite a number of years, others are of recent creation, but none has proved to be of significant help in the reduction of unemployment.

THE SICK AND INJURED

Work-related sicknesses and injuries have been increasing steadily. Cases filed with the State Insurance Fund (Workmen's Compensation), increased from 46,832 in 1981-2 to 55,189 in 1986-7. Of the 52,777 claims reported in 1985-6, 52 per cent were public employees (FSE 1986, pp.1-3).

A similar increase in claims was noticed with the No-fault Automobile Insurance. In 1985-6 a total of 50,911 claims were reported. That number increased to 51,502 in 1986-7 and is expected to reach 54,482 in 1987-8 (ELA 1987, Section 72, p.4).

Puerto Rico

Social Security

Worker's Compensation. Covered workers suffering
a temporary disability are entitled to weekly
compensation equal to two-thirds of the wage
received by the worker at the time of the
accident. Maximum weekly payment is US$65.00,
while minimum is US$20.00. This payment is for a
minimum period of 312 weeks and for an additional
26 weeks when the injured worker is referred to
Vocational Rehabilitation for training in other
occupations, being unable to perform in their
previous job. Free medical care is also provided.

Automobile Accident Compensation No-fault
Automobile Insurance. This has as its main
objective the reduction to a minimum of the
economic and social effects produced by automobile
accidents on the family and dependents of the
victims, no matter who suffers or causes the
accident.
 The programme provides medical and hospital
services, as well as compensation to persons
injured as a result of accidents of motor drawn
vehicles which occur within the Commonwealth of
Puerto Rico.
 Any person who becomes physically injured,
sick or dies as a result of a motor drawn vehicle
accident is covered by the insurance.
 The injured in an automobile accident
(drivers, passengers, pedestrians) have the right
to receive medical and hospital services for two
consecutive years in public or private facilities
established within the territorial limits of
Puerto Rico, which have a contract with the
Automobile Accident Compensation Administration.

Dismemberment (loss of parts of the body). In
case of dismemberment the maximum compensation is
US$5,000.00 which is paid weekly or in a lump-sum
when necessary.
 When the injured person cannot work and
produce income, the compensation is equal to 50
per cent of the previous salary, or average income
up to a maximum of US$100 a week for up to 52
weeks. If by that time the victim is still
disabled, they will receive 50 per cent of the
salary or average income up to a maximum of US$50
a week for not more than 52 weeks. This provision
applies to cases where the injured person had a

paid job at the time of the accident, or 6 to 12 months prior to the accident.

If the victim is a housewife the compensation is US$25.00 per week, for up to 12 consecutive weeks. This benefit will be provided in case of total and continuous disability to perform her job.

The dependents of a victim in case of death can be compensated up to a maximum of US$25,000. This compensation is distributed according to the degree of dependency of spouse, children, parents or any other person under or over 18 years with physical or mental defects, not able to function independently.

The funeral and burial expenses are covered up to a maximum of US$500. This is paid after it is established that the victim died as a consequence of an automobile accident. The cost of living indexation results in periodic increases in benefits, which are also excluded from income taxes.

Fiscal Welfare. Exempt from income taxes is the economic benefit received under sickness or injury insurance or laws which provide compensation to workers, such as compensation for personal injuries or sickness, plus any indemnity received in a judicial procedure or transaction, due to such injuries or sickness.

Personal Social Services

Department of Health. Created by the Constitution of the Commonwealth of Puerto Rico in 1952. The Department of Health is normative and monitoring in character. Through its units it supervises, evaluates and advises the entire health system.

The two programmes which mostly apply to the sick and injured are medical emergencies and hospital services. The former provides 24-hour service, the objective of which is to provide assistance and medical care to severely injured persons or in critical metabolic conditions, reducing mortality and possible physical and mental conditions which may limit the productive and useful life of the patient.

Hospital services include the most complex and specialised services in the public health system of the Island. Attention is given to emergencies, hospitalisation and ambulatory treatment. Services are provided in the area and sub-regional hospitals.

Puerto Rico

Evaluation

Workmen's Compensation extends universal
protection to virtually all employed persons in
the public and private sectors. In fiscal year
1985-6 Workmen's Compensation covered 777,000
employees, which is 79.53 per cent of the labour
force (977,000); 33.78 per cent of the population
16 and over (2,300,000); and 23.67 per cent of the
total population (3,282,500). These numbers
indicate that this social insurance rates high in
coverage.

It is difficult to evaluate the compensation
benefit as it varies according to different
factors associated with the accident. But, of the
social security programes in Puerto Rico,
Workmen's Compensation provides the highest
economic benefits and greatest diversity of
medical services.

The State Insurance Fund's major problems are
the massive evasion of coverage by liable
employers; high administrative costs (US$34.1
million in 1985-6); serious delays in the
processing, adjudication and payment of claims (an
average of six years in a case of total and
permanent disability); inconsistencies within the
programme and in relation to other programmes; the
growing incidence of cases of total and permanent
disability, particularly psychiatric disorders,
especially amongst government employees; and
coordination problems with other programmes which
cover sickness and disability.

The Administration of Compensation for
Automobile Accidents has none of the usual
problems associated with the collection of premium
income since all car drivers pay their compulsory
contribution along with the annual car
registration fee. Victims of automobile accidents
are not subjected to delays in adjudication of
claims involving medical and hospital services
provided at the time of the accident. The
Administration does have, however, serious
shortcomings in its operations as they pertain to
financial management and control. It fails to
vigorously pursue the recoupment of over-payments
and other recoverable amounts.

Personal social services for the sick and
injured are mostly the responsibility of the
Department of Health. There is undoubtedly an
almost unanimous concern about public health
services in Puerto Rico.

242

Puerto Rico

ASSESSMENT OF THE PUERTO RICAN WELFARE SYSTEM

The second effort to establish a comprehensive
social security system in Puerto Rico was in the
1970s. The Commission on an Integral Social
Security System was charged with the
responsibility to work towards a goal that few if
any countries have yet reached: a comprehensive
and integrated social security system that would
provide the entire population with an adequate and
supportable level of protection against all common
economic risks. The Commission reported to the
Governor and the Legislative Assembly in 1976.
Eleven years have passed and no action has been
taken on the Report. The Commission considered
(CISSS 1976, pp.1-2):

> The strengths of the system are framed in the
> commitment of Puerto Rico to the development
> of an economic and social system that would
> advance the general welfare of all its
> people. Many of the existing social security
> programmes were innovative and forward looking
> when they were introduced. Puerto Rico had a
> school lunch programme long before there was a
> federal programme. The social insurance
> programme for no-fault automobile insurance
> pre-dated those few programmes that now exist
> in the United States. The Workmen's
> Compensation programme is broad in coverage
> and administered with a concern for the
> injured worker that has in the past led
> experts from other countries to come to Puerto
> Rico to study its methods and achievements.
> Puerto Rico has a temporary disability
> programme for non-work-connected illnesses
> that provides protection of a kind available
> in few states of the United States. The
> federal OASDHI programme provides broad and
> generally adequate benefits. The
> federal-state unemployment insurance uses
> sounder social insurance principles than those
> in state programmes in the United States.
> Puerto Rico has an established public
> assistance system to help needy families. In
> addition, the availability of publicly
> provided medical care and of a variety of
> personal social services backup the cash
> income security benefits. In fiscal year
> 1975, the expenditures for social security
> (social insurance, public aid and related

243

programmes, and the food stamp bonus) amounted to $1.7 billion. The total represented 24 per cent of the Gross Domestic Product, nearly twice as high a ratio as in the United States as a whole.

The main problems pointed out by the Commission were (CISSS 1976, p.7):

the low benefit levels in a number of programmes; the number of separate programmes, particularly those covering the risk of disability, is confusing and results in excessive administrative costs; the absence of adequate work programmes for the unemployed, especially the youth; a disturbing laxity in tax collections and in correction of under-reporting of payrolls; a woeful lack of continuous and reliable data on even the most elementary aspects of the operations of the individual programmes, let alone on the functioning of the system as a whole; and finally there is no adequate provision for participation of the beneficiaries in administration and decision-making.

The Social Report (JP 1985) makes an observation which is also relevant to this assessment:

a high participation in the social welfare system may be positive as an external physical component, as an indicator of the availability of services. High participation may be considered also a negative factor as it might indicate low levels of social integration and participation in the productive process, and as a consequence, an excessive dependency on social welfare services.

The negative element that prevails in Puerto Rico is excessive dependency on social welfare services. Social security as well as personal social services which are designed to provide benefits in transitory life situations have become permanent solutions to personal and social problems in Puerto Rico. From a critical perspective, not a few of the social welfare provisions have contributed to the maintenance of the status quo, disguising the social reality of the country. The structural deficiencies of the socio-economic order have been absorbed by the social welfare system. Clear examples are the unemployment and the nutritional assistance programmes, the subsidy policies, and above all the excessive dependence on federal funds, which performs an ideological function affecting national solidarity.

The social welfare provisions have not made a significant contribution towards the eradication of poverty and the creation of an egalitarian and just society. The 1970 Census revealed that 40 per cent of the poor families received 8 per cent of the total income while 10 per cent of the rich families received 35 per cent of the total income (Villamil 1979). The 1980 Census demonstrated that 62.4 per cent of the population lived below the poverty line (DSS 1987, p.3). In 1987, 91,000 families were living in extreme poverty due to a complete lack of income. The creation of an egalitarian and just society is difficult to achieve with most of the values that are underlying the social welfare system as well as the whole social structure in Puerto Rico. A truly egalitarian, humanistic social system that visualises social welfare provisions as a right and not as residual concessions is the challenge.

ACKNOWLEDGEMENT

I want to express my appreciation to Dr Eduardo Rivera Medina, Dean of Academic Affairs; Dr Saul Pratts, Dean of the Faculty of Social Sciences; and Professor Josefa R. Rios de Caraballo, Director of the Graduate School of Social Work, who endorsed this project as one of the innovative academic alternatives to be worked out by professors at the Rio Piedras Campus of the University of Puerto Rico during the summer of 1987. Their support and encouragement throughout the whole process has been of considerable value in the production of this chapter.

My appreciation also goes to Miss Wanda L. Rivera, a social work graduate student who collaborated in the collection of data, and to the dedicated clerical staff of the Graduate School of Social Work, most particularly Mrs Carmen Sanjurjo, who typed the document.

I want to dedicate this study to the graduate and undergraduate students to whom I have taught the courses in the Social Welfare Policy and

Puerto Rico

Services Sequence. Their critical observations have stimulated my concern for the study of the Puerto Rican social welfare system within the Latin American context.

REFERENCES AND FURTHER READING

Administracion de Compensaciones por Accidentes de Automoviles (ACAA) (1986), Causas y Efectos de los Accidentes de Transito en Puerto Rico, San Juan: ACAA.

Autoridad Acueductos y Alcantarillados (1987), Memorando Explicativo: Presupuesto de Gastos Funcionales 1987-88, San Juan: Autoridad de Acueductos y Alcantarillados.

Carnivali, J. & Vazquez Calzada, J. L. (1985), Perfil Socio-demografico de la Poblacion de Edad Avanzada de Puerto Rico, CIDE (5), San Juan: Escuela de Salud Publica, Recinto de Ciencias Medicas, Universidad de Puerto Rico.

Castro, J. (1987), Datos Estadisticos sobre el SINOT, San Juan: Departamento del Trabajo y Recursos Humanos.

Collazo, M. L. & Umpierre, J. M. (eds) (1987), Taller del Gobernador sobre la Instrumentacion de la Politica Publica de Servicios a los Envejecientes de Puerto Rico, San Juan: Recinto de Ciencias Medicas, Universidad de Puerto Rico.

Commission on an Integral Social Security System (1976), Report to the Governor and the Legislative Assembly - Commonwealth of Puerto Rico, San Juan: Commonwealth of Puerto Rico.

Departamento Servicios Sociales (1987a), Memorial Explicativa paro Gastos de Funcionamiento y Mejoras Permanentes, San Juan: Departmento de Servicios Sociales.

_____ (1987b), Resumen Sobre el Memorial Explicativo - Ano Fisca 1987-88, San Juan: Departamento de Servicios Sociales.

DTRH a (n.d.), Que es Seguro Choferil? San Juan: Departamento del Trabajo y Recursos Humanos.

246

Puerto Rico

_____ b (n.d.), <u>Seguro por Incapacidad No</u>
<u>Ocupacional: Guia para el Trabajador</u>, San
Juan: Departamento del Trabajo y Recursos
Humanos.

_____ c (n.d.), <u>Seguro por Incapacidad No</u>
<u>Ocupacional: Guia para el Patrono</u>, San Juan:
Departamento del Trabajo y Recursos Humanos.

Diaz, M. E. (1956), 'La asistencia publica en
Puerto Rico: estudio de caso de una
institucion social transplanda', <u>Revista de</u>
<u>Servicio Social</u>, XVII, (3).

Estado Libre Asociado (1987), <u>Presupuesto para el</u>
<u>Ano Fiscal 1987</u>, Tomo II, San Juan: Estado
Libre Asociado de Puerto Rico.

Fondo del Seguro del Estado (1986), <u>Boletin</u>
<u>Estadistico 1981-82 al 1985-86</u>, San Juan:
Oficina de Planificacion, FSE.

Geigel Polanco, V. (1936), <u>Legislacion Social de</u>
<u>Puerto Rico</u>, San Juan: Departamento del
Trabajo.

Junta de Planificacion JP (1985), <u>Informe Social-</u>
<u>Puerto Rico</u>, San Juan: Junta de Planificacion
de Puerto Rico.

_____ (1986a), <u>Informe Economico al Gobernador</u>,
San Juan: Junta de Planificacion de Puerto
Rico.

_____ (1986b), <u>Proyecciones de Poblacion por Edad,</u>
<u>Sexo y Municipio: Puerto Rico 1980-2005</u>, San
Juan: Junta de Planificacion de Puerto Rico.

Mesa Lago, C. (1978), <u>Social Security in Latin</u>
<u>America</u>, Pittsburgh: University of Pittsburgh
Press.

Oficina de Presupuesto y Gerencia (1984), <u>Manual</u>
<u>de Organizacion del Gobierno de Puerto Rico</u>,
San Juan: Estado Libre Asociado de Puerto Rico.

Parrilla, C. (1987), <u>Comportamiento Suicida en</u>
<u>Ninos y Adolescentes</u>, San Juan: mimeografiado.

Pratts, S. J. (1987), <u>La Politica Social en Puerto</u>
<u>Rico</u>, San Juan: Ediciones Porta Coeli.

Puerto Rico

PRMA (1985), Fringe Benefits Survey 1985, San Juan: Puerto Rico Manufacturers' Association Manual, Industrial Relations Series.

Ribera, J. C. (1987), Hallazgos del Proyecto de Epidemiologia Psiquiatrica de Ninos, San Juan: mimeografiado.

Rivera, A. (1985), El Papel del Estado Espanol en la Beneficencia de Puerto Rico del Siglo XIX, Madrid: Universidad Computense, Facultad de Ciencias Politicas y Sociologia.

Rivera, L. N. (1987), Sistema de Bienestar Social: Incapacitados e Impedidos, San Juan: Universidad de Puerto Rico.

Sanchez, C. D. (1987), Politica Publica en Torno a los Ciudadanos de Mayor Edad en Puerto Rico y su Impacto en la Familia, San Juan: mimeografiado.

Seda, R. M., Diaz, G., Garcia, V. & Rodriguez, C. (1984), Crisis Economica, Politica, Social y Perspectivas del Trabajo Social en Puerto Rico, San Juan: Universidad de Puerto Rico.

Seda, R. M. (1987), El Desarrollo Integral del Pueblo Puertorriqueno: Peto al Trabajo Social, San Juan: mimeografiado.

Social Security Administration (1987), Puerto Rico: State Statistics, Washington: US Department of Health and Human Services.

Villamil, J. J. (1979), 'Puerto Rico 1948-1976: The Limits of Dependent Growth', Transnational Capitalism and National Development, Humanity Press.

URUGUAY
Rodolfo Saldain

THE WELFARE SYSTEM ENVIRONMENT

Ideological Environment

Batlle's Conception of the Protective State Idea.
The politicians who governed Uruguay during the
first two decades of the twentieth century
questioned strongly the economic and social
relationships prevailing in Uruguay at that time
(Barran-Nahum 1981, p.13). Jose Batlle y Ordonez
Colorado, who was president from 1903 to 1907 and
again from 1911 to 1915, chose the state as the
appropriate instrument for achieving his reformist
conception. Indeed it was the state that had to
arbitrate in the conflict between labour and
capital and that had to defend the weaker groups,
irrespective of the influence of the vested
interests. The people of Uruguay have thus come
to perceive the state as having the role of a
strong arbitrator and their expectation is that
the state is able to solve all of Uruguay's social
and economic problems.

Social and Political Control Objectives. In
Uruguay the state has the basic aim of preventing
and avoiding social conflicts. In order to
achieve this it has sought to lessen social
inequalities. Thus de-regulation of working
conditions and the introduction of social
insurance early in the development of Uruguay is
considered a strong mechanism for achieving
political and social control, as well as lessening
social inequalities.
The social and labour legislation evidences
the influence of developments in Bismarck's
Germany in the 1880s and 1890s. It sought to

consolidate traditional institutional structures, and at the same time protect the underprivileged masses and provide a means by which class conflict could be effectively mediated (Finch 1980, p.216).

Middle-class Welfare Ideology. During the first decades of the twentieth century Uruguay evolved a middle-class welfare ideology. Although all classes were receiving protection from the social welfare system, emphasis was placed on the small industrial sector and on civil servants (Finch 1980, p.20). Social policies in general, and social security policy more specifically, has long been dominated by the strong demand for economic security expressed by the middle-classes. This, together with the total absence of an indigenous population and the achievement of economic prosperity has meant that Uruguay was socially and psychologically distant from the rest of Latin America, at least until the 1970s.

Historical Origins

Since independence from Spain was gained in 1925 Uruguayan history has been dominated by two political parties: the Colorados (liberals) and the Blancos (conservatives). Their rivalry resulted in frequent outbreaks of civil war in the nineteenth century. Thanks to the progressive policies of Batlle, president during the first two decades of the twentieth century, Uruguay became the first welfare state in Latin America. Details of the historical evolution of Uruguayan public welfare programmes are given in Table 1.

TABLE 1: HISTORICAL ORIGINS OF PUBLIC WELFARE IN URUGUAY, LEGISLATIVE AND PROGRAMME DETAILS

1829	Law relating to invalidity, widowhood and orphanages for people who fought for independence.
1830	First constitution enacted, article 81 of which required the executive branch to provide retirement pensions for civil servants and military personnel.
1838	Protection against long-term social security risks granted to state employees.
1892	Work-related disability protection given to policemen and firemen.

1896	Social security protection given to teachers. Tripartite financing established for the first time.
1904	Social security protection extended to all state workers.
1914	Work accident risk prevention measures introduced.
1919	Social security protection extended on limited basis to private sector workers. Non-contributory age and invalidity pensions established.
1920	Work accident compensation established.
1925	Special social security programme provided for public and private sector bank clerks. Special social security system established for political staff.
1933	Reorganisation of social security administration and the creation of the Retirement Pension Uruguayan Institute established.
1934	Social security protection given to workers dismissed from employment in industry and commerce.
1936	Family allowance payments provided by individual companies appear.
1940	Creation of a non-government organisation to provide social security protection to notaries. Social security protection extended to self-employed and employers.
1943	Family allowances for employees in commercial and industrial enterprises introduced.
1944	Special social security programme for seasonal workers of cold-storage plants established.
1945	Special social security programme for workers in wool and leather sheds established.
1948	The Retirement Pension Uruguayan Institute is abolished and three decentralised institutes established.
1950	Women who are mothers eligible for retirement pensions after 10 years employment, irrespective of age.
1951	Special retirement benefits created.
1953	Pension eligibility conditions for working women more liberal than those for working men.
1954	A specific institute established to provide social security protection to university personnel. Old age,

invalidity and death benefits provided to all workers. Family allowances extended to rural workers.

1958 A general strike insurance covering employees in industrial and commercial enterprises initiated. Maternity benefits programme initiated. Paid maternity leave established. Family allowances paid to the unemployed and pensioners.

1960 Sickness benefits introduced for construction workers. Coverage extended to harbour workers in Montevideo.

1961 Survivors' pensions established. Cost of living adjustments to pensions introduced. Creation of compulsory insurance for occupational accidents, through the State Security Bank.

1964 Sickness benefits extended to workers in the wood industry and in metallurgy industry. Supplementary survivors' pension provided in respect of children. Additional benefits provided under family allowance programme for families establishing a home. Marriage benefits established. Birth allowances extended to all workers. Pre-natal benefits extended to all workers. Holiday camp established for the benefit of all workers. Unemployment benefits extended to workers in rural cold-storage plants. Sickness benefits extended to car industry workers, textile industry workers, workers in cargo and fishing boats, workers in the graphic industry and to needle workers.

1967 The Social Security bank is created.

1972 Sickness benefits extended to beverage industry workers, leather industry workers and confectionary industry workers.

1973 Tripartite management of social security institutions abolished, replaced by direct government control.

1975 A decentralisation of social security administration occurs and a new benefits system created.

1979 Rationalisation of social security administration initiated.

1981 Eligibility requirements for family allowances made more restrictive.

	eligibility conditions for unemployment benefits made more restrictive and coverage reduced.
1984	Sickness benefits extended to rural and domestic workers.
1985	The Social Security Bank is re-established.
1986	Sickness benefits extended to small rural producers. Eligibility for non-contributory age and invalid pensions liberalised. Special social security system for self-employed workers redesigned.

Political Environment

The Eastern Republic of Uruguay lies on the south-east coast of South America, with Brazil to the north and Argentina to the west. From 1973 to 1985 Uruguay was ruled by a military-backed regime. During this period the government tried to initiate socio-economic strategies to reduce labour costs (that is salaries, benefits and social liabilities), to reduce the state's budget and to suppress redistributive policies designed to tax capital and profit. In the mid-1980s the government of Uruguay returned to civilian control following the economic crisis experienced by Uruguay in 1984. To legitimise the new democratic regime all Uruguayan forces sought to establish a new political, economic and social consensus (Rial 1984, p.133). The thrust of this consensus was the establishment of the Concertacion Nacional Programatica (CONAPRO), which sought to establish agreement on a range of reforms amongst a diversity of political parties. The practical outcome of this strategy was modest, for negligible social legislation was enacted.

Socio-economic Environment

In 1986 Uruguay had a population of 2.9 million and a low population density (15.6 people per square kilometre). More than 85 per cent of its population live in urban areas. There are no significant ethnic minorities. The economically active population totals 1.2 million (some 41 per cent of the total population). It should be noted

253

that the workforce participation rate has been declining in recent years. The age structure of the Uruguayan population reveals a growing rate of demographic dependency. A combination of a low birth rate and a relatively long life expectancy has resulted in Uruguay having an ageing population trend (Finch 1980, p.200). Uruguay has also faced an endemic emigration of its population over the last 25 years (Aguir 1982, p.77).

The Uruguayan employment structure reveals a strong emphasis on the tertiary sector which constitutes almost 50 per cent of the workforce. Seventy per cent of the workforce is in the private sector.

The Uruguayan economy suffered serious stagnation in the 1960s and 1970s. It confronted formidable problems. The 1980s, however, have seen the beginnings of a recovery, although serious problems remain.

Uruguay has long suffered a chronic inflation condition with the inflation rate fluctuating between 30 and 66 per cent a year, over the period from 1975 to 1984, with the rate reaching 83 per cent in 1979. The early 1980s saw a marked reduction in the inflation rate which fell to 20.5 per cent in 1982. Since 1985 however, the inflation rate has dramatically increased to between 70 and 85 per cent per annum.

Unemployment increased rapidly in the 1980s from 7.3 per cent in 1980 to 13.1 per cent in 1985. The following year, however, saw the unemployment rate fall to 10.7 per cent. The number of unemployed in 1986 was 128,833 people.

THE WELFARE SYSTEM: AN OVERVIEW

Administration of Social Security

More than 98 per cent of those protected by social security measures are covered by compulsory social insurance programmes, which are administered by the state (see Figure 1). The trade unions and employer organisations share in the management of compulsory social insurance programmes for bank clerks, university professionals and notaries against long-term social security risks. The substitute and complementary occupational welfare programmes, which are not very significant, are administered by trade unions and, in some instances, employers.

FIGURE 1: SOCIAL SECURITY ADMINISTRATION IN URUGUAY

Social Security Programme	Administrative Arrangements
Old Age, Invalidity and Death	Social Security Bank
Sickness, Maternity, Unemployment and Family Allowances	Social Security General Directorate through the Directorate of Family Allowances, Sickness and Unemployment Insurance, under the general supervision of the Ministry of Labour and Social Security.
Occupational Injury and Death	Social Security Bank
Maternity Allowance	Mother and Child Protection Services.

SOURCE: US Department of Health and Human Services 1986.

By middle of the 1960s the management of old age, invalidity and death benefit programmes was the responsibility of four institutions, each responsible for particular occupational groups (rural workers, employers, domestic servants and those eligible for non-contributory age and disability pensions; workers and employers of industry and commerce; state workers, except for bank clerks and military personnel, political staff and educational personnel; and finally, military personnel). Each of these institutions is responsible for administering specific legislation.

With the adoption of the 1967 constitution there was a centralisation of social security administration under the auspices of the Social Security Bank (Banko de Prevision Social (SSB)) which is an autonomous body, in order to coordinate social security administration. From 1967 to 1979 it coordinated only those institutions concerned with administering old age, invalidity and death benefits for non-military personnel (the administration of age, invalidity and death benefits for military personnel has always remained independent). For short-term contingencies, the state's role has been relatively minor in comparison to that of trade unions and employer organisations. More radical centralising impulses were experienced in the early 1970s when the executive branch of government took on the administration of sick pay, family allowances and maternity benefits programmes in 1973.

In 1979 the Social Security General Directorate (DGSS) was created for the purpose of further centralising the administration of social security. Under its auspices came old age, invalidity and death benefit programmes for all occupational groups except for police, military personnel and Jockey Club staff, family allowance programmes, non-occupational sickness benefits programmes and unemployment benefit programmes.

With the introduction of democratic government in the mid-1980s came the recreation of the Social Security Bank in 1986. Its structure comprises a Board of Directors and four decentralised councils which are in charge of long-term risks, short-term risks, general management and services and revenue collection respectively. It should be noted that these decentralised councils have not been appointed as yet and they are unlikely to emerge in the near future. This development is the first step towards a reversal of the centralisation tendencies of the 1970s.

Social security institutes administering programmes for university professionals, notaries and bank clerks also received full managerial autonomy in the mid-1980s.

The Administration of the Personal Social Services

The personal social services are hardly developed in Uruguay. Those relating to children and the provision of supplementary food are administered by the state through the Childs Council and the National Feeding Institute respectively. There are also private initiatives providing services targeted at children.

In the countryside and small towns and villages there are some personal social services administered by community volunteers.

Uruguay

Financing Social Security

Social security programmes are financed by contributions from workers, employers and the state, supplemented by income from general taxes and investments. Table 2 provides details of the contribution rates payable. Over the last 15 years the relative importance of employer and employee contributions has diminished whilst that of the state contribution has increased (see Table 3).

TABLE 2: SOCIAL INSURANCE CONTRIBUTION RATES IN URUGUAY

Insured Person	• 16-19 per cent of earnings for covered workers in industry and commerce.
	• 12 per cent of earnings for rural workers.
	• 16 per cent of earnings for public employees.
Employers[1].	14-18 per cent of payroll in industry and commerce.
	• 14 per cent of payroll in respect of rural workers.
	• 10 per cent of payroll in respect of public employees.
Government	• Defined financing of social security institutions from government revenue.

Note: 1 Employers all pay entire cost of occupational injury and death benefits through compulsory insurance premiums with the Social Security Bank

SOURCE: US Department of Health and Human Services 1986.

TABLE 3: SOCIAL SECURITY BANK'S SOURCES OF FUNDS (in percentages)

	1979	1980	1981	1982	1983	1984	1985	1986[1]
Worker's and employer's contribution	87.1	73.2	60.9	48.3	54.7	58.0	66.7	70.9
Government subsidies	7.4	24.4	34.8	50.7	44.7	41.4	31.5	24.9
Investments	5.5	2.4	4.3	1.0	0.6	0.6	1.8	4.2
TOTAL	100.0	100.0	100.0	100.0	100.0	100.0	100.0	100.0

Note: 1 Preliminary data.

SOURCE: Based on SSB data.

Uruguay

The non-contributory age and disability benefits, family allowances, maternity benefits and unemployment benefits are financed directly by the state.

In total more than 50 per cent of social security expenditure in Uruguay is paid for by the state, although this has been systematically reduced.

It should be noted that the principal source of government revenue in Uruguay is a broad-based consumption tax in the form of a value-added tax.

In 1986 rural employers' contribution rates were diminished, substituted by a contribution rate based on the extension and productivity of country estates.

Financing the Personal Social Services

The state institutions providing personal social services finance their programmes by means of state allocation. In some instances beneficiaries pay a modest price for goods and services consumed so as to cover part of the cost incurred. This principle applies to the National Feeding Institute.

The personal social services provided by the community are financed by general donations, although in some cases they receive state allocations or grants from international institutions. Moreover recipients with an income beyond particular levels are required to contribute to the cost of benefits received.

THE AGED

The contingency of old age is covered by means of a system of contributory and non-contributory pensions. By this means social security protection for this target group is almost universal.

Social Security

<u>Contributory Pensions</u>. To qualify for an earnings-related contributory pension covered workers must have attained the retirement age (64 for men and 55 for women) and have 30 years of coverage. There is no mandatory retirement age,

259

except for public employees who must retire at the age of 70. Workers engaged in hazardous occupations and in teaching have a right to a pension with fewer years of employment and at a younger age. A reduced pension is available to workers with 10 years of service upon reaching the age of 70, for men, or 65, for women. Early retirement is available to politicians and judges, after 20 years of service, the last three involving political or judicial posts, and for teachers after 25 years of service or upon the attainment of age 50 and 20 years of service.

The pension payable is equal to 60 per cent of average earnings achieved by male workers in the four years prior to retirement, plus 5 per cent for each additional five years of work, up to 75 per cent of earnings. For women the pension is equal to 65 per cent of average earnings in the last four years plus 5 per cent for each additional five years of work, up to 75 per cent of earnings. The minimum pension is specified as 85 per cent of the minimum wage prevalent at the date of retirement. The maximum pension is seven times the minimum wage at the time of retirement.

The reduced and early pensions are equal to 40 per cent of average earnings in the last four years prior to retirement, plus 1 per cent of earnings for each year of service up to 70 per cent of earnings. (Teachers receive a reduced pension equal to 50 per cent of average earnings in their last four years prior to retirement, plus 2 per cent of earnings for each year of service beyond 20 years, up to 70 per cent of earnings.)

There are automatic annual adjustments to all pensions for wage changes.

Separate pension arrangements apply to military and police personnel.

Dismissal Pensions. In 1985 a special programme was created for state civil servants who had been dismissed for illogical reasons during the period of dictatorship. They obtained a pension provided they had 10 years of service prior to the time of their dismissal. No age limit applies.

Non-contributory Age Pensions. Means-tested pensions are available to workers with a minimum of 10 years service upon reaching the age of 70 if male, or 65 if female. This pension is available to foreigners who satisfy a 15 year residency requirement. In December 1986 this non-contributory pension benefit was 45.6 per cent of the average pension granted by the Social Security Bank.

Funeral Subsidies. Deceased contributory pensioners attract a funeral subsidy of up to four times the minimum wage, unless the deceased pensioner qualified for certain types of prepaid funeral insurance.

Personal Social Services

Uruguay lacks a systematic and significant development of the personal social services targeted at the elderly. However, some services are provided.

Homes for the Elderly. A number of homes for the elderly have been built outside the capital, upon the initiative of volunteers from the local community. There are approximately 40 such homes catering for about 1,200 elderly.

Concessional Transport Costs. A number of transport companies provide concessional fares for the elderly.

Concessional Cultural Entertainment Activities. Several organisations providing cultural entertainments provide concessional rates for pensioners.

Nutritional Food Supplements. This programme is administered by the Department of Labour and Social Security and was established in 1985 to provide additional food for low income pensioners. This has been provided to about 150,000 elderly.

Evaluation

A combination of an ageing population and the generosity of the eligibility conditions has made the contributory pension system financially unstable. The situation has been exacerbated by the relative low age of current pensioners. As a result the funding of contributory pensions has become more dependent on government subsidies.

Uruguay

The contributory pensions provided to the elderly are generally most inadequate to maintain them above subsistence level. Pension indexation has not been able to maintain the purchasing power of pensions.

Because there is no widespread mandatory retirement, contributory pensioners can continue to remain in remunerative work. This needs to be reviewed and the impact of non-mandatory retirement on the labour market must be studied carefully.

Support for the personal social services is minimal and there is no commitment to developing such services in the foreseeable future. Those voluntary activities that do exist seem to provide an adequate level of support to the elderly although their coverage is quite minimal.

THE HANDICAPPED AND DISABLED

The handicapped and disabled are considered to be largely a family responsibility in Uruguay.

Social Security

Contributory Invalid Pensions. All workers who become totally and permanently work-incapacitated qualify for an invalidity pension provided they have attained 10 years of contributions, are in residence at the onset of invalidity and not in receipt of any other pension. If the disability precludes the performance of the disabled person's usual work then the pension is payable for a maximum of five years, after which the pension ceases unless the beneficiary attains retirement age, or unless the disability is such that the beneficiary is unable to engage in any type of employment. If the disability precludes any type of employment, then the invalidity pension continues until the attainment of retirement age. Foreigners must satisfy a 10-year residency test to qualify for this benefit.

The amount of the pension payable is equal to 70 per cent of average earnings over the last three years, or if appropriate the period of employment actually undertaken. A minimum pension equal to 85 per cent of the minimum average wage is specified, along with a maximum pension rate equal to seven times the minimum wage. The

Uruguay

invalidity pension is subject to automatic annual adjustments for wage changes.

Non-contributory Invalid Pensions. Means-tested pensions are payable to needy invalids. In 1986 eligibility conditions associated with this pension were liberalised allowing its coverage to be extended.

Permanent Disability Pensions (Work Injury). Under the Uruguayan workmen's compensation system all workers employed in industry and commerce, as well as agricultural and domestic workers, qualify for a disability pension if the disability is work-related. If the disability is total and permanent then the pension is equal to 100 per cent of earnings. In the event of a partial disability the pension payable is determined on a pro rata basis.

Medical and surgical care, hospitalisation, medicines and appliances are provided.

Personal Social Services

There are no specific programmes designed to provide personal social services to the disabled and handicapped.

Evaluation

The social security protection provided to the disabled is most inadequate. The contributory invalid pension programme is inequitable because its beneficiaries are permitted to engage in new work activities. Moreover, the lack of any rehabilitation services restricts the reintegration of the disabled into the workforce. Thus workers who are disabled lose their jobs once they qualify for an invalid pension and after five years they may also lose their pensions, but without proper rehabilitation they find it very difficult to re-enter the workforce. This has created a group of fringe workers. The lack of suitable rehabilitation programmes to allow disabled workers to re-enter the workforce should be treated as a matter of high priority.

Uruguay

CHILDREN AND YOUTH

About 27 per cent of Uruguay's population is aged
under 15, some 796,000 children. Those aged
between 14 and 18 constitute 6.5 per cent of the
population, or some 192,000 youths.

Social Security

Specific social security programmes targeted at
children and youths are administered by the Social
Security Bank (SSB), the Ministry of Public Health
(MSP) and the Child's Council and the National
Feeding Institute (INDA).

Family Allowances. All employed persons,
including domestic workers, and contributory
pensioners receive a family allowance if they have
at least one child under the age of 14, 18 if a
student, or no age limit if invalided. The family
allowance is no less than 8 per cent of minimum
monthly wage per child.

Maternity Allowances. Health assistance is
available to young children of employed women.
This programme provides about 45 per cent of the
health services given to infants and covers more
than 75 per cent of the population aged under six
years.
    For children under the age of 90 days the
assistance rendered under the family allowance
programme encompasses all medical care required.
This is provided without cost to eligible babies.
Approximately 25 per cent of all children in this
age group receive this protection.
    For children aged between 91 days and six
years the services provided include ambulatory
assistance, developmental monitoring and control,
as well as various forms of medication. Until
1987 these benefits were exclusively provided in
Montevideo, although since then geographic
coverage has been extended into the rural areas
and has expanded by some 90,000 children. Thus
this programme services 4.6 per cent of the
eligible population.
    The maternity allowance programme also
provides assistance to families with congenitally
handicapped children, in the form of free
essential medical care. This benefit is provided
to children of any age.

Uruguay

Personal Social Services

Services Provided by the Child's Council. This institute provides a range of services for children. It provides institutional care to some 3,700 children a year. Such children may be placed in institutional care as a result of their families lacking adequate income or providing inadequate care (52 per cent), abandonment (10 per cent) and criminal behaviour on the part of parents (20 per cent).

In 1986 the Children's Council financed 464 paid foster care homes which provided assistance to 998 children.

In order to achieve the major goal of the Child's Council, which is to provide preventative care for children, a number of programmes have recently been developed to provide early assistance to children at risk. This includes the establishment of emergency placement homes designed to assist children confronting crises; this service has a very limited coverage. Moreover, a programme of financial aid for needy families is being developed.

Services of the National Feeding Institute. A national programme of food supplementation has assisted 181,000 children. Some 11,000 children have their daily lunch at one of its refectories. This supplements the assistance given by the Primary Education Board which, through the school refectories, provides food supplementation to a further 100,000 school age children, 82 per cent of whom live outside Montevideo.

The longer-standing food supplementation programme administered by the INDA involves the encouragement of milk consumption. This programme is administered by state and private institutions and covers some 150,000 individuals (Terra & Hopenhay 1986, p.142).

Private Sector Services. Community initiatives, with state support, have developed some 170 institutions that provide day-nursery services as well as support services at the time of confinement. In total these initiatives service some 9,000 children.

Uruguay

Evaluation

Child poverty in Uruguay is a serious social problem. It has been estimated that some 31.7 per cent of all children under 14 years of age are in poverty (Monteverde 1985, p.5).

The social security programmes are targeted at children employed in the formal sector. Coverage is very limited in the countryside.

The services provided by the Child's Council have a very limited impact on the welfare of children as a consequence of budgetry and infrastructure constraints. The recent initiatives taken by that institution are still at the experimental stage and they are very difficult to evaluate.

Supplementary feeding programmes, although not extensive in coverage, are specifically targeted at children in need and have contributed significantly to the improvement of nourishment levels.

In the context of the crises that have faced Uruguay over the last 15 years the welfare needs of children in Uruguay are self-evident. The need for further state support of children in poverty is essential as needy families face a serious lack of public services (Terra & Hopenhay 1985, p.93).

With youths there is a complete lack of welfare programmes targeted at this age group. The state is however just beginning to evidence interest in this matter, due largely to the impact of some pilot programmes initiated by the private sector.

Despite the evident need for social support targeted specifically at children the trend in public expenditure on that target group has diminished during the first half of the 1980s as a percentage of Gross Domestic Product and of central government expenditure.

NEEDY FAMILIES

The family unit in Uruguay has been in a state of transformation over the last decade because of a marked increase in the female workforce participation rate. This is the challenge confronting the Uruquan welfare system.

Uruguay

Social Security

Survivors' Pensions. Earnings-related survivors' pensions are payable in the event of non-occupational and occupational death.

Dependents of workers covered by Uruguay's worker's compensation programme who die as a result of a work injury or illness qualify for survivors' pension. For widows or invalid widowers the pension is equal to 50 per cent of the deceased worker's earnings. Orphan's benefits of between 20 and 100 per cent of the deceased worker's earnings are provided to dependent children under the age of 16, or invalided children of any age. In the absence of direct dependents these benefits are granted to parents and grandparents of the deceased worker.

Dependents of deceased old age or invalid pensioners, unemployment benefit recipients, or deceased persons who were insured workers within one year of their death qualify for survivors' pension. Widows may receive up to 75 per cent of the deceased worker's average earnings in the last four years. This pension is also available to divorced wives receiving alimony, dependent invalid widowers, or unmarried daughters aged 45 who cared for their parents. Other eligible beneficiaries include invalid parents, adopted children and children from previous marriage. Full orphans receive a pension equal to 66 per cent of average earnings of the deceased person in the last four years. These pensions are subject to automatic annual adjustments for wage changes.

Funeral Grants. In the event of a non-occupational death survivors' pension recipients receive a funeral grant of up to four times the prevailing minimum wage.

Maternity Benefits. All employed and self-employed women who are currently in covered employment or receiving unemployment benefits receive a maternity benefit equal to 100 per cent of their earnings for up to six weeks before and six weeks after confinement. Medical assistance is also provided during pregnancy.

Personal Social Services

Pregnant women, whether working or not, who qualify for a family allowance have a right to

267

integrated assistance during their pregnancy and confinement. Medical care is provided at polyclinics, hospitals under the auspices of the Social Security Bank or medical institutions contracted by the Social Security Bank. About 25 per cent of all births are covered by this programme.

Evaluation

The Uruguayan social welfare system is not able to adequately promote family welfare. The system of survivors' pensions is most inequitable. In 1980 the highest survivors' pension was 15.1 times the lowest survivors' pension. Although this proportion has subsequently decreased to 10.6 in 1985 and to 8.7 in 1986 the inequalities still exist. Moreover, the survivors' pension now constitutes a significant financial burden, aggravated by the fact that 30 per cent of beneficiaries are of employment age.

The number of people covered by the maternity programme is significantly higher outside the capital, with nearly 70 per cent of births receiving assistance from this programme.

THE UNEMPLOYED

Unemployment is a serious social problem in Uruguay. In the mid-1980s the unemployment rate was 10.7 per cent, or some 129,000 people.

Social Security

Employees in industry and commerce who have paid social security contributions for two to six months and who have at least two years of residency qualify for unemployment benefits provided their unemployment is not due to their participation in a strike, or their dismissal for disciplinary reasons. Such unemployed workers must apply for unemployment benefits within 30 days of becoming unemployed.

In the event of total unemployment the unemployment benefit is equal to 50 per cent of past earnings received over the six months prior to becoming unemployed.

Uruguay

Day labourers who experience a 25 per cent
reduction of the usual working hours over the
period of a month qualify for the benefit that is
equal to the difference between their actual
earnings and the amount they would have been paid
had they been the recipients of unemployment
benefits. In fact, this benefit is insignificant
for the benefits are low and the number of
applications is virtually nil.

Unemployment beneficiaries also have the right
to receive a supplement of 25 per cent of the
benefit payable if they are married or caring for
a disabled relative.

Unemployment benefits are paid for a period of
180 days after which it automatically ceases.

Special supplementary occupational
unemployment schemes exist for workers in
cold-storage, wool and leather industries. These
provide supplementary benefits to day labourers.

Personal Social Services

Under Uruguayan law totally or partially
unemployed workers may not be evicted from their
homes by their landlords for as long as they
remain unemployed.

Evaluation

Income replacement is the clear purpose of
unemployment benefits in Uruguay. The most needy
sectors of the population, those in the formal
sector, do not qualify for unemployment benefits
and thus remain unprotected, at a time when the
unemployment rate is notoriously higher than the
historically prevalent rate.

THE SICK AND INJURED

The welfare of the sick and injured has received
priority attention from the Uruguan government in
recent years. Both programme coverage and funding
for services targeted at this group have increased.

Social Security

Sickness Benefits. Since 1984 all private sector
wage earners have been eligible for an earnings-

related sickness benefit, provided they have three months' contributions, or 75 days' contributions in the last 12 months. This benefit is payable from the fourth day of illness for up to one year, but it may be extended for an additional year. The sickness benefit is equal to 70 per cent of last earnings, with a maximum rate equal to three times the minimum monthly wage.

Comprehensive medical services are available through special mutual systems. Employers are required to join an appropriate institution, which provides medical assistance to covered workers.

If a sick worker is reported to be disabled, then sickness benefits are paid for 181 more days, so as to allow the beneficiary to apply and to procure a special invalidity pension.

A voluntary mutual system of general sickness insurance exists for particular occupational groups. The voluntary approach is strongly backed by Uruguay trade unions. In December 1986 some 50,000 workers were covered by these systems.

Occupational Disability Benefits. Under Uruguay's workmen's compensation scheme employees in industry and commerce, agricultural work and domestic service receive, in the event of a temporary occupational disability, a benefit equal to 50 per cent of earnings in the first month, increasing to 66.66 per cent of earnings thereafter. If the disability is due to occupational sickness then the disability benefit is 100 per cent of last salary. Workers suffering a work injury as a result of an occupational accident are provided with medical assistance through the SSB. This assistance is also provided to uncovered workers, in which event the SSB brings repayment action against the employer.

Employment Protection. The employer must maintain a position for the sick or injured worker during his period of temporary disability. Moreover, upon returning to work such workers cannot be discharged for a period of 30 days. In the event of a partial disability the employer must provide a suitable position, unless they can prove that that is impossible. If an employer violates this obligation then severance pay payments payable to the discharged worker are increased from two to 12 months' salary. If the discharged formerly sick or injured worker was temporarily disabled as a result of an occupational illness then the indemnity upon dismissal is calculated at the rate of three months' salary for every year of service.

Personal Social Services

There have been three attempts to establish worker rehabilitation programmes in Uruguay. These occurred in 1958, 1974 and again in 1983. Currently there are no such programmes.

Evaluation

The coverage of Uruguay's sickness benefits programme increased dramatically between 1984 and 1986, when the number of beneficiaries increased by over 66 per cent. This increase in beneficiaries has resulted in an acute shortage of funding. Reflecting this is the increase in the government's subsidy from 0.7 per cent of GNP in 1983 to 0.2 per cent in 1986. In 1986 sickness benefits accounted for 7 per cent of the government's social security subsidy.

Although the provision of sickness benefits has substantially improved the welfare of the lower income groups in Uruguay, as well as extending access to medical assistance, there are many sectors in the economy that are outside its coverage, including state workers and workers employed in the informal economic sector. Indeed, only 50 per cent of the economically active population are covered by the sickness benefits programme.

The level of protection provided to workers in the event of occupational illness or injury was sufficient four decades ago, but currently it is clearly inadequate.

AN ASSESSMENT OF THE URUGUAYAN WELFARE SYSTEM

The Uruguayan social security system has a very extensive coverage in relation to both the population and the social security risks. It fundamentally focusses on salary workers from the formal economic sector. The informal sector, however, has very limited coverage only.

The lack of any significant development in the personal social services is strongly indicated. There is no global state policy or significant private action in this area. Demands are very weak, in spite of the fact that Uruguay's ageing population suggests the necessity of developing specific personal social services for the elderly.

The role of the family in Uruguay has changed over the last couple of decades. Yet government support for the family, which peaked in the 1960s with the introduction of family allowances, has not been forthcoming.

In terms of its impact on distribution of income, Uruguay's social security system has tended to redistribute income towards the lower income groups (Davrieux 1987). This has been the result of the benefit eligibility criteria and the specification of benefit ceilings.

It is clear that the Uruguayan social security system's main objective is income replacement, which is typical of the values pertinent to a society dominated by interests of the middle-class. Poverty alleviation, as a social security objective, has never been taken seriously. It is evident that in the last decade poverty has increased markedly and most alarmingly.

Uruguay's serious problem of inflation has reduced the capacity of its social security system to provide income support in the longer term. Over the period from 1962 to 1986 social security beneficiaries have maintained only 25 per cent of their purchasing power. This situation reflects badly on Uruguay's social security systems.

It is clear that individual needs and expectations with respect to social security are not being met. The fact that social security focusses on those in the formal economic sector has hindered the development of a national solidarity, as a substitute for corporate solidarity. This has occurred in spite of significant government subsidies to the social security programme. Indeed Uruguay is facing a serious problem with regard to its social security system, which is not being properly addressed by academics, those in the social sector, or politicians. It must be remembered that politicians are blocked from taking action to address the problems of Uruguay's social security system as a result of the feared electoral repercussions of any reform.

There is a need for Uruguay's society to redefine its social welfare objectives, particularly in the context of Uruguay's current economic difficulties, which are quite different

Uruguay

to those that set the context for the introduction
of social security in Uruguay. In essence, there
is a need for social welfare policies that meet
Uruguay's present social needs.

ACKNOWLEDGEMENT

This chapter was written by Rodolfo Saldain under
the guidance of Ariel Gianola, Associate
Researcher of the Centre for Latin American
Studies at the University of Pittsburgh.

REFERENCES AND FURTHER READING

Aguir, C.A. (1982), Uruguay: Pais de Emigracion,
    Montevideo: Coleccion Temas del Siglo XX, No.3.

Argenti, G. et al. (1984), 7 Enfocues sobre la
    Concertacion, Montevideo: CIESU/EBO.

Barbegelata, H.H. (1978), Derecho del Trabajo,
    Montevideo: FCU.

Barran-Nahum, A. (1981), Batlle, los Estancieros y
    el Imperio Pritanico, T.2, Montevideo: EBO.

CEPAL (1985a), La Evolucion de la Sociedad y las
    Politicas Sociales en el Uruguay, 85-3-398.

_____ (1985b), La Evolucion de la Economia y la
    Politica Economica en Uruguay en el Periodo
    1981-1984, 85-4-542.

CLAEH (1983), Uruguay, Indicadores Basicos,
    Montevideo: CLAEH.

Davrieux, H. (1987), 'A quien beneficia el gasto
    publico social?' In SUMA, Montevideo:
    Cline-EBO, 2(2).

DGEC (1986), Recuentos Preliminares. VI Censo
    General de Poblacion v IV de Vivienda. 1985,
    Montevideo.

Emida Uriarte, O. et al. (1985), La Concertacion
    Social. Estudios en Homenaje al Prof. Americo
    Pla Rodriguez, Montevideo: AMF.

Uruguay

Errandonea, A. & Constabile, D. (1969), Sindicato y Sociedada en el Uruguay, Montevideo: FCU.

Finch, H. (1980), Historia Economica del Uruguay Contemporaneo, Montevideo: EBO.

Fortuna, J.C. (1985), El Sistema de la Seguridad Social en el Uruguay, CIESU/DT 116/85.

Frances, A. (1983), 'Seguridad social'. In 'El ocaso del Estado Benefactor', El Uruguay de Nuestro Tiempo, No.10, Montevideo: CLAEH.

Gianola Martecani, A. (1983), 'Nuevas estrategias para el estudio de la seguridad social'. In Cuadernos, No.26, Montevideo: CLAEH.

Gonzalez, L.E. (1986), 'Los Partidos y la Redemocratizacion en Uruguay', in Cuadernos, No. 37, Montevideo: CLAEH.

INDA (1987), Impacto de la Situacion sobre el Estado Nutricional de la Familia y Fundamentalmente de la Ninez en el Uruguay, Montevideo: mimeo.

Monteverde, J.P. (1985), Estado de la Infancia, Montevideo: CLAEH.

Prebisch, R. (1978), 'Planificacion, desarrollo y democracia'. In Desarrollo y Democracia, Estudios No.9, Montevideo: CLAEH.

Real de Azua, C. (1964), El Impulso y su Freno, Montevideo: EBO.

Rial, J. (1984), 'Estado, partidos politicos y concertacion social en el Uruguay de la transicion'. In 7 Enfoques sobre la Concertacion, Montevideo: CIESU/EBO.

Terra, J.P. & Hopenhay, M. (1986), La Infancia en el Uruguay, Montevideo: CLAEH/UNICEF EBO.

United States, Department of Health and Human Services (1986), Social Security Administration, Social Security Programs Throughout the World - 1985, Washington, DC: Department of Health and Human Services.

APPENDICES

SOCIAL SECURITY PROVISIONS

COUNTRY	SERVICE PROVIDERS	THE AGED	THE DISABLED AND HANDICAPPED	CHILDREN AND YOUTH	NEEDY FAMILIES	THE SICK AND INJURED	THE UNEMPLOYED	METHODS OF FINANCING	RESPONSIBLE GOVERNMENT ADMINISTRATIVE AGENCIES
ARGENTINA	Central government administrative agencies	. Contributory wage-related pension . Social assistance	. Temporary disability pensions . Constant attendance allowances . Lump-sum permanent disability grant . Contributory wage-related invalidity pension . Social assistance . Medical care . Rehabilitation	. Orphans' pension . Family allowance . Birth grants . Adoption grants	. Survivors' pension . Maternity leave on full pay . Pre-natal care . Birth benefit . Marriage grants	. Sick leave	. Severance grant	. Contributions from: employers employees government	. Ministry of Labour and Social Security . National Institute of Health and Social Insurance

PROVISION OF PERSONAL SOCIAL SERVICES

COUNTRY	SERVICE PROVIDERS	THE AGED	THE DISABLED AND HANDICAPPED	CHILDREN AND YOUTH	NEEDY FAMILIES	THE SICK AND INJURED	THE UNEMPLOYED	METHODS OF FINANCING	RESPONSIBLE GOVERNMENT ADMINISTRATIVE AGENCIES
ARGENTINA	Central government administrative agencies	. Nursing homes		. Foster care . Institutional care	. Legal aid	. Health care	. Employment centres	. Government allocation	. Ministry of Public Health and Social Action . National Institute of Social Services
	Regional government administrative agencies	. Nursing homes						. Government allocation	. Provincial welfare department
	Local government administrative agencies	. Nursing homes . Recreational centres . Hot meals	. Homes for disabled . Special schools	. Day-care	. Recreational services		. Employment centres	. Government allocation	. Municipal welfare department
	Voluntary agencies	. Nursing homes	. Homes for disabled	. Orphanages			. Employment centres	. Donations . Government allocation	
	Private enterprise	. Nursing homes						. Service charge	

SOCIAL SECURITY PROVISIONS

COUNTRY	SERVICE PROVIDERS	THE AGED	THE DISABLED AND HANDICAPPED	CHILDREN AND YOUTH	NEEDY FAMILIES	THE SICK AND INJURED	THE UNEMPLOYED	METHODS OF FINANCING	RESPONSIBLE GOVERNMENT ADMINISTRATIVE AGENCIES
BRAZIL	Central government administrative agencies	. Contributory wage-related pensions . Free health care . Flat-rate pensions in rural areas	. Contributory wage-related invalidity pensions . Invalid allowances . Work injury disability pensions . Free health care . Rehabilitation	. Family allowances . Orphans' pensions . Fiscal welfare	. Survivors' pensions . Maternity benefits . health care	. Sickness allowances . Rehabilitation . Free health care	. Unemployment allowances . Free health care	. Contributions from employers, employees, government	. Ministry of Social Insurance & Assistance . Social Insurance & Assistance National System (SINPAS)
	Regional government administrative agencies								
	Voluntary agencies								
	Private enterprise	. Occupational retirement pensions	. Occupational accident pensions			. Occupational sickness benefits			

278

PROVISION OF PERSONAL SOCIAL SERVICES

COUNTRY	SERVICE PROVIDERS	THE AGED	THE DISABLED AND HANDICAPPED	CHILDREN AND YOUTH	NEEDY FAMILIES	THE SICK AND INJURED	THE UNEMPLOYED	METHODS OF FINANCING	RESPONSIBLE GOVERNMENT ADMINISTRATIVE AGENCIES
BRAZIL	Central government administrative agencies (shared responsibility with states)	. Counselling	. Counselling . Job placement services	. Institutional care . Food programmes . Delinquency programmes . Nurseries	. Local community action programmes . Food assistance	. Counselling	. Job placement services	. Social insurance contributions . International aid . Government allocations	. National Social Insurance Medical Assistance Institute . Social Insurance and Assistance Financial Administration Institute . Brazilian Assistance Legion's Foundation . Department of Community Action . Food and Nutrition National Institute
	Voluntary agencies	. Institutional care . Free food	. Institutional care . Free food	. Institutional care . Free food	. Free food . Institutional care			. Government allocations . Tax exemption . Donations	. National Social Service Council
	Private enterprise	. Occupational welfare benefits		. Vocational training			. Job placement services	. Fee for service	

SOCIAL SECURITY PROVISIONS

COUNTRY	SERVICE PROVIDERS	THE AGED	THE DISABLED AND HANDICAPPED	CHILDREN AND YOUTH	NEEDY FAMILIES	THE SICK AND INJURED	THE UNEMPLOYED	METHODS OF FINANCING	RESPONSIBLE GOVERNMENT ADMINISTRATIVE AGENCIES
CHILE	Central government administrative agencies	. Old system: Wage and contributions related pensions. Age 65 male, 60 female . New system: Individual capitalisation fund related pension. Age 65 male, 60 female . Welfare pension equal to one-third of minimum pension to the indigent	. Mandatory private insurance . Welfare pension equal to one-third of minimum pension to the indigent	. Flat-rate allowance per child up to 18 yrs, students up to 24 yrs and adopted children (no age limit if invalid)		. Public health system comprehensive medical and hospitalisation benefits . Private health system medical and hospitalisation benefits as contracted	. Welfare pension equal to one-third of minimum pension to the indigent . Emergency programmes for unemployed breadwinners . Milk and food programmes	. 19.2 per cent of wages paid as pension contribution by employee (old pension system) . Employee's individual compulsory savings: 13 per cent of wage or salary (new pension system) . 6.9 per cent of wages paid as public health care by insured . 7 per cent of wage paid as private health insurance premium . General revenues (family allowances and welfare pensions)	. Superintendency of Social Security (administration of old pension system) . Pension Funds Managing Corporations (Private) (administration of new pension system) . Compensatory Family Allowance Fund . National System of Health Services . Private Health Insurance Companies
	Local government administrative agencies	. Support for indigent aged	. Support for indigent invalids				. Support for indigent unemployed		. Municipal Authority (in conjunction with central government agencies)

PROVISION OF PERSONAL SOCIAL SERVICES

COUNTRY	SERVICE PROVIDERS	THE AGED	THE DISABLED AND HANDICAPPED	CHILDREN AND YOUTH	NEEDY FAMILIES	THE SICK AND INJURED	THE UNEMPLOYED	METHODS OF FINANCING	RESPONSIBLE GOVERNMENT ADMINISTRATIVE AGENCIES
CHILE	Chile has no system of personal social services								

SOCIAL SECURITY PROVISIONS

COUNTRY	SERVICE PROVIDERS	THE AGED	THE DISABLED AND HANDICAPPED	CHILDREN AND YOUTH	NEEDY FAMILIES	THE SICK AND INURED	THE UNEMPLOYED	METHODS OF FINANCING	RESPONSIBLE GOVERNMENT ADMINISTRATIVE AGENCIES
COLOMBIA	Central government administrative agencies	. Contributory wage-related pensions . Health care	. Contributory wage-related invalidity pension . Health care	. Family allowances	. Survivors' pension . Maternity leave		. Severance indemnity		. Ministry of Labour and Social Security . CAJANAL . ISS
	Regional government administrative agencies	. Funeral grant	. Constant attendance allowance . Funeral grant . Rehabilitation						
	Private enterprise	. Non-contributory wage-related pension . Funeral grant	. Non-contributory invalidity pension . Constant attendance allowance . Funeral grant . Rehabilitation		. Survivors' pension . Maternity leave				. Ministry of Labour and Social Security

PROVISION OF PERSONAL SOCIAL SERVICES

COUNTRY	SERVICE PROVIDERS	THE AGED	THE DISABLED AND HANDICAPPED	CHILDREN AND YOUTH	NEEDY FAMILIES	THE SICK AND INJURED	THE UNEMPLOYED	METHODS OF FINANCING	RESPONSIBLE GOVERNMENT ADMINISTRATIVE AGENCIES
COLOMBIA	Central government administrative agencies		. Rehabilitation . Orthopedic appliances		. Vocational training . Health services			. Social security contribution	. Ministry of Labour and Social Security . CATANAL . ISS
	Private enterprise		. Rehabilitation	. Nurseries . Child-care centres				. Employee allocations	. Ministry of Labour and Social Security

SOCIAL SECURITY PROVISIONS

COUNTRY	SERVICE PROVIDERS	THE AGED	THE DISABLED AND HANDICAPPED	CHILDREN AND YOUTH	NEEDY FAMILIES	THE SICK AND INJURED	THE UNEMPLOYED	METHODS OF FINANCING	RESPONSIBLE GOVERNMENT ADMINISTRATIVE AGENCIES
CUBA	Central government administrative agencies	. Wage-related pensions and allowances at age 60(M)/55(F) . Free health care	. Free health care and institutional care	. Free health care	. Wage subsidies	. Cash benefits . Free health care	. Free health care	. State allocation . Enterprise contributions . State allocation	. State Committee of Labour and Social Security (CETSS) . Ministry of Public Health (MINSAP)
	Regional government administrative agencies	. Survivors' pensions	. Wage-related disability pensions		. Cash/in-kind benefits . Funeral grants			. State allocation	. Organs of People's Power Provincial (OPP)
	Employers						. Cash benefits of 70% of base salary	. State allocation . Absorbed as operating expenses	

PROVISION OF PERSONAL SOCIAL SERVICES

COUNTRY	SERVICE PROVIDERS	THE AGED	THE DISABLED AND HANDICAPPED	CHILDREN AND YOUTH	NEEDY FAMILIES	THE SICK AND INJURED	THE UNEMPLOYED	METHODS OF FINANCING	RESPONSIBLE GOVERNMENT ADMINISTRATIVE AGENCIES
CUBA	Central government administrative agencies	. Retirement homes . Day-care	. Special education . Day-care		. Food . Housing . Children's day-care subsidies			. State allocation . State allocation . State allocation . User charges	. Committees for Defense of Revolution . Federation of Cuban Women . Cuban Workers Ctrl (general supervision) . Ministry of Public Health . Ministry of Education . National Commission for Prevention and Social Care (general supervision)
	Regional government administrative agencies	. Counselling	. Counselling	. Counselling . Counselling . Institutional care	. Counselling	. Home help . Counselling . Health education . Community services		. State allocation . State allocation	. CDR, FMC and CTC (provincial and municipal offices) . National Commission for Prevention and Social Care (provincial and municipal offices)
	Voluntary agencies	. Residential homes				. Institutional care		. Donations	. Roman Catholic Church

NOTE: Since there is no 'professional' social work in Cuba, trade union cadres, community leaders and FMC workers involve themselves in providing a variety of interpersonal helping and personal services.

SOCIAL SECURITY PROVISIONS

COUNTRY	SERVICE PROVIDERS	THE AGED	THE DISABLED AND HANDICAPPED	CHILDREN AND YOUTH	NEEDY FAMILIES	THE SICK AND INJURED	THE UNEMPLOYED	METHODS OF FINANCING	RESPONSIBLE GOVERNMENT ADMINISTRATIVE AGENCIES
GUATEMALA	Central government administrative agencies	. Limited retirement pensions at 65 for government workers	. Invalidity pension . Accident insurance . Cash benefits . Medical care . Some rehabilitation	. Child labour regulation . Maternity benefits	. Maternity benefits . Limited low-cost housing . Emergency relief	. Free and low-cost medical care . Survivors' pensions . Funeral grant . Disability grant	. Limited severance pay for government and industrial workers	. Half of funds provided by employers; one quarter from government and one quarter from workers . State funds by direct taxation	. Guatemalan Institute of Social Security . Ministry of Labour . Ministry of Health
	Employers	. Variable retirement pensions	. Some health care provisions	. Some free health care		. Some free medical care and rehabilitation	. Limited severance pay for industrial workers in urban areas	. Operating expenses	

PROVISION OF PERSONAL SOCIAL SERVICES

COUNTRY	SERVICE PROVIDERS	THE AGED	THE DISABLED AND HANDICAPPED	CHILDREN AND YOUTH	NEEDY FAMILIES	THE SICK AND INJURED	THE UNEMPLOYED	METHODS OF FINANCING	RESPONSIBLE GOVERNMENT ADMINISTRATIVE AGENCIES
GUATEMALA	Central government administrative agencies	. Housing and medical care for the aged without families . National home for the aged	. Rehabilitation programme . Institutional care	. Institutional care . National orphanage	. Resettlement programme . Some food provisions	. Free medical care . Low cost and subsidised care	. Registration for public works projects . Limited referral service	. State allocation . Taxation	. Ministry of Health (MOH) . Ministry of Labour (MOL) . Ministry of Agriculture . National Health Planning Unit
	Regional government administrative agencies			. Nutrition and education programmes	. Community development programmes			. International aid	
	Local government administrative agencies		. Education programmes						
	Voluntary agencies	. Some personal services food and clothing through charitable agencies		. Vocational training . Counselling . Recreation programmes	. Emergency relief programmes	. Free and low-cost medical care	. Assistance to unemployed workers' families	. Public donations . User fees . Government subsidies	. Coordination through MOH, MOL, and National Health Planning Unit
	Private enterprise			. Aid programmes in education and nutrition					

287

SOCIAL SECURITY PROVISIONS

COUNTRY	SERVICE PROVIDERS	THE AGED	THE DISABLED AND HANDICAPPED	CHILDREN AND YOUTH	NEEDY FAMILIES	THE SICK AND INJURED	THE UNEMPLOYED	METHODS OF FINANCING	RESPONSIBLE GOVERNMENT ADMINISTRATIVE AGENCIES
MEXICO	Central government administrative agencies	. Age pension (old age seniority) . Health benefits	. Permanent disability pension . Temporary disability pension . Health care . Rehabilitation . Prosthetic services	. Survivors' pension . Lump-sum when no pension granted . Maternal/ infant health care	. Widow's pension . Paid maternity leave . Lump-sum when no pension granted . Maternal health care . Day-care . Subsidised or low rental housing	. Paid sick leave . Medical, preventive, hospital, rehabilitation, prosthetic devices	. Pay-off lump-sum . Pension if insured and 60 years old	. Taxes . Employee/ employer contributions	. ISSTE . IMSS . Ministry of Health

288

PROVISION OF PERSONAL SOCIAL SERVICES

COUNTRY	SERVICE PROVIDERS	THE AGED	THE DISABLED AND HANDICAPPED	CHILDREN AND YOUTH	NEEDY FAMILIES	THE SICK AND INJURED	THE UNEMPLOYED	METHODS OF FINANCING	RESPONSIBLE GOVERNMENT ADMINISTRATIVE AGENCIES
MEXICO	Central and regional government administrative agencies	. Nursing homes . Medical care . Food . Shelter	. Rehabilitation services . Prosthetic services . Education	. Legal services . Shelter/ housing . Information referral . Social services . Medical care . Psychological and other diagnostic services . Mental health . Maternity benefits . Day-care	. Information and referral services . Shelters . Boarding homes for children of working mothers . Emergency funds . Boarding homes for working women . Funeral home services	. Medical and rehabilitative services	. Information and referral . Food kitchens . Shelter for homeless	. Taxes . General revenues . General revenues . Taxes	. National System for the Integral Development of the Family (DIF) . National Council for the Confirms of Youth (Insure) . Department of Community Development . Secretariat of Health and Public Assistance . COPLAMAR (rural development) . Centre for the Integral Assistance of the Elderly
	Voluntary agencies	. Medical care . Nursing home . Property and buildings for government clinics, social services		. Boarding homes . Temporary shelter . Day-care . Medical care clinics . Orphanages . Adoptions				. Donations . government allocations	. Office of Community Development . Office for the Protection of women and Children
	Private enterprise	. Medical care . Hospitalisation		. Day-care . Adoption				. Absorbed operational expenses	

SOCIAL SECURITY PROVISIONS

COUNTRY	SERVICE PROVIDERS	THE AGED	THE DISABLED AND HANDICAPPED	CHILDREN AND YOUTH	NEEDY FAMILIES	THE SICK AND INJURED	THE UNEMPLOYED	METHODS OF FINANCING	RESPONSIBLE GOVERNMENT ADMINISTRATIVE AGENCIES
PUERTO RICO	Central government administrative agencies	. Cash benefits on retirement and death . Hospital and medical insurance . Lump-sum payment on death of insured person	. Cash benefits on temporary or permanent disability and death . Hospital and medical service . Maternity benefits	. Cash benefits to dependent children of retired, disabled or dead insured person	. Wage-related pension benefits	. Medical and hospital services . Compensation . Housekeeper . Per diem and transportation payment . Medical equipment . Lawyer's fee . Funeral grant	. Cash/in-kind benefits	. Employer/ employee contributions . Employer contributions . United States funds . State funds . Loans (USA) . Flat-rate annual tax	. Social Security Administration and Health Care Financing Administration, USA . Department of Labor and Human Resources, Puerto Rico . State Insurance Fund, Puerto Rico . Administration of Compensation for Automobile Accidents, Puerto Rico
	Private enterprise	. Wage-related pensions . Hospital and medical insurance	. Cash on disability	. Pension plans and life insurance benefits		. Hospitalisation . Major medical		. Employer/ employee contributions	
	Employers	. Wage-related pensions	. Medical plan . Workmen's compensation	. Paid maternity leave	. Paid maternity leave	. Medical plan . Workmen's compensation . Paid sick leave		. Employer/ employee contributions	

PROVISION OF PERSONAL SOCIAL SERVICES

COUNTRY	SERVICE PROVIDERS	THE AGED	THE DISABLED AND HANDICAPPED	CHILDREN AND YOUTH	NEEDY FAMILIES	THE SICK AND INJURED	THE UNEMPLOYED	METHODS OF FINANCING	RESPONSIBLE GOVERNMENT ADMINISTRATIVE AGENCIES
PUERTO RICO	Central government administrative agencies	. Information and referral . Day-care . Home-care . Housekeeper . Substitute homes . Rehabilitation . Cash payments . Low-cost subsidised housing	. Counselling . Rehabilitation . Medical services . Cash benefits . Residential institutions . Evaluation and treatment services . Support services	. Counselling . Housekeeper . Day-care . Foster home and adoption . Group homes . Institutional care . Cash benefits . Nutritional and health services . Recreational services	. Economic assistance . Nutritional assistance . Subsidies . Housing . Work incentives . Health services . Training and employment . Rehabilitation	. Health services . Medical emergencies . Hospital services	. Orientation . Referrals . Job placement . Training . Remedial employment and skill development . Nutritional assistance	. State allocations . United States government allocations . User charges	. Social Services Department . Health Department . Housing Department . Public Education Department . Anti-addiction Department . Recreation and Sports Department
	Voluntary agencies and Private enterprise	. Day-care . Residential care	. Day-care . Residential care . Special schools . Counselling	. Day-care . Residential care . Counselling		. Health services . Medical emergencies . Hospital services	. Job placement . Employment and training . Referrals	. Government subsidies . User charges . Donations . United funds of Puerto Rico	

SOCIAL SECURITY PROVISIONS

COUNTRY	SERVICE PROVIDERS	THE AGED	THE DISABLED AND HANDICAPPED	CHILDREN AND YOUTH	NEEDY FAMILIES	THE SICK AND INJURED	THE UNEMPLOYED	METHODS OF FINANCING	RESPONSIBLE GOVERNMENT ADMINISTRATIVE AGENCIES
URUGUAY	Central government administrative agencies	. Contributory wage-related pension . Means-tested pension	. Contributory wage-related invalid pension . Means-tested invalid pension . Work injury pension . Health care	. Family allowances . Health care	. Maternity benefits . Survivors' benefits . Funeral grant	. Contributory sickness allowances . Health care	. Contributory unemployment allowances . Severance pay . Dismissal pension	. Contributions from: employers employees government	. Ministry of Labour and Social Security . Social Security General Directorate . Social Security Bank . Mother and Child Protection Services

PROVISION OF PERSONAL SOCIAL SERVICES

COUNTRY	SERVICE PROVIDERS	THE AGED	THE DISABLED AND HANDICAPPED	CHILDREN AND YOUTH	NEEDY FAMILIES	THE SICK AND INJURED	THE UNEMPLOYED	METHODS OF FINANCING	RESPONSIBLE GOVERNMENT ADMINISTRATIVE AGENCIES
URUGUAY	Central government administrative agencies	. Transport concessions . Food supplements		. Emergency placement homes . Institutional care . Food supplements	. Pre-natal care . Health care			. State allocation	. Child Council . National Feeding Institute . Ministry of Labour and Social Security
	Voluntary agencies	. Homes for the elderly . Cultural activities		. Day-care centres . Nurseries				. Government allocation . Service charges . Donations	. Municipal authorities

INDEX

adoption
    Argentina 11; Puerto Rico 228
adoption grants, 19
age allowance, 34
aged, personal social services
    Argentina 13-14; Brazil 35; Cuba 119; Mexico 187; Puerto Rico 217-18; Uruguay 261
aged, social security
    Argentina 11-13; Brazil 33-4; Chile 63; Colombia 80-1; Cuba 118-19; Guatemala 154-5; Mexico 186-7; Puerto Rico 216-17; Uruguay 259-61
aged, the
    Argentina 10-11; Brazil 33; Chile 62; Colombia 79; Cuba 118; Guatemala 154; Mexico 186; Puerto Rico 215-16; Uruguay 259
ageing population
    Argentina 10, 11; Brazil 29; Chile 62; Cuba 108, 118; Puerto Rico 215-16; Uruguay 254, 261, 272
automobile accident compensation, 213, 227, 240, 242-3

birth benefits, 17, 19
burial assistance see funeral grants

capitalism
    Cuba 100; Guatemala 140; Puerto Rico 203
children and youth
    Argentina 18; Brazil 42; Chile 64; Colombia 90; Cuba 122; Guatemala 157; Mexico 189-90; Puerto Rico 226-7; Uruguay 264
children and youth, personal social services
    Argentina 18-19; Brazil 44-5; Chile 65; Colombia 90-1; Cuba 123-4; Guatemala 158-9; Mexico 190; Puerto Rico 228-32; Uruguay 265

Index

Index

personal social services, administration
Argentina 9; Brazil 32; Chile 61; Colombia 78;
Cuba 109; Guatemala 148-51; Mexico 186; Puerto
Rico 209-13; Uruguay 256-7
personal social services, financing of
Argentina 10; Brazil 32; Chile 61; Colombia
78; Cuba 117; Guatemala 152; Mexico 184-5;
Puerto Rico 213-15; Uruguay 259
political environment of welfare systems
Argentina 6-7; Brazil 28; Chile 58-9; Colombia
73-4; Cuba 106; Guatemala 144; Mexico 180;
Puerto Rico 207-8; Uruguay 253
Portuguese influence, 25
poverty
Brazil 30, 39; Cuba 125; Guatemala 160; Mexico
191; Puerto Rico 202, 205, 218, 230, 235, 245;
Uruguay 266, 272
pre-natal care
Argentina 17, 19; Chile 65; Cuba 123;
Guatemala 160, 161-2; Uruguay 265, 267, 267-8
provincial government welfare services
Argentina 7, 10, 14; Brazil 31; Cuba 108, 109;
Mexico 182, 184-5
public assistance see social assistance

recreational activities and centres
Argentina 14, 15, 17, 18; Colombia 89;
Guatemala 159-60; Mexico 187; Puerto Rico 218,
225, 230; Uruguay 261
rehabilitation services
Brazil 37, 38, 39, 46-7; Colombia 80, 85, 92;
Cuba 108, 121; Guatemala 156-7, 164; Mexico
188, 189; Puerto Rico 222, 223, 224, 225;
Uruguay 263, 270
retirement age
Argentina 11-12; Brazil 33; Chile 63; Colombia
80-1; Cuba 118; Guatemala 154-5; Mexico 186;
Puerto Rico 216; Uruguay 259, 260
retirement benefits
Argentina 11-13; Brazil 34; Chile 63; Colombia
80-1; Cuba 118-19; Guatemala 155; Mexico 186;
Puerto Rico 216-17; Uruguay 259-60
retirement, compulsory
Brazil 33; Uruguay 259-60, 262
Roman Catholic Church, influence of
Argentina 2, 6; Brazil 26; Colombia 74;
Guatemala 139; Mexico 175, 181, 198, 199
rural social security
Brazil 28, 34, 37, 38, 43, 46; Cuba 110;
Guatemala 161; Mexico 179; Puerto Rico 220;
Uruguay 259, 263